WHAT HAPPENED TO AMERICAN PRISONERS OF WAR IN KOREA

compiled by
Sandy Strait

Royal Fireworks Press

Unionville, New York

Royal Fireworks Press
First Avenue, PO Box 399
Unionville, NY 10988-0399
(914) 726-4444
FAX: (914) 726-3824
email: rfpress@ny.frontiercomm.net

Royal Fireworks Press
78 Biddeford Avenue
Downsview, Ontario
M3H 1K4 Canada
FAX: (416) 633-3010

ISBN: 0-88092-275-3

Printed in the United States of America on acid-free recycled paper
using vegetable-based inks by the Royal Fireworks Printing Company
of Unionville, New York.

TABLE OF CONTENTS

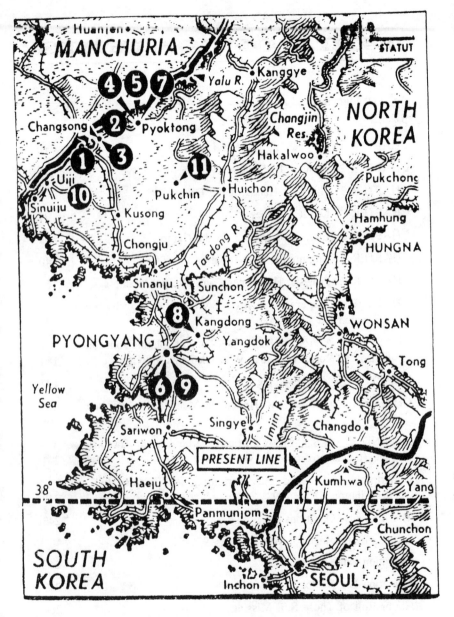

Prisoner of War Camps in North Korea

The Mining Camp
    Believed to have been in various locations; temporary
    transit camp.
Camp 1 Changsong
Camp 2 Pi-Chong-ni
Camp 2 Annex, Ōbul
Camp 3 Changsong
Camp 4 Wiwon
Camp 5 Pyokdong

Camp 6 Pyogyang
Camp 7 Pyokdong
Camp 8 Kungdong
Camp 9 Pyongyang
Camp 10 Chonma
Camp 11 Pukshin--Camp Kanggye
Camp 12 Pyongyang
Camp Manpojin--a transit camp
Pak's Death Palace, Suan--Interrogation center

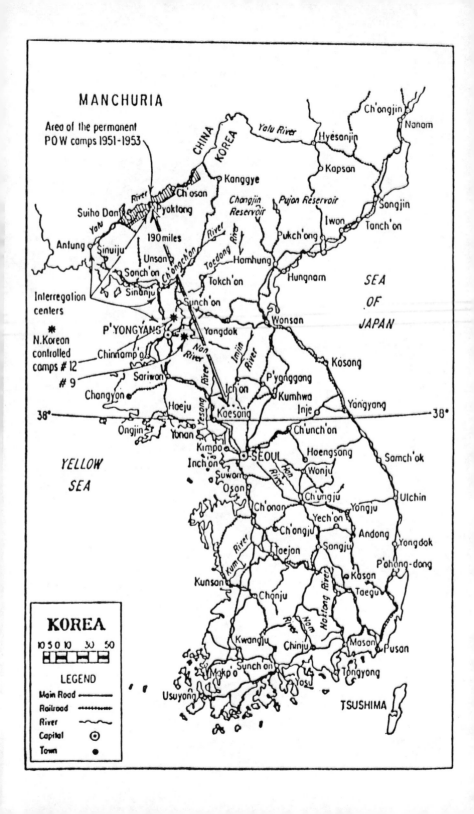

ACKNOWLEDGMENTS

I would first like to thank my wonderful friend, Richard Rook, for encouraging me to start this project. His answers to the questions got me hooked on the idea, as I found them to be insightful, moving, and very real. And then he kept me going for more than two years, never letting me get discouraged. He wrote many, many letters and made phone calls introducing me to his beloved friends, his fellow POWs, urging them to join us. He made it impossible for them to say 'No' to me. (But I don't know how anyone could say 'No' to a terrific guy like him anyway!) He has been the 'heart' behind this book. You were right, buddy, this is a book that needed to be written. Thank you for everything, Dick! (And a big thanks to your lovely wife, Joan, for all her help as well.)

A huge debt of thanks is due Jack Chapman, who right from the start unselfishly offered us everything he had accumulated over years of researching the plight of the Korean War POWs. His outstanding manuscript, "If Captured," is the backbone of the entire book. He also sent photos, maps, and other resource materials, and conferred at length by phone and e-mail with Richard and me about the book. It would not have been possible to complete this project without you, Jack. I'd like to say that you are the 'brain' behind this book, and sincerely thank you for everything you sent and for all you've done to help.

Another friend who contributed so much to the book is Andrew Aguirre, and I'd also like to thank him. His answers to the students questions were exceptional, and certainly enhanced this book. Also, the many, many hours of work compiling the listings of those who came home in both Operation Big Switch and Operation Little Switch are certainly appreciated and add so much to the book.

Harold Kaschko is another veteran who sent in not only his own story, but maps, charts, lists of resources, and important

I

documents, including the certificate and letter pertaining to 'Circular 131.' This was invaluable. Thank you, Harold.

An additional source of help was the POW Network, directed by an old friend of the family, Chuck Schantag, and his hard-working wife, Mary. This is a non-profit organization founded to research and distribute information about prisoners of war. They were most eager to help and we certainly appreciate their time and effort.

I would also like to thank Linda Calvin, my co-author of the first book in this series, *What Was It Like In Vietnam? Honest Answers From Those Who Were There.* As my good friend and a dedicated high school history teacher, she has encouraged me to continue this series, and authorized the use of the original questions from her students to help veterans tell their stories in detail. She continues to advocate the use of 'authentic curriculum' in our classrooms. Linda's students at Urbandale High School in Urbandale, Iowa, with their enthusiasm and concern for America's veterans, are truly the inspiration for the entire series.

My family came through for me again, as they always have. My husband Jerry, a Vietnam combat veteran, answered countless 'military type' questions that we civilians always have and gave his wholehearted support to this project. My daughters Heather and Lori both had an active role in the book, with both suggestions and some editing help. My son-in-law, Morgan Toal, offered invaluable technical help with the computer problems that popped up, by way of the Internet from their home way up in Barrow, Alaska. (Thank you for putting up with me—I love you all so much!)

I have had the support and encouragement of many friends and would like to thank them also. They are Carol Distaso, Chris Francis, Becky Johnson, Michelle Gregory, Kathy Martino, and Carroll Strauss. Also, all our friends in our vets groups, Vietnam Vets Reunited have been wonderful. Thanks!

I would like to finally thank each of the courageous heroes in the book, those I mentioned above, as well as Jim Ransier,

Edward Sheffield, Richard Makua, Joseph Wilson, Theo Baudoin, and Johnnie Johnson. Your answers were very personal, very real, and very important to an understanding of what really happened. Your stories touched me deeply. You are what heroes are supposed to be. I have enjoyed working with all of you. Your letters and phone calls have supported and encouraged me all along the way. I consider each of you gentlemen among the finest people I've ever met and as an American I would like to genuinely thank you for your service to our country and to say to all of you:

Welcome Home, my friends.
I am so glad you made it!

PREFACE

The men whose stories you are about to read have reached into their souls to bring out memories that are harrowing and unrelenting. Their experiences were nothing short of horrific. It was a time in their lives that they would much rather be able to forget ever happened. But they cannot forget, and neither should we.

They served at a time when America was exhausted from one war and wanted nothing to do with another. While most of the country was busy trying to get back to work, they were struggling just to stay alive. Their stories are deeply moving and inspirational.

We are now at a time in our history when our young people need heroes. A hero is defined as a person of distinguished valor, a person who shows courage and bravery in the face of overpowering adversity. These men are heroes. They survived a living hell and helped one another to survive. They should never be considered the forgotten prisoners of a forgotten war, for they have important lessons to teach us all....

This series of books started with a book about the Vietnam War, called *What Was It Like In Vietnam?* written by me and my good friend and fellow teacher, Linda Calvin. In that book, Vietnam vets answered questions that Linda's high school classes had asked during panel discussions with veterans in their community, Urbandale, Iowa. The questions were given to vets throughout the country and resulted in this collection of oral histories to be used as "authentic curriculum" in high school classes. (When the book came out in 1995, we soon found out that high school students were not the only ones interested in knowing what is was like in Vietnam. It seemed most people had the same questions in mind, and had always wanted to know the answers.)

After the Vietnam book came out, Linda was not available to co-author, so I decided to continue on my own researching and developing a series of books to include WW II, Korea, Vietnam, and Desert Storm. I started out by posting messages to veterans on message boards in America Online's Military and Veterans centers, inviting veterans of these wars to answer the students' questions. (Linda Calvin suggested I continue to use the same questions in order to have continuity in the series and I certainly agreed.)

Around Christmas of 1994, I received my first letter from a former Korean War POW, Richard Rook. He told me he wanted to answer all the questions, more than 100 of them, not just some, but that it would take him awhile to type them into his computer because of a challenge he has in his life. He went on to explain that he has a service-connected disability that has left him with the use of only one finger on one hand. When I got his letter I called him right away to tell him I'd gladly take his answers on an audio cassette, as I do for anyone who asks. But he insisted on writing himself. I was amazed by his determination and inspired by it.

Richard explained to me in our first conversation that there weren't many books out about Korea, and hardly any about the POWs from that war. I became interested in knowing more about these 'forgotten POWs.' (At the time I was flooded with e-mail from Desert Storm vets and really didn't know how I could handle another book, but I was fascinated by the need.) He assured me he could introduce me to the POWs if I was willing to compile their stories. That's how we got started in what has become a group effort.

One issue that stunned me, and further emphasized the need for this book, came up in the beginning of this project. It was the issue of "Circular 131." Harold Kaschko sent me a copy of a certificate he had been told to sign when he was repatriated in September of 1953, during Operation Big Switch. Being eager to return home after years of captivity, he signed the certificate, like everyone else who was asked. He was able to produce a copy of it and send it with his answers. "Circular 131" was an official document denying the returnees the right to speak about their military experiences, either at that time or later on in civilian life. Being the kind of men that they were, they honored this vow, and for the most part did not divulge their experiences to anyone. Harold also sent a letter, dated July 29, 1993, from the Department of Defense, finally relieving the POWs of their obligations under the certificate. There were nearly 40 years between the dates on these two documents. [Please see the Appendix for actual copies of these documents]

One of the first POWs Richard Rookk referred to me was Jack Chapman. Jack had written a manuscript about his experiences in 1964 and wanted to send it to me as his contribution to the book. (He told me that he and another former Korean POW had used parts of it in lectures given to Army Rangers and the ROTC at Fort Lewis, Washington.) When I received it I was amazed at the detail and comprehensive quality of it. Dick had written an outstanding manuscript. I suggested to him that he add to it and try to have it published on his own, but he said that he wanted us to use it in any way we could in this book in order to educate the public about what really happened in the Korean War prison camps. His manuscript has become a very important part of this book, not only because it tells his personal and touching story, but because it serves as historical background for the beginning of most of the chapters.

I feel it most fitting to include the original introduction to Jack Chapman's manuscript at this point.

"If Captured" by Jack Chapman, 1964

"There is certainly no glory in being captured by the enemy and while there is no disgrace, it is yet a traumatic, frustrating and often humiliating experience to be forced, through circumstances beyond your control, to lay down your weapon and surrender to the foe.

The ordeal of a prisoner of war was once very aptly described by Sir Winston Churchill, who wrote:

"It is a melancholy state, you are in the power of the enemy. You owe your life to his humanity, your daily bread to his compassion. You must obey his order, await his pleasure, possess your soul in patience. The days are long, hours crawl by like paralytic centipedes. Moreover, the whole atmosphere of prison is odious. Companions quarrel about trifles and get the least possible enjoyment from each other's society. You feel a constant humiliation in being fenced in by railings and wire, watched by armed guards and webbed about with a tangle of regulations and restrictions."

This factual, chronological story is written without malice toward anyone. "If Captured," taken from the Soldier's Creed and Fighting Man's Code, is an unimaginative prepositional phrase until it actually rears its horrible, ugly head. My only thought at this writing is the hope that no other American serviceman will ever have to endure the suffering of a prisoner of war.

This story is dedicated to the hundreds of valiant, ex-Korean prisoners of war, who, though captured in 1950 and ill-treated in the Communists tactics of torture and brainwashing, survived and resisted, until finally, in 1953, they were returned to United Nations control at Panmunjon, South Korea.

This book, unlike the others in the series, was written completely in narrative form and taken directly from two kinds of sources. The first source was the set of questions and answers themselves, and the second source consisted of the stories and manuscripts written by the former POWs. (The only exception is the section on Johnnie Johnson.) The choice on what to submit was left up to the individual. Most chose to answer the students'

questions, some offered their own writings, and some chose both. This accounts for the diversity in the length and detail of the stories.

Every effort was made to keep these memories intact for the sake of future generations. As each veteran's individual experience is unique and different, so are his dialect, vocabulary, and grammar. Very little editing was done because I wanted to keep each individual's voice, emotions, and expressions. No concessions have been made to political correctness; these men had thousands of reasons to speak ill of their captors, and some of them do so forcefully.

This material is presented as I received it. I have not added anything from my own viewpoint, with the exception of the introduction to Chapter Eleven. The opinions expressed are those of the respondents.

It was very difficult to obtain the listings found in the back of the book. The rosters of names in the final section of the book are not meant to be a definitive listing, they should be seen, rather, as an attempt to honor all those who served.

The title of the final chapter of this book comes from some of the information sent to me by Harold Kaschko. It is contained in a letter that was sent by Dr. William Shadish in response to the article, "POWs: Quiet Heroism in Ambiguity," by Col. Robert Berens, published in the December 1992 Ex-POW Bulletin, reprinted from ARMY Magazine. In his letter, Dr. Shadish, himself a Korean War POW, refutes claims made by certain sources that the majority of POWs from the Korean War "cooperated in indoctrination and interrogation questions..."

He goes on to say, "I have heard this garbage over and over again, and at this point I have had enough. There is literature to point out that the prisoners of war in Korea cooperated less than any other prisoners of war in other wars. They were subjected to more intensive pressures than in other wars. It is grossly unfair to label them as collaborators, actively or passively..."

"They have, for whatever reason, deliberately damaged the reputation of good and honorable men and they have never had the decency to apologize..."

"I feel it is time that someone clearly and forcefully states this so that the world will know that men who were prisoners of war in Korea were courageous, loyal fighting men and defended their country, many of them to their last breath, while they were prisoners."

It is with utmost respect that this book is dedicated to all who were held as Prisoner of War during the Korean War. We have so much to learn from their courage in the face of such terror.

CHAPTER ONE

INTRODUCING THE SURVIVORS

P.F.C. Jack Chapman

Jack served in Korea with the Army's Seventh Infantry Division. He became a member of Task Force Drysdale, which consisted of U.S. Army personnel, U.S. Marines, and members of the 41st Independent Commando, British Royal Marines. Jack took part in the Inchon Landing and the Iwon Landing. On November 30th, 1950, after being wounded seven times, Jack was captured at the Chosin Reservoir along with 143 other survivors of the original 900 man Task Force Drysdale, when it was overrun by thousands of Chinese Communist forces. This area became known as "HELL'S FIRE VALLEY." Jack was to spend his 19th, 20th, and 21st birthdays in Communist prisoner of war camps. He was released on August 20th, 1953.
[Jack's story is featured in Chapters 2, 3, 4, 5, 6, 7, 8, 10 & 11]

Sgt. First Class Richard Rook

Richard was sent to Korea when President Truman called in the Reserves in June of 1950, leaving behind a wife and infant daughter, who waited for him. He served as a rifleman with the 2nd Infantry Division. Richard was captured on May 19, 1951, during the spring offensive. He spent his 23rd, 24th, and 25th birthdays in North Korea. Two weeks before the war ended he and a few others were removed from their camp and isolated, being referred to as "bad elements" by their captors, due to their rejection of Communist indoctrination. They thought this was the end for them, but peace finally came, and Richard was released on August 25, 1953.
[Richard's story is featured in Chapters 2, 3, 4, 5, 6, 7, 8, 10 &11]

Lt. Col. Harold Kaschko (Retired)

Harold was drafted into the Army in 1942 and went to Officers Candidate School at Ft. Sill, Oklahoma. In 1944 he was assigned CO (Commanding Officer) of Battery A, 241st FA Bn., under General Patton's 3rd U.S. Army, where he spent 263 consecutive days in combat in the European Theater. Harold held the rank of Captain when he was shipped to Korea in August of 1950, and there served as Commanding Officer, Battery "C," 38th Field Artillery Battalion, 2nd Infantry Division. He was captured on December 1, 1950 near the Chinese roadblock just miles from Kunu-ri. He spent 1,011 days in captivity and was released in Operation Big Switch in August of 1953.
[Harold's story is featured in Chapters 2, 3, 8, 10 & 11]

Sgt. Edward Sheffield

Edward was stationed with the 24th Infantry Division at Camp Hakata, Japan, only 200 miles from Korea when the war started on June 25, 1950. "It all happened so fast and unexpected," he says. By the 5th of July he found himself on the front lines, watching column after column of Chinese troops go by, in full combat dress. He was captured on July 14, after taking a bullet in the leg. Edward is a survivor of the infamous death march lead by the brutal North Korean major known as the "Tiger."

During the death march he watched the "Tiger" murder 125 men. Edward was released on August 30, 1953, in Operation Big Switch.
[Edward's story is featured in Chapters 2, 3, 4, 5, 6, 8 & 11]

Cpl. James Ransier

James was assigned to the 7th Infantry Division, 32nd RCT, 3rd Battalion, "I" Company, as an infantryman when he reached Korea in January of 1951. On the morning of March 2nd, 1951,

he and his friend, Don Faudskar were captured by a small group of North Koreans who shot them both in the feet, as they took them into custody. Two other soldiers with them were killed. They were taken to a North Korean colonel for questioning. The two soldiers were held for several days and then released as the North Koreans were being forced to retreat from the area. Being seriously wounded, they had to crawl back to their outfit, helped along their way by both South Koreans and Americans.
[James' story is featured in Chapters 2, 3, 8, 10 & 11]

Sgt. Andrew (Chief) Aguirre

Andrew joined the Marine Corps at age 18, looking for adventure and excitement as young men do. He soon found it. He was in WW II for two years and three months. He served at Guadalcanal, the Russell Islands, Okinawa, and later was stationed in Tientsin, China, and Kobe, Japan. He was an experienced combat Marine by the time Korea came along. He left a girlfriend behind then, who is his wife today, more than 40 years later. Andrew was with B Company, 1st Tank Battalion, 1st Marine Division. It was his job to fire the main turret gun. His knowledge of the Japanese language helped him and his men out of several risky situations. He was held POW for two years and nine months, being released during Operation Big Switch.
[Andrew's story is featured in Chapters 2, 5, 10, & 11]

Staff Sgt. (E-6) Richard Makua

Richard is a man of few words, but much emotion. During the war he was a forward observer with the Army's 7th Division. He held the rank of staff sergeant, and was an infantryman with a heavy mortar company. Richard does not like to talk about his experiences as a POW where he faced starvation and death every day. He was repatriated during Operation Big Switch in 1953 and returned home to Hawaii.
[Richard's story is featured in Chapters 2, 3, 5, 10 & 11]

P.F.C. Joseph Wilson

Joseph served for 5 years after WW II as a merchant seaman, helping to rebuild Europe. He was only in the Army for 6 months before going to Korea. He served as a rifleman with the all black Company K, part of the 25th Infantry Division. He was a POW for 27 months, being captured on April 22, 1951, after being wounded twice. He tells of facing racial prejudice from the Chinese. He feels blessed to be born in America where as he says, "We are all one people." He was released during Operation Big Switch. Since then, he has found that his experiences dealing with wounded POWs during the war has given him great incentive to work with needy veterans in his community.
[Joseph's story is featured in Chapters 2, 3, 5, 10 & 11]

P.F.C. Theo Baudoin, Jr.

Theo volunteered for the Army at age 17. He served with the 2nd Engineer Combat Battalion, 2nd Infantry Division on the front line in Korea. He helped build pontoon bridges, cleared mines, and did demolition work, helping troops to cross the Nacktong River on their way north. He personally witnessed atrocities committed by the North Koreans. Theo was taken prisoner by Chinese Communist soldiers on December 1, 1951, at Kunu-ri and released in August of 1953 in Operation Big Switch. He is now active in writing and speaking about his experiences in Korea. A North Korean propoganda photo taken of his capture appears on the cover of this book.
[Theo's story is featured in Chapters 2, 3, 5 & 11]

P.F.C. Wayne A. (Johnnie) Johnson

Johnnie enlisted in the Army and was sent to Japan in May, 1949, where he was a scout in "L" Company, 21st Infantry Regiment, 24th Infantry Division. During only his first week in Korea, his unit was overrun, and he was captured on July 11, 1950. He was held as prisoner for more than three years, finally being released during Operation Big Switch. As a prisoner, he was also a survivor of the brutal North Korean guard known as the "Tiger." During his entire captivity, Johnnie worked diligently, at great personal risk, to record secretly the names of hundreds of people he saw die. He smuggled out his list inside an empty toothpaste tube when he was repatriated. His work has enabled many families to know the truth about the death of a loved one. Johnnie has just recently been awarded the Silver Star for his valiant effort more than 40 years ago.

[Johnnie's story is featured in Chapters 2, 9, 10 & 11]

CHAPTER TWO

PRELUDE TO CAPTURE

Jack Chapman

On June 25, 1950, came the news of Communist aggression into the Republic of South Korea, a young struggling democracy formed after World War II. Next came the news that the North Koreans had overrun the City of Seoul and were pushing further south toward Pusan like a horde of locusts. Not really knowing what it meant, we spoke of it and proclaimed our hope and belief that United Nations action would settle the matter. However, simultaneously came the rumors that United States forces were to be deployed to halt the aggression before the United Nations could begin their deliberations.

Soon there was speculations as to which units would do what, causing commanders to inventory equipment on hand and to attempt to make up the shortages in manpower, which they learned was not possible in the peace-time United States Far East Command.

Armed with Soviet weapons, North Korean Communist forces invaded South Korea on June 25th, 1950. Six days later a battalion of the United States Army's, 24th Infantry Division was rushed to Korea from Japan. The Division was soon in action against the enemy on the outskirts of Seoul. Within weeks, United States forces in Japan were being reinforced by South Korean Army troops to make up for the shortage of manpower in our units. Half of our reinforcements were South Korean. They were hard to understand, and we had to have an interpreter for everything. However, they were good people.

Also came the news that the early American reinforcements in Korea were being virtually annihilated and that more were needed. My division, the Seventh Infantry Division, with its three

15

regimental combat teams and support units (of which my unit, the 31st Regiment, also known as "The Polar Bear Regimental Combat Team," was an integral part) was soon to be on its way from Japan to the "United Nations Police Action."

Time became an important factor; shortage of equipment, personnel, and compliance with training schedules were forgotten as assembly for shipment began. Then came the long array of convoys (their equipment and ships all being of World War II vintage.) The hours of loading and getting underway were long, dismal, tiring, and nearly unbearable for the young and inexperienced troops at hand.

Then, I invariably relapsed into my own dilemma of the past. Life was good for me, a boy growing up in the middle and far western half of America. I recalled all of the family customs, traditions, the outdoorsman, and the other qualities of life that are part of the American heritage. I recalled the yearning to venture forth, this time as a young man, away into a man's world, as a soldier of my country. Military life for me came naturally; after all, I was brought up to do what was directed and to do it to the best of my ability. Korea was a country that few of us young troops had ever even heard of or talked about. We'd ask ourselves, "Where is Korea located?"

My childhood years rolled vividly before me, school years, the Pledge of Allegiance to the American flag each morning before class, the study of early American patriots, of the forward drive and succeeding greatness of our country's sovereignty. At the time I was there I understood what I was fighting for—to help the South Korean people, whose country had been overrun by the North Koreans. We were briefed on what lay ahead, but our superiors had no idea what we eventually would encounter since American forces had never before met hard-core Communist elements in battle.

The United Nations launched a powerful counter-offensive in September 1950, with the First Marine Division and the Seventh Infantry Division making an amphibious landing at Inchon, on the west coast, approximately 200 miles north of Pusan, South

Korea, thereby cutting the communication lines of the North Koreans. Though resistance from the Communist elements was small, resistance by natural elements was great, impeding every effort. Surprisingly though, the landing was expeditious for most of our units, with the reassembling and subsequent southward advance to trap the North Korean Army being rapid.

Our first real enemy engagement came in the mountainous Suwon area. After several heavy encounters, our leaders assumed that the arrival of the second wave of United Nations forces would convince the North Korean commanders to lick their wounds and high-tail it back north. This, they did eventually, by skirting though and/or around the widely spread United States and South Korean Army units, leaving behind an array of guerrilla units. Around the end of September the United Nations Assembly authorized the crossing of the 38th parallel. The middle of October 1950, the Seventh Division was pulled out of action and moved southward to the huge, overcrowded city of Pusan for reinforcement.

In October 1950, as the United Nations forces 'mopped up' the Southern resistance, plans were being launched for another landing. This one would be a backbreaker, landing in the North Korean heartland, to isolate the North Korean Army units from logistical support and to force the surrender of the entire North Korean Army.

The X-Corps consisting of the Seventh Infantry Division and the First Marine Division, was to affect an amphibious landing at Wonsan on the east coast of North Korea, making juncture with the Eighth Army which was to attack across the 38th parallel with its main effort on the North Korean capital, the city of Pyongyang. At the time that this proposed action was being initiated, little did we know that simultaneously, the Communist Chinese People's Army was preparing hundreds of thousands of screaming hordes to pour over the Yalu River in support of North Korea.

The Seventh Division, assembling near Suwon, commenced its motor-march southward to the huge, over crowded (with refugees and United Nations Army Units) city of Pusan, South Korea on or about October 5th, 1950. We utilized our own trucks, plus some of those of the Eighth Army and the Marines. We were ordered to take a round-about 350 mile inland route from Suwon to Pusan (Suwon-Chongju-Kumchon-Taegu). The 31st RCT reached Pusan about October 8th, 1950.

On or about October 10th, 1950, the X-Corps's mission was changed to advance northward instead of westward from Wonsan. General Almond decided to land the Seventh Infantry Division as close as possible to its axis of advance inland toward North Korea's northern border. The Seventh Infantry Division was to land at Iwon, about 105 miles northeast of Wonsan, North Korea, in the enemy's industrial region, then proceed north to the Yalu River, which separates North Korea from Communist China.

By October 16th, our division and its equipment had been packed aboard the transports. On or about October 27, 1950, the LSTs and ships sailed north from Pusan up the coast for Iwon, in preparation for the landing that was to end the United Nations Police Action in Korea and have the American GIs home for Christmas. The fleet set sail and proceeded north into the chilling, wintry waters off the eastern coast of north Korea.

We were again briefed on the "Gung Ho" American type, World War II landing, only this time it was supposed to be comparatively easy, the psychological effect of mass United Nations forces landing in North Korea, doing the final job. Two days later (October 29, 1950) we landed at Iwon. The landing itself was not as difficult as the Inchon assault landing had been. The beach was rocky and water was much colder, but the terrain much kinder than before.

The Division landed at Iwon, the 17th Regiment charged inland to take Pungsan with the 31st Regiment on the 17th left in the Division's center, moving northward on the left of Pungsan. The Seventh Division was to strike north to Pukch'ong though Pungsan and Kapson to the Yalu River at Hyesanjin. The "roads" in this area were non-existent. We spread out, mostly on foot, into the mountains, holding or advancing in the Division's center.

After moving inward, our morale was high, still believing the "Home for Christmas" slogan; we began to make a tragic error, by spreading ourselves too thinly over the northern most part of North Korea. The 3rd battalion of the 31st encountered a few Chinese Communist Forces. These Communist Forces fought desultorily or not at all, leading our commanding officers and others unwisely to regard all Chinese with contempt.

All of our units were moving helter-skelter toward the Manchurian border, close behind the retreating North Korean Army. We skirted some straggling Communist forces, in the belief that rear echelon units would make short work of these groups.

October 1950, the U.S. Eighth Army hit the city of Pyongyang. The ground troops assaulted from the south and a parachute drop by the 187th Regimental Combat Team north of the city completed its envelopment. Pyongyang was the enemy's capital, and its fall symbolized the complete defeat of North Korea. Practically all organized resistance came to an end. The enemy army had ceased to exist as an effective fighting machine and the way seemed open to a speedy end to hostilities.

By mid November, elements of the X Corps had advanced to the Yalu River. Our instructions was, "under no circumstances were we to cross the Yalu River."

As the bitter cold North Korean winter came upon us, the word came that we would not cross into Manchuria, and that pending negotiations were to end the "Police Action." The North Koreans had learned their lesson, and we could still be home for Christmas.

However, in conjunction with talks of supposedly ending the police action, and in view of the forthcoming negotiations, we heard rumors of a tremendous build up of North Korean lines, bolstered by the Chinese Peoples Army. The word was that this was just a "save face" maneuver by the Communist elements and that these elements, having recently been driven northward by the United Nations forces would not dare try it again, but would as stated, negotiate.

Daily our patrols began to report that an one estimated million Chinese Peoples Army troops were massed along the opposing lines, however, they seemed to have only manpower and no heavy equipment. These hard-core Communists elements had been thoroughly brainwashed that their first weapons would come from captured stocks taken from the United Nations forces.

Thursday, November 23rd, 1950 (Thanksgiving Day). Today we had our Thanksgiving meal as promised, (turkey dinner and it was great and wonderful.) The next day or so after Thanksgiving Day, my unit, two heavy weapons squads of Company "D," 31st was again assigned to Captain Charles Peckham's Company "B," 31st Infantry Regiment. We were given orders to advance to the Changjin (Chosin) Reservoir.

We moved out for Hamhung, North Korea, and arriving there sometime around midnight a couple days or so after Thanksgiving Day. We remained at Hamhung until about 12 p.m., on the 28th of November, getting supplies and replacement equipment. We then continued northward to the First Marine Division Command Post, which was located at or near Koto-Ri, a few miles south of the reservoir.

Monday, November 27th, saw the first of many Communist Chinese attacks in and around the reservoir. The Chinese had thrown seven divisions around the reservoir, and one of the greatest epics of the war took place at the reservoir. On this night the Chinese cut roads in all sectors. West of Yudam-ni where the 5th Marines had been attacking, they had about 37 roadblocks in the first six miles of road. Between Koto-ri and Hagaru-ri they erected about 11 roadblocks. Most of the bridges were blown, damaged or destroyed.

The first battalion of the 31st Infantry Regiment (with Charlie Company of the 57th Field Artillery attached) was ordered to continue present mission (Pukchong area.) The second battalion

20

was ordered to close without delay and be prepared to attack north on order.

We (Baker Company) arrived at the First Marine Division Command Post on the evening of November 28th, having traveled from Hamhung the better part of the afternoon. We were bone tired, nervous, and tried to get some rest in the freezing cold weather without success. Throughout the evening there was gunfire off in the distance.

We were poorly prepared for the icy weather that had already laid a mantle of frost on the ground and capped the highest peaks with snow. At dusk the temperature dropped abruptly for the second day in a row, this time a numbing 20 degrees below zero. With two pair of pants, two shirts and a field jacket on, I was still freezing. Man was it something. I had received training at Camp Hale, near Leadville, Colorado at the old home of the 10th Mountain Division, where I learned to ski and mountain climb. During the winter of 1949 I was on maneuvers in Alaska where we slept outside and most of our time there was in the field, skiing and snowshoeing. However we were equipped with adequate clothing. The only other time that I can remember being so cold was on our return trip from Alaska to Camp Carson, Colorado, we made a stop in Cut Banks, Montana. The temperature was around 50 below zero with the wind chill factor, and it was cold.

Having received cold weather training in Colorado and Alaska, I had an advantage over many of my fellow soldiers. But here the supply of winter clothing which was scheduled for us, somehow did not reach us before we left Hamhung. If we had adequate clothing maybe we would not mind the cold so much, but boy, we were cold, it was something! As anyone can see, we went into Koto-ri (Chosin Operation) without proper clothing and equipment. Our C-rations were frozen, and we did not stop long enough to thaw them out.

With the coming of darkness and intense cold, thousands of Chinese began to move over the crusted snow. Three divisions of the Chinese closed in on two regiments of the Marines. Two divisions of the Communists struck Yudam-ni and the third slipped south to cut the 14 miles long route which led southeast to Hagaru.

Toktong Pass was the most vital terrain along the entire 14-mile route. The pass was located approximately six miles southeast of Yudam-ni. Company F, 7th Marines commanding officer had required his men to dig in before erecting any tents. They had completed their task as darkness fell on the 27th. The perimeter remained quiet past midnight. However, around 2:30 a.m. on the 28th, the Chinese struck from three directions. In their first assault from the high ground to the north the enemy swarmed over the forward positions of a Marine platoon. The Lieutenant in charge had deployed his men with two squads forward and one slightly to the rear in supporting positions. Fifteen Marines were killed and nine were wounded in the initial onslaught. The eight remaining Marines fell back slightly.

A head count later revealed that three Marines were missing. They were Corporal Wayne A. Pickett and Private First Class Robert L. Batdorff and Daniel D. Yesko.

(Source; 1st Provisional Historical Platoon Interviews, April 17, 1951, No. 1, G-3 Historical Branch Archives, Headquarters, U.S. Marine Corps. 1st Marine Division, Casualty Bulletin 89-50, December 27, 1950.

Richard Rook

When I found out that I was going to war, naturally I was frightened because I was old enough to realize that there was a possibility that I might not come back. It certainly wasn't my idea to go, but I was in the Reserves, and when the North Koreans came across the 38th parallel on June 25, 1950, President Truman called in the Reserves. Because I was in the Army Reserves, I only went through a three week refresher course before going.

I left a wife and a 7 month old daughter behind. That's why I was so frightened. Being in a war is a combination of being frightened, lonely, disgusted, and it is terribly bloody. The person who said, "God is in every foxhole" certainly knew what he was talking about. I had three reasons to keep my cool. They were God, my wife and my daughter.

Of course my opinion of the war wasn't very good because of my particular circumstances. I wasn't there because I wanted to be, but I fully understood why I was there and why I was needed along with the thousands of others. My opinion changed somewhat after I learned what would have become of the South Koreans if we weren't there.

One of the first things I remember after landing in Korea was a lecture we all had to listen to about why we there and what we were fighting for. It was at this lecture that they told us about some of the strange customs of the Korean people. The one that stands out most in my mind is that we should be very careful while driving in Korea because people will dart out in front of you the last minute so that you almost hit them. They think their evil spirits are right behind them and they, the evil spirits, will be killed if you run over them.

I had Engineer training, and was a heavy equipment operator, but when I arrived in Korea, they were in dire need of riflemen, so I landed in an infantry outfit. I was assigned to the weapons squad of the 3rd platoon in Baker Co., using the A6 light machine gun, 3.5 Bazooka, M1 Grand rifle, M1-A1 carbine, Thompson Sub-machine gun, and the .45 Automatic. Our objective was to seek and destroy.

After the squad leader got hit, I took over the squad for about two months. Then the assistant platoon sgt. got hit, and I was moved into that position where I remained until I was captured. I was "on line" (in combat) with Baker Co, 38th Regt. of the 2nd Infantry Division, from the 1st of January 1951 until May 19, 1951 at which time I was captured and spent the remainder of the "police action" in North Korea.

I can't remember exactly when it was, but my worst or most frightening experience was very early in my combat career. We were the reserve platoon and after the 1st and 2nd platoon had been cut up pretty bad, they moved us into attack position. We were crouched down behind a rice paddy wall with the bullets "snapping" over our heads when we were given the command to "fix bayonets." Well, that was enough for me right there. I was so frightened that I started to shake. It made such an impression on me that to this day it still frightens me. We didn't have to use bayonets that day or any other for that matter, but I'll never forget how I felt that day.

There was another time. In Korea we were able to call in an "air strike" if needed. If in the process of reaching a particular objective, we needed help to knock out a heavy concentration of troops or maybe a machine-gun nest or for any reason whatsoever, we'd call in the Air Force. To protect our own troops, every unit carried "air panels." An air panel was a bright colored piece of cloth 3 feet by 8 feet with different colors on each side. Every day the angle that we would lay the panel out and the color would change. It was one of my duties, as assistant platoon sergeant, to contact the company CP (command post) every morning to receive the password and air panel lay-out for the day.

On this particular day, we had taken a hill and then were pushed off. Earlier, we had called in an air strike, and, of course, we had our air panel displayed properly. In the process of being pushed off the hill, the air panel was picked up and taken down with us. When we were charging up the hill to retake it, two or three Corsairs began to strafe, what at the time, we thought was us.

We were just below the crest of the hill (about 10 feet) when they came in spitting 50 cal. bullets just over the crest. They were so close that the expended "brass" (spent shells) was almost falling on us. After we took the hill with very little opposition, we discovered what had happened. It seems that the alert pilots spotted the Chinese coming back up the other side of the hill, and without being directed to do so, they decided to make one more pass. It's a good thing they did too, because we found about a hundred bodies on top. Through radio contact, the pilots said that even though we didn't have our air panels displayed, they knew where we were. Incidentally, the pilots were all sergeants. They were commonly known as the "flying sergeants."

One more incident I remember was when we were in a defensive position and were "dug in" quite well. We were "front-line" and had been for over a week. There had been a lot of infiltration lately where the Chinese would get behind our lines at night and "bayonet" guys sleeping in their sleeping-bags. We had had plenty of time to booby-trap and set flares down in front of our respective holes. I know one thing for sure, nothing, not even a rabbit, could survive a midnight stroll down in front of my hole. In the process of setting up my booby-traps in front of my hole, I noticed a tree stump, about 10 feet high, down about 15 feet in front of my hole. In addition to the fragmentation and WP grenades set up as booby-traps, I had set up two flares which were angled so that they would light up a large area. Now that I've set the scene, I'll get on with my story.

It was a cold, dark night in the middle of April. This night was no different than any other—we were on a 50% watch. In a two man hole this meant, 2 hours on and 2 hours off. It was around midnight, and I was on guard. At that time I was carrying a 45 automatic which I carried in a shoulder holster. When I was on guard I switched the holster so that it put the weapon on my chest. I had my sleeping bag up over my shoulders while standing when I dozed a little. About that time I heard a real loud, HOOT HOOOOOOO! My heart jumped up into my throat and I started firing my 45. I then tripped my two flares and by this time every G.I. on that hill was shooting at nothing. It's a good thing that the enemy wasn't around because we had sure given our positions away. The next morning, the C.O. wanted to know who started that little "fire-fight."

Thankfully, everyone was just as scared as I was, and nobody knew how it started. Also, the next morning, I discovered a family of owls living in that tree stump, which was hollow. It was with great difficulty that I made the decision that had to be made, I dropped a grenade into the tree. I certainly didn't want a reoccurrence of the events of the night before.

Harold Kaschko

I was drafted into the Army on January 9, 1942 and went to OCS (Officers Candidate School) CS at Ft. Sill, Oklahoma in May, 1942. I graduated as artillery second lieutenant, August 1942, and was assigned to the 241st FA Bn. at Camp White, Oregon, and remained with this unit throughout W.W.II.

In August of 1944, I was assigned CO (Commanding Officer) of Battery A, 241st FA Bn., which was assigned to General Patton's 3rd U.S. Army. The 241st FA Bn. had 263 consecutive days in combat supporting XX Corps, commanded by General Walto H. Walker. The 241st was the first artillery battalion in the 3rd U. S. Army to fire from German soil (Nov. 20, 1944).

I served in the 1st Cavalry Division in Japan in 1947 and in the Iwate Military Government Team as economic officer and detachment commander. Upon returning to the U.S. from Japan in 1949, I was assigned to Btry C, 38th FA Bn., 2nd Inf. Div., Ft. Lewis, Washington.

On 25 June 1950, when the North Koreans invaded South Korea, our battalion was still centered at Fort Lewis, Washington. I was battery commander there. Our battalion was NOT combat trained nor ready for combat. I had a T/O & E strength of about 70 men, out of an authorized 128. The U.S. Army at Fort Lewis was restricted in funds to buy gasoline, so we could not drive our trucks to move our howitzers for training. We had to push the pieces by manpower around the area where they were parked. Training was not as high a priority as the Post Household Details and other cost saving jobs for soldiers. Louis Johnson, the Secretary of Defense, announced that he was cutting the fat out of the military.

(About May of 1950, I had been asked to rate our combat effectiveness. I turned in a report that we were 35% effective, which I believed was honest. I was told that the Division Artillery Commanding General changed my report to 75%. I served in World War II for nine months as a Battery Commander of a 105 mm artillery battery in General Patton's 3rd U.S. Army in Europe and was qualified to make the judgment of 35%.)

The Division was alerted on 9 July 1950 for shipment to Korea. About 5,000 replacements were needed to bring the Division up to strength. We worked many long hours getting the equipment repaired or replaced, packed and crated, and also welcoming our replacements. While we were enroute to Korea, crossing the Pacific Ocean, we had our men practice firing their carbines and weapons into the ocean to get them acquainted with their firearms.

On a personal note, going to Korea meant leaving my wife of four years and our 20 month old son. Like everyone else, I was scared. However, in spite of the fear of being killed or wounded by enemy fire, we did our job. I have talked to many soldiers, officers and enlisted men, of World War II and Korea, and I have never met one who said he was not scared or afraid of dying. However, throughout both wars, I did not know of anyone in my unit, including myself, who ever thought about deserting.

During the Korean War, I held the rank of Captain and was Commanding Officer, Battery "C," 38th Field Artillery Battalion, 2nd Infantry Division, U.S. Army. The 38th FA Battalion had eighteen 105mm Howitzers and the men necessary to operate and support the firing battery. Battery "C" had six 105mm Howitzers. The mission of the artillery is to provide close artillery fire on enemy targets for the infantry. We do that by sending forward observers to live and work with the infantry units. We also had two light airplanes to provide observation and direct artillery support to the infantry. Our battalion destroyed howitzers and equipment and attempted to get back to friendly lines by foot. Some made it and others were killed or captured. I was in combat from August to December of 1950, before I was captured.

Edward Sheffield

The 25th day of June 1950 the war started in Korea. It all happened so quickly and unexpectedly. We were alerted immediately. The 24th division was stationed at Camp Hakata, Japan, less than 200 miles from Korea. We were occupation forces in Japan using and maintaining the same old equipment that was used in World War II. For the first six days, we helped evacuate the military establishments and dependents of the personnel from Korea. We were restricted to the post—all passes pulled.

On the 2nd day of July, the air raid sounded again. All men were ordered to report to their company and wait further instructions. Our instructions were to pack our equipment and combat gear, load all weapons and ammunition. We were told that we would load on LST's the next morning for Puson, Korea, and anyone who wanted to write home better do it then. We landed in Puson the 4th of July and transferred our equipment to railroad cars.

The morning of the 5th of July we were on the front lines with our obsolete equipment. Some of the 24th Division had been flown over two days before and had been fighting with the South Korean troops. Our mission was to delay and hold the North Korean Army as much and as long as we possibly could or until the authorities could get more divisions of fighting men in Korea.

One division of ill-equipped soldiers can't hold out long against an army the size of the North Korean army. I was with an artillery unit which normally supports the infantry front line soldiers with big guns, but the situation in Korea was quite different. By the third day, nearly all infantry units were wiped out so we started pulling back from one position to another firing a few rounds at a time, sometimes point blank at enemy tanks, with 105 Howitzers.

In that country there are only a few substandard roads and two or three railroads. It was very difficult for us to move our big guns and find positions for them in the mountain terrain.

James H. Ransier

Having been 12 years old just prior to the Japanese bombing of Pearl Harbor on December 7, 1941, I became caught up in the war effort and the patriotic feeling that everyone had. As a Boy Scout, I can remember being assigned as a messenger at the town hall and during the practice blackouts would deliver messages by bicycle to various points in town, as would other Scouts, while the Civil Defense people went through various exercises. Like others our age, we wanted to enlist as soon as we could and would even worry that the war would end before we could enlist.

In 1948, and not yet knowing what exactly I wanted to do in the future, I enlisted in the U.S. Army for a period of one year of active duty followed by six years in the reserve. I took basic training at Camp Hood, Texas, home of the 2nd Armored Division, and was then assigned to an armored infantry company. About one week later I decided to audition for the 2nd Armored Division Band. I was accepted as a drummer and spent the rest of the year on a tour of several concerts and parades and was the drummer in a six-piece combo playing dance jobs at the officer's club, enlisted men's club in camp and every Saturday night at the U.S.O. Center in Waco, Texas.

At the end of my one year of duty in July of 1949, I went home and decided to attend college. In September on my second day at school as a sophomore, I received word from my parents that I had received a letter from the War Department, and I was to report to Fort Campbell, Kentucky, for refresher training prior to being sent to Korea.

The result was mixed emotions when the notice to report came. I did not want to postpone my education, but I was anxious to serve my country like so many others had done. I also felt the

29

invasion of South Korea, a country in the process of becoming a democracy, by North Korea, a Communist country, was wrong, and we should help South Korea prevent it from happening.

When I arrived in Korea, I was assigned to the 7th Infantry Division, 32nd RCT, 3rd Battalion, "I" Company, as an infantryman. As such I carried an M-1 Rifle, a bayonet and two hand grenades. We were in the mountains on the east side of the Korean peninsula and about four to six miles below the 38th parallel. Each day fighting was very much the same. At dawn we would fight our way up a hill to drive the North Koreans off. If this was accomplished, we would then dig in to defend against a possible counter attack. The terrain of each hill often differed greatly as did the North Korean's effort to defend it.

When I arrived at and joined "I" Company, it was after dark. I was taken to the top of the ridge they took that same day and was shown a shallow foxhole to get into and told I was now on guard duty until relieved. I can honestly say I had no trouble staying awake. I was there for two hours and then my relief man came and took over. Then when I got into my sleeping bag at the bottom of the hill, I had no trouble staying awake wondering what the morning light would bring and how would I react.

The next morning we awoke just prior to the sun beginning to light the dark sky. We were to eat our "C" rations as fast as possible so as to be back up the hill and start down the other side to be ready for our advance up the next slope. (This might be a good time to mention the weather. It was either cold or colder.) We then advanced to the top of the ridge and started down the other side. Then we started up the hillside to the next ridge. It did not take the North Koreans long to see that we were coming. Mortar rounds started to come down around us and as we continued to move up the slope, small arms fire also could be heard. The noise and the confusion continued to increase. There were times when I was so excited, I would think to myself, "You are crazy."

In looking up at the ridge we were trying to take, I could see heads pop up and then disappear. Rifle barrels would rest on the ridge and then fire along with burp guns (an automatic weapon similar to the tommy-gun used by Chicago gangsters during Prohibition). I soon decided just to keep firing at the top of the ridge, and keep the bullets as close to the top of the ridge as I could. I thought if they kept hearing bullets zinging close to their heads, they might not look to see what they were shooting at. I don't have the slightest idea as to the success of my theory but I do know it kept me and my mind busy as we continued to move up. As we got nearer to the top of the ridge, the North Koreans' firing became less and less.

Then, they rolled a few concussion grenades down the hill. At that moment two of them stood up with their hands in the air. Just as I was thinking that we had it won, someone yelled, "They have hand grenades," and at that moment their hands came down as they threw four of our own grenades (taken from dead American soldiers) at us. I didn't react fast enough to think of shooting them, but others did as I dropped to the ground. When we reached the top, the two who threw the grenades were dead along with a good number of other dead and wounded. The medics would be there soon, as they worked their way up the hill taking care of our own wounded. Once all of our own had been attended to, they would take care of the North Koreans.

We then started to dig in so as to repel any counter attack they might try. That night as I lay on the ground in my sleeping bag with the temperature well below zero, I could not help but think of how warm our house always was when it was cold outside. (Even now, as my wife and I sit in our warm home on a cold night and feel the warmth of our wood-burning stove, I often think of Korea and just how cold everyone was all the time, both night and day. There was just no place to go and really get warm.)

For the six weeks or so that I was with the 32nd RCT, our days and nights were very similar. There were a few times the squad I was in had to go on patrol. I hated going on patrol. Excitement in a fire fight was probably a mix of adrenaline and fear, but patrol was all fear. Being cold and dirty and sweaty was our life style. We each were smelling like a can of garbage in August that hadn't been emptied for three weeks. At least no one could complain! We were all in the same can.

An old saying—that I believe to be true—goes, "You'll find no atheist in a foxhole." While in Korea, I believe I prayed every night. As a young boy, I had the good fortune to have parents who went to church and Sunday school on a regular basis. As a result, I grew up not questioning the existence of God. He was the Living God, the one who created heaven and earth and us. As I grew older, I still believed in God, but I did not know him. This was a fact that I did not become aware of until after I returned home from Korea and had time to dwell on all that had happened.

Andrew (Chief) Aguirre

My reaction to finding out I was going to war the first time, in 1944, when I was drafted into WW II, was casual as I had been on my own since I was 14 years old working out in the fields doing stoop labor. I had been forced to discontinue school when in the eighth grade.

I first left home when I was fifteen when I joined a group of box makers. We used to follow the crops in California, Washington, Oregon and Idaho. We made boxes for tomatoes, lettuce and other vegetables, so I was used to being away from home and did not mind it a bit as I loved being independent.

One of my good friends had joined the Marine Corps and urged me to join also. At 18 years of age, I looked forward to all the adventure and excitement that the Marine Corps was offering. I was in WW II for 2 years and 3 months, in Guadalcanal, the Russell Islands, Okinawa and Tientsin, China. I was stationed in Kobe, Japan, before going to Korea.

By the time Korea came along, I had already been in one assault landing in Okinawa and had spent one year in Tientsin, China. So, by 1950 I was quite mature (25 years old) and took going to war in Korea as just another adventure. After WW II,

I had joined the Marine Corps Active Reserve, and I had no choice about going. When I left for the Korean War, I left a girlfriend behind who waited for me. To this day, after 42 years, she is still my wife.

During WW II, I was an operator in an amphibious tractor battalion. An amphibious tractor is a tractor/tank that can travel and move on land and sea and capable of carrying troops, equipment and supplies. I was driving one of these during the assault landing in Okinawa in April of 1945. When I went to Korea in 1950, I was in a tank battalion. I was a gunner and fired the main turret gun which was a 90 mm that was fired in conjunction with a 30 Caliber machine gun. I came out of WW II as a corporal and later came out of Korea a three stripe Sergeant.

In WW II, our objective was to take in infantry troops and secure the beaches, then take supplies and ammunition to the front. In the Korean War, our objective was to support the infantry in taking towns and cities like Seoul and Inchon and other important objectives like airfields. In Korea, we were always on the move and never stayed in one place long enough to interface with the population, consequently I never made friends with any of the locals. Since we did not trust any of the adult locals, we kept them at bay and at a distance. The only ones we got a little friendly with were the street waifs who were always following us for whatever we would give them. It was heart wrenching to see them cry and carry on when we had to leave them behind, knowing there was nobody to care for them, and they had a long war to survive.

It was very exciting in combat, and one never knew what the new day would bring. Usually in combat one never has time to think too much, and one acts by instinct relying on one's past training and experience. It is after the battles that one thinks about it. In spite of all that happened in the battle, one never thinks he is going to get killed. It is always the other guy who will get killed, not me. It is always in a laughing manner that combatants will discuss the happenings of the day's battle. Fear is put aside by the excitement and the movement of the battle.

When you get a group of young men together, they will always find a way to jest and joke about each other or life in general. They will laughingly relate what they did or what some one else did and make a big joke of practically everything. Serious situations will be downplayed by joking and making smart remarks about them. So in regards to the question about having any good times, yes, we did have good times with many moments of bizarre, unconventional fun.

I relied on my training, experience, upbringing, the companionship and camaraderie of my fellow Marines to keep going. One does not go insane just because one is in a war. In fact, it is your sanity that keeps you going in spite of the many adversities. The strenuous training of boot camp will cull out any recruit with the potential for going insane in combat. I never ran out of coping skills. I coped with each situation as the situation demanded. The survival instinct within all of us instinctively finds the ways and means to cope and survive. I never adjusted to being there. What I did do was resign myself to being there, knowing it was only a temporary condition and would not last forever.

Was I scared? Everybody is a little apprehensive and tense before going into combat, and this might be mistaken for fear. Fear can be controlled by reasoning. By this I mean you can reason what is coming and what the outcome will be if you remember your training and do as you're told. Fear is different from being apprehensive and tense because even if you are tense and apprehensive, you will perform and obey orders. Those with fear will not perform and obey, but seek an escape from the reality of the noise and sights of war which has overwhelmed them. Many of these individuals seek protective shelters and stay in them, hoping they will not be detected until the battle ends or moves beyond them.

It was not my job to try to understand why I was there and what I was fighting for. I was there because my country wanted me there, and I was fighting because the Marine Corps had trained me to fight and expected me to fight well and uphold the Marine Corps fighting tradition.

I did not have an opinion of the war at the time. I joined the Marine Corps expecting to fight and that was exactly what I was doing. I was trained and raised that when my country and the Marine Corps wanted me to fight, that is exactly what I would do. In other words "Mine was not to question why, mine was just to do or die." The Marine Corps and all the training they had given me kept me going throughout the war. Also, it would have been a disgrace for me to give up in front of my Marine peers. Every man has a certain amount of pride, self-esteem and ego which he must maintain and uphold.

I never had any personal problems that I could not handle. I was at the age where there really is no personal problems and what problems there were lost in the company of my fellow Marines. Deserting was the last thing on my mind. It may be hard to believe, but most of the American fighting men unconsciously like combat. Why? I do not know. Perhaps it is expecting the unexpected; perhaps it is a challenge that we accept to see if we can measure up to it and are able to handle it. Then, perhaps it is the training we were given and the weapons we possessed that made us feel invincible, with the power of life or death over other individuals. Perhaps it is that we were brainwashed by the Marine Corps. After I got out of the Communist prisoner of war camps; many people asked me if the Chinese had brainwashed me. I said, "No. The Marine Corps beat them to it."

I feel that a deserter is the lowest and most detested person in the military because he has not only let himself down, but worse, has let his buddies down. In the event he did succeed in deserting, he could never live with himself and most likely would commit suicide in disgrace. No, it is better to fight and take your chances on getting killed and the possibility of getting a million dollar wound (a combat wound that they will send you home) and going home feeling that you did your job (I was never wounded in spite of all the exposure to combat. While others around me did, I never even received a scratch. I guess I was one of the lucky ones who had someone watching over me.)

What was it like to have someone die in front of you? If the dying person was a gook enemy, then it was a feeling of apathy, and one did not get too concerned as that was what the game was all about, to have as many of them die as possible. If he was one of ours, then it was like part of ourselves was dying, and we acted accordingly, trying to make the individual as comfortable as possible, consoling him all we could.

I never experienced any prejudice in the Marine Corps even though I was of Mexican descent and looked more like a Native American. I was nicknamed "Chief," and I liked it, as "Chief" identified me with the American Indian for whom I had a great respect. Prejudice exists when lack of respect for your fellow Marines exists. In the Marine Corps you gain respect by your performance. Everybody likes a good performer.

In Korea, I and my fellow tankers lived wherever we happened to find ourselves. Sometimes we were in rear areas where we slept in tents, while other times, near the front or at the front, we slept inside the tank or underneath it, depending on the situation. We did not have regular hours for eating or sleeping and being tankers, we had many time consuming chores to perform every day to keep ourselves and our equipment in fighting readiness. A typical day started with washing up a little, using the steel helmet to wash with, then making a fire to warm up the canned breakfast and to make coffee. After eating we would check things such as weapons, ammunition, make sure the canteens were full of water as one consumes much water in combat because your mouth gets very dry with the excitement and anxiety of battle. To help alleviate the thirst, I would always have a large wad of chewing gum in my mouth. I would relieve some of the tension and excitement by constant chewing.

It isn't long before the word comes out, "Wind them up." This means start the tanks and stand by to move out, which we soon did, moving in a tank column toward the front. Arriving at the front we were greeted by the infantry who was always glad to see us, and they always inquired as to how many tanks we have. The greater the number, the happier they were. The tank commanders would usually attend a briefing of what was expected in the day's push, then they would return and mount the tanks, and soon we were moving out ahead and in front of the infantry.

When asked if I ever killed anyone and how it felt, I can say that I, as a gunner on a tank, did kill many gooks, but they were not kills that were real close. Most of them happened while I was inside the tank, and the gooks were out in the fields, houses, or trenches on the hillsides. I never felt anything; it was the normal thing to do, and I did it. It was expected of me. This is what I had been trained to do. These gooks were abstract individuals whom I had never seen before, had nothing to do with them prior to this encounter, did not know them or would ever know them, so in a way, for me, they did not exist. They were just abstract individuals; the quicker we got rid of them, the quicker we could go home. This was the way I felt when the kills were from inside the tank, but it was a little different when the kill was face to face.

As I said, most of my battles, with the exception of a few which occurred on foot patrols, were fought from inside of a tank. My first tank battle was when we were pushing toward the capital of South Korea, Seoul. We stopped pushing to refuel and re-supply and were doing this when, all of a sudden, mortars and lots of small arm fire started to come in. Some of our tank crew was socializing, but managed to get back into the tank. With all of our crew in position, we went to the enemy. Most of them were in this village in front of us and were hidden well.

I spotted an electrical transformer on a post in the middle of the village so I fired a 90mm into it making it explode and the explosion set all the electrical wires on fire which raced down to the huts setting them all on fire. It was amidst the fighting that the loader says, "Chief, look over to the left by those trees. There seems to be some tires there."

I traversed the turret and saw the tires were part of an anti-tank gun which was firing at the tank in front of us. I opened up with the turret machine gun killing all the people manning the gun. After this, I switched to other targets and again the loader says "Chief, there are some gooks crawling toward the gun. "

I turned the 90 mm toward the anti-tank gun and told the loader to load me a heavy explosive shell. I fired at the anti-tank gun, blowing it to pieces. The gooks retreated and when we started to back off, the tank in front of us drove off the left track, which had been chewed up by the anti-tank gun. We got the crippled tank out of the fire zone and wasted no time going after the retreating gooks. Some of the enemy soldiers were retreating among the panic stricken civilians so I could not get them without killing some civilians. I waited until a large number of enemy soldiers separated themselves from the civilians and were far enough away from the civilians for me to fire. I fired the 90 mm, killing all of them.

In this same area, the following day, we were pushing and all was quiet as we passed many fields of corn and other plantings. The tank commander says "Chief, fire a white phosphorous shell into that field and see what you can scare up." When a white phosphorous shell explodes it splatters white phosphorous all over and will set fire to whatever it makes contact with. In humans, it will stick to the skin and start to burn through the flesh. Shortly after the shell landed, a large number of enemy soldiers got up and started running for this house nearby. Instead of dispersing themselves, the soldiers ran in a group. I fired a 90 mm into the group, killing most of them. The remaining few regrouped, and again I fired into them. By this time only a few remained, and these managed to make it to this house nearby. I poured about three 90mm shells into the house, blowing it all to pieces and killing the remaining soldiers.

On another occasion, we were pushing to Seoul and were going through an area which supposedly had been cleared of enemy soldiers. We had five tanks and a flame throwing tank and a platoon of engineers with us. The terrain was hilly, and we were moving on a railroad track. Everything was going good without any firing, until we came to a small railroad station. Then we started to receive a tremendous amount of small arms fire. Off to our left was a cave, and in front of it was a series of ditches which were full of enemy infantry. It was hard to determine how many there were, but there were many. So many that our 60 man engineer platoon could not attack them. The terrain also was such that our tanks could not get to them, so it was a stand off for awhile. We could keep them at bay with our tank fire power so they could not attack us, but we did not have enough infantry for a frontal attack.

Then the flame-throwing tank moved up and managed to get close enough to reach the cave and the ditches. After taking care of the cave, he placed a great amount of burning flames on top of the ditches. The flames suspended for a few seconds then dropped into the ditches on top of the enemy soldiers. They soon came out of the ditches with their clothes burning and their hands in the air, and many were rolling on the ground screaming and trying to rid themselves of the burning material that was burning through their flesh. The infantry wasted no time in collecting their weapons and stripping off their clothes, leaving them naked. It was then that we saw that there were two women with them. Some Marines gave them a couple of field jackets to cover themselves. The men remained naked. The count revealed we had captured 250 prisoners. I never did find out how many were left dead or wounded in the cave and in the ditches.

We continued our trek to Seoul, still going on the rail road tracks. It was a strange procession as the naked prisoners were in front followed by some engineers, who in turn were followed by our six tanks, then some more engineers. We were moving sort of relaxed, pondering the recent engagement when the radio became alive. Everybody seemed to be yelling at the same time to say enemy gooks were running toward a village nearby. It seems that about three hundred of them had been waiting and hiding in the tall grass, adjacent to the rail road tracks, waiting to ambush us, but must have gotten scared at the sight of the six tanks and in a wild panic and in disarray left their hiding places and were running in the open fields toward the village. It did not take long for the tanks to start chopping them down. It was a turkey shoot, and very few made it to the first houses in the village. These houses were soon systematically destroyed and were burning as we poured shell after shell of 90 mm's into them. While all this was going on, the naked prisoners we had were made to lie down on the ground. We finally made it to Seoul where we were relieved of the prisoners, and we went to support a regiment that was going to jump off into Seoul.

There were many more engagements and to tell them all would take a long time but those described above were typical of much of the action in Korea for us in the tank battalion. One more that I could tell about here was the closest I came to being killed. It was when I was on a patrol trying to find the North Koreans (the enemy), and we had a stupid lieutenant leading the patrol. We were walking abreast through this open valley in a rice paddy which was surrounded on both sides by a thick forest, when suddenly an enemy machine gun opens up on the patrol and soon has it pinned down. My sergeant jumps to his feet and starts to run in the direction of the machine gun. As he is running, he turns and hollers at me to follow him. I could see the bullets hitting the ground at his feet as I was running behind him. The sergeant made it to the edge of the forest, and the enemy machine gunner then turns his weapon on me. I could see the ground jumping in the air around my feet as if an invisible shovel was scooping it up. I could also hear the bullets whining as they ricocheted by my feet. I stumbled and fell. Instinctively, I rolled to the side and as I was lying there, I looked where I had fallen and I could see the spot being splattered with machine gun fire. I managed to make it to the edge of the forest and joined my Sergeant. We then crawled close enough to the enemy machine gun to knock it out with concussion grenades. My sergeant was awarded the Silver Star for this action.

I remember many things and incidents, but mostly I remember the guys I served with and with the many great guys I interfaced with. Each person I remember is associated with some incident or incidents which I remember vividly and a certain place or a certain time. Those people I remember most were my three crew men who I was caught with. My loader was a small 18 year old kid who never questioned an order and would perform as expected of a Marine. The driver was kind of jittery and would scare easy; he required cussing and swearing to make him perform to par. He refused to drive when we most needed him. The assistant driver was a kid who was in a band as a saxophone player and did not know a thing about tanks. He was a replacement for a 17 year old in our crew. Shortly before making the assault landing in Inchon, Korea, all 17 year olds were removed from front line combat units.

I never saw my friends die. When I saw them, they were already dead. Even so, I got sad and empty, like part of me had died, and all my active association with my dead friends kept coming to my mind. I always thought they had died because they had not had the experience and the knowledge of warfare to have survived and had no business being in this war. In Koto-Ri, a plateau near the Chosin Reservoir, I attended a mass burial of dead members of the Army, Marine Corps and British Marines who were killed during the Chosin Reservoir battle and could not be brought out with us when we would break out of the entrapment. It was tearful seeing all those frozen bodies in the frozen positions they died in. Many had outstretched arms and legs. Some of them were curled up while some were in the fetal position. They were frozen in these positions and could not be re-positioned by moving the arms and legs. Many of these men had suffocated on their own blood as they were bleeding from the mouth and nose. After getting hit, the blood just kept freezing until it finally it finally sealed off the air channels. They were laid side by side followed by burial services conducted by a Baptist, a Catholic, a Jewish rabbi, and a British chaplain. After the services, a bulldozer covered them up for eternal sleep in the God forsaken frozen mountains of North Korea.

Richard Makua

During the war I was a forward observer with the Army's 7th Division. I was a staff sergeant, an infantryman with a rifle company. We were a heavy mortar company, using 4.2 mortars. I had about 3 months training before going to Korea. Yes, I do feel that training helped prepare me for combat.

I had no choice about going off to war, as I was drafted. When I found out I was going to Korea, I got drunk. But I didn't regret going since it was for my country.

When I went off to the war, I had a girlfriend I had to leave behind; at least I thought she was my girlfriend! She got married while I was in Korea. It really broke my heart, but after awhile I got over it and got myself together as time passed.

I was in the war about a month before being captured. What was my opinion on the war at the time I was there? It was, "What in the hell am I doing here?" Yes, I was scared. And it felt like hell to see my friends die.

What kept me going during the war was the knowledge that I was fighting so my children wouldn't have to come here or go through anything like this.

There was close friendship in my squad. I tried to keep my squad close, but then there were blacks and whites in my squad, and sometimes you got to keep 'em in line. Nobody wanted the job, so I was chosen. There was a little bit of prejudice among the troops I was with at first; then everyone got adjusted to one another. I had to give medical aid when one guy had a leg wounded and no one wanted to help him, so I helped him with his wounds.

Joseph Wilson

I didn't react too good when I found out I was going to Korea. I didn't know anything about Korea. They didn't say anything. I changed. I was not happy before I was sent to Korea. I had been in the Army about 6 months before I went to Korea. I had been drafted and had about 14 weeks of basic training. I left behind a wife and son, Charley. My wife's name was Rose Heereas; we had been married 6 years. We were living in Honduras, Central America.

42

I was in the all black Company K, of the Army's 25th Infantry Division serving as a rifleman, with the rank of P.F.C. I carried an M-1 rifle. Our objective was to take a hill and hold it. Did I fully understand why I was fighting and what I was fighting for? No, not at all.

Theo Baudoin, Jr.

The war in Korea was from June 25, 1950 to July 26, 1953. It lasted three years, one month and two days. I was a prisoner of war there for 33 months. I was 17 when I volunteered in the Army. One year later I was on the front line in Korea. I was with the 2nd Engineer Combat Battalion, 2nd Infantry Division.

I was in Headquarters and Service Company. We were a bridge company that built pontoon bridges, cleared mines, and did some demolition work. We also had a water purification unit, and sometimes we did some reconnaissance. We also had five Sherman tanks equipped with bulldozer blades. That was our assault squad. During the time I was in Korea, I had been assigned at one time or the other to each one of these units.

I was at Ft. Lewis, Washington when the Korean War broke out. We were immediately put on alert, and then sent to Korea. We went to Korea aboard the Victory troop ship named the *General S.S. Greely*. It was a 14 day sea voyage, very crowded aboard this ship. We ate and slept in 8 hour shifts.

When we arrived in Pusan, Korea, the situation was that we only had a perimeter of about 50 miles held by South Koreans, and Americans. The North Korean Armies were ready to make their final assault and completely take over South Korea.

We were moved to an area outside Miryang to prepare us to ready a pontoon bridge to cross the Nacktong River. We finally got a bridge built, but the North Koreans made an all out assault and sent our infantry retreating through our lines. The 2nd. Engineers rifle companies held until a Marine Brigade was sent in to assist. With the Marines, we again retook lost ground. We built our bridge, and the 9th Infantry and support units crossed the Nacktong River and moved north.

The enemy was now retreating. It was here we discovered the atrocities the North Koreans had committed. Twenty-six American soldiers had their hands tied behind their backs with communication wire and had been lined up shoulder to shoulder and machine gunned with burp guns. Their feet were bare and bloody from having been forced to walk on the rocky terrain.

By the middle of September, United Nations Forces had landed at Inchon. Seoul, the South Korean Capital, was recaptured. UN troops moved northward. We had moved up through the North Korean Capital, Pyongyang, and set up our command post in Sunchon, North Korea in a silk mill.

We were told that on October 20th, hundreds of paratroopers of the 187th Airborne Regimental Combat Team were dropped from C-119 flying box cars. This was to cut the fleeing North Korean Army's escape route. Also to try and intercept about 370 American prisoners the North Koreans had and were moving north by rail. Outside of Sunchon, the bodies of 73 Americans were found. They had been dumped from box cars they had been packed in. They had died of dysentery, starvation, and exposure. The trains were hidden by day in the many tunnels. There, in a tunnel, 100 Americans were found shot as they waited for their meal. Two days later, near Kujang-dong about 30 miles northeast of Sunchon, 28 more Americans were found.

Wayne A. (Johnnie) Johnson

I was born December 16, 1931, in Lima, Ohio. I am the son of Archer L. (deceased) and Elizabeth Johnson. I have two brothers, Roger L. and Dean R. Johnson and a sister, Karen Thomas of Lima. I have a son, Johnnie W. Johnson and a daughter, Rachelle J. Weitz of Lima. I attended Lima Central High School.

At 17 years of age I enlisted in the Army and was sent to Fort Knox, Kentucky, then overseas to Camp Wood, Kumamoto,

Japan, in May, 1949, where I was a scout in "L" Company, 21st Infantry Regiment, 24th Infantry Division.

Then when the Korean War broke out, and my Division was sent and during the first week of fighting, my unit was over-run, and I was captured on July 11, 1950. I was listed as Missing in Action for one and a half years; my family was then notified that I was a Prisoner of War, which I remained for three years, one and a half months.

CHAPTER THREE

"INTO THE HANDS OF THE ENEMY"

Jack Chapman

On November 29th, 1950, a platoon of heavy weapons, from Dog Company, 31st Regiment, with Lieutenant White as our Platoon Leader, under the commander of Baker Company, 31st Infantry, Captain Charles Peckham was made part of "Task Force Drysdale," (named for Lieutenant Colonel Douglas B. Drysdale, Commanding Officer of the British 41st Independent Commando, Royal Marines.)

This Task Force included 235 members of the Royal Marines, about 205 US Marines of Captain Carl Sitter's "G" Company, some 190 soldiers of Captain Peckham's Baker Company, 31st RCT, and about 82 U.S. Marines (clerks, truck drivers, military policemen, and several U.S. Navy corpsmen attached to the 1st Marine Division.) Task Force Drysdale numbered around 900 men with armor support. Its mission was to cut through the Chinese Communist forces along the 10-14 miles of road between Koto-ri and Hagaru-ri.

Task Force Drysdale was formed when General Smith ordered Colonel Puller on November 28th, to send him "desperately needed reinforcements, to hold Hagaru-Ri." General Smith wanted reinforcements, although it meant that they would suffer heavy casualties in reaching Hagaru-ri.

Colonel Puller's 1st Marines still had the job of opening the road and reinforcing Hagaru. At the same time they had their hands full defending the Koto-ri perimeter. Colonel Puller could spare only one rifle company of his own units to reinforce the Marines to the north. Clearly this was insufficient, particularly in light of the action fought by Dog and Fox Companies that

46

same day. Therefore a composite unit was formed on November 28th consisting of personnel from ten different organizations.

The 41st Independent Commando, Royal Marines, had just arrived at Koto-ri these 250 Royal Marines had come up to join the American Marines. They had only recently arrived in Korea and had not yet seen any combat. Lieutenant Colonel Douglas B. Drysdale, commander, 41st Commando was assigned to lead the composite force which bore his name.

After commencing the move north, the task force was reinforced with 29 tanks, 76 vehicles and trailers, and 210 Marines from four different Marine units. Their arrival made the task force virtually to a battalion size. The official Marine Corps history of the operation accounts for approximately 922 men, plus vehicles, trailers and tanks. In spite of its impressive numerical total, the heterogeneous make-up of the unit rendered much of it ineffective as a fighting organization. This fact soon became evident.

Wednesday morning, November 29, 1950, in the still bitter cold of North Korea, we, the newly formed Task Force Drysdale, engaged enemy elements of the Communist Chinese People's Army. We did not realize how extremely perilous our position was or that soon the "Million Hordes" of latter day Genghis Khans were to come screaming down upon us.

November 29, at 0945 hours, the mist hung low over the snow covered country side as Task Force Drysdale attacked toward Hagaru-ri. Slight resistance was encountered a few hundred yards beyond Koto-ri. Resistance increased steadily thereafter, and our progress was slow. The column inched its way northward, with constant halts and starts.

The snow lay deep on the hills, and it was bitter cold as our convoy moved out for Hagaru-ri. Behind the British Commandos came Baker Company, 31st Infantry. Huddled in the trucks, our heads were buried deep in our field jackets against the biting cold, and at first we did not hear the sharp crack of small-arms fire, and then mortars rounds began to fall and the machine guns opened up and a truck about one third of the way along the mile long column began to burn.

As the brakes slammed on and the trucks skidded to a stop on the icy road, we came to a halt on the narrow road, a hand grenade landed in the bed of our truck near my feet and without thinking, I grabbed the grenade and tossed it out of the truck toward the railroad. We jumped from the vehicles and dove for the ditch on the side of the road. It was not really a ditch, but a low place between the railroad embankment on one side and the roadbed on the other.

The Chinese began to lob a steady rain of mortar shells, and from the hills, they raked the ditch banks with machine gun fire. They did not come in close then. Our aircraft, seeing the burning truck on the road, swooped back and forth all day, rocketing and strafing the Chinese.

The resistance that we had encountered earlier stopped, and we mistakenly believed that the Communists had withdrawn and that we were in the clear. The head of the column, which included the 41st Commandos, a Marine rifle company and several tanks pushed their way on to Hagaru-ri.

The center of the column was barred by the damaged truck and the Chinese small arms fire and mortar fire prevented its removal. Our communications had been lost because of the weather, distance, terrain, and other circumstances, so neither the front nor the rear of the convoy realized that the center of the column had been cut off. Included in the center column was some 41st Commandos, most of Baker Company, Marine Military Police Detachment and some Marines from service and support units.

As darkness set in, the center portion of the task force came under increasing heavy fire. The Chinese had succeeded in splitting the task force even further, reducing it to one large perimeter and three small sections. Casualties mounted, and bodies were stacked around the hastily formed perimeter. Freezing temperatures threatened to take an even greater toll. We made an attempt to turn our vehicles around and get back to Koto-ri. This attempt was unsuccessful for the section of the convoy that I was in and darkness found us cut off from both Koto-ri and Hagaru-ri.

On November 29/30, 1950, as soon as darkness put an end to the Marine air strikes, all hell broke loose. As the night came on, the Chinese became increasingly bold; they started firing again, just enough to keep us on our toes. There was no attempt for several hours to close within grenade throwing distance.

It was a clear, bright, starlit night, and the truck burning in the road made more light, and you could see them coming by the hundreds across the snow. They had our convoy zeroed in, and we had only the dubious cover of our vehicles and the shallow ditches on either side of the road and the narrow railway for our protection from their rifle fire and grenades. They did not bother to creep or crawl, but just came on, walking, and from the ditch we kept up a steady fire.

Early during the evening of November 29th, I received my first wound, a shrapnel wound to the left arm, nothing serious. My wound was cared for and I refused to return to Koto-ri. I returned to my squad and shortly thereafter, I was again wounded, a shrapnel wound to my right leg. This time I returned to the Aid station, only to find that the corpsman was too busy treating more serious wounded men. I returned to my position. Around 2100 hours, November 29th, the gunner, a sergeant, from my squad jumped down from the weapon and refused a direct order from Captain Peckham, Commander of Baker Company, to reassume his position. This sergeant got down on his hands and knees in front of the vehicle and started praying.

The fighting was pretty bad at this time. One of the men standing next to me, got a bullet in the forehead. The bullet went through his skull and embedded itself in his helmet.

Captain Peckham finally told the sergeant that he was going to recommend him for a court martial, however, the sergeant still refused. Captain Peckham tried to find someone to take over the rifle, without success. Finally, I told Captain Peckham that

I would take over the rifle. Captain Peckham then stated, "You are to be commended and cited for valor."

During this action, I received shrapnel wounds to the left leg, and a bullet wound to the right arm and right leg. What was left of my 75 mm recoilless rifle crew continued to fire the rifle at any enemy gun/mortar flashes until I was shot in the forehead and the gun put out of action. I had just finished reloading the rifle when I was hit in the head, right above the right eye and I did not get a chance to fire it. Sergeant Charles Hrobak from Baker Company, had just informed me that this was the last 75 mm round.

I had a pack of Phillip Morris cigarettes (C-ration cigarettes from World War II) in the left breast pocket of my field jacket. It was about two days after being captured that I noticed a hole in my field jacket pocket. When I pulled the cigarette pack out, I found a burp gun bullet in the pack. This pack of C-ration cigarettes had saved my life.

The Chinese ambushed Task Force Drysdale about one half-way to Hagaru-ri, in what became known as "HELL'S FIRE VALLEY" and cut us to pieces. The higher ground rose sharply on the right of the road, while on the left a frozen creek wound through a field several hundred yards wide, bordered by the Changjin River.

This was "HELL'S FIRE VALLEY," name applied by Colonel Drysdale, and it was the scene of an all-night fight by more than half of Task Force Drysdale. The valley was about one mile long, covered with a frozen crust of snow and did not afford much cover, it offered the enemy a convenient approach to the rear by the Communists having the advantage as they were entrenched on the upper regions of the precipitous slope.

We had a railroad to our right that was covered with Chinese, and an open field to our left with a small stream and the Changjin river running through it, with the Communists dug in and a mountain to cross.

About fifty to one hundred yards ahead of us was what was left of Colonel Drysdale's 41st British Commandos, who were getting cut to pieces. They withdrew to our position sometime around 2000 hours (8 p.m.).

The Chinese Communists made screeching blasts on their damn whistles and bugles that made your flesh crawl as the sound reverberated through the chilled night air. After several minutes, the sound of gunfire, bugles and whistles died down and stopped.

The Chinese were clever, they were well trained and had perfect discipline. They enjoyed the comfort of the darkness, and during this time they would crawl in close and then with the sounds of the damn whistles, the blare of bugles, the night silence was suddenly shattered. The night was a turmoil, broken constantly with the sound of bugles, the loud blast of a whistle, and then the onslaught of the attack.

For what seemed like eternity, a death-like silence hovered over the bitter cold darkness. We listened and waited. Suddenly the eerie sounds of the bugles and whistles could be heard again, only this time much closer. We gripped our weapons, pointing them into the darkness that cloaked everything. Mortar rounds and grenades slammed into the ground close by, spraying a shower of shrapnel over us.

Here we were, United States and United Nations forces getting the hell shot out of us, running out of ammunition, with malfunctioning weapons caused by the extremely cold weather, and about half of our men either dead or seriously wounded, while wave after wave of Chinese Communists soldiers, screaming and blowing their damn bugles and whistles descended upon us. The killing was so savage that the Chinese had to climb over the bodies of their own men.

We'd shoot down a whole line of them and another line would be right behind them. They would stop to pick up the weapons of the ones who had fallen, and then they would come on like the first ones. We would shoot then down, and they just formed another line and kept on coming.

51

We had no weapon larger than our single 75mm recoilless rifle, in addition to our rifles, carbines and some grenades. What 60 and 80 mm mortars we had were without ammunition. We were nearly out of ammunition and no way of getting air support. You've got to understand what if feels like to be in combat and not have enough ammunition, or have a weapon that doesn't work. The feeling is helplessness.

Major McLaughlin assumed command of the ill-fated segment of Task Force Drysdale. It was his ill fortune to be traveling to Hagaru-ri in the capacity of liaison officer to the 1st Marine Division. He accompanied the only convoy scheduled to make the trip at that time. Initially his role was simply that of a passenger with the column. As November 29th faded into a new day, he assumed command of the battered center portion of the task force. Before November 30th was five hours old, he and his command were prisoners of the so-called Chinese Communist People's Volunteers.

Captain Peckham's Baker Company was caught in the ambush and cut to pieces. Baker Company losses were more than 100 killed or missing in action and 19 known wounded, who managed to get back to our lines. Our two squads of heavy weapons lost greatly.

Captain Peckham was taken prisoner along with Lieutenant George Snipan from Baker Company. Our platoon leader and sergeant was killed along with many of the squad members. Our assistance platoon sergeant and one squad leader were taken prisoner along with myself. Approximately 143 of us were taken prisoner during this encounter with the Chinese Communist Forces.

We were near the outskirts of the Village of Pusang-ni, and was led by Major John N. McLaughlin. Our group consisted of Captain Charles Peckham's Baker Company and attached heavy weapons squad from Dog Company, 31st. RCT, a group of Marine Military Police, some Commandos, Associated Press photographer Frank Noel and a few more Marines.

During the time that I was the gunner, I received gun shot wounds to both arms, right leg and forehead and shrapnel wounds to the hip and legs. When I got hit in the head, it felt like my head had exploded. When I came to, there was blood over my right eye. I had been hit just above the right eye. (Note: The bullet stayed there until 1964 when a young Air Force Doctor removed it to relieve my constant terrible headaches.)

All the guns were silent, and Major John McLaughlin came down the line of quiet, waiting men. He said that the Chinese had captured a mm and sent him back with the word that, if we did not surrender in fifteen minutes, we would be wiped out. Major McLaughlin was taking a poll of the men to see what they wanted to do. If we said stay and fight, he would fight. If we said give up, he would go back and tell the Chinese that, if they would give safe conduct to the wounded back to our lines, the unit would surrender. We had some hope at first that the tanks of Baker Company, 1st Tank Battalion, would come to our rescue. But they had ran into heavy opposition along the road which had been cleared only a few hours before by Task Force Drysdale.

There was some debate, for a few men wanted to hold out until day light, when our planes would come back. However, the Chinese were so close now that the planes could not strike them without hitting us. This would have meant sure death to the wounded, for by now eight out of ten men were hurt and bleeding or numb from concussion shock, and we were beginning to freeze. Ammunition dwindled and by 0300 hours, November 30th, only a hand-full of ammunition remained.

The temperature had fallen to 20 degrees below zero, and with most of our men wounded and in dire need of shelter and medical care, Major McLaughlin had no choice but to consider the Chinese demands for surrender. Our Army Medical personnel had provide what treatment they could for the wounded.

When it became obvious that further resistance by our group would be fruitless, and when the word was passed that surrender was imminent, most of the men with Major McLaughlin rendered their weapons useless by throwing vital parts into the snow or by breaking the stocks of their rifles and carbines.

Major McLaughlin went away and in a few minutes, all along the railroad bank and across the narrow road and on the hills beyond, the Chinese stood up. The Chinese had continued slipping in close during the surrender demands and when the surrender was agreed upon, many of the Chinese soldiers sprang to their feet from positions all around our perimeter and at distances as close as 20 to 30 feet away. Many of the first Chinese to enter our position weren't paying much attention to us. They were swarming over the unburned trucks, looting happily at whatever they could find.

The Chinese Communist forces who followed the first group, surprised the U.S. Marines and British Commandos by their friendly attitude. They smiled, shook hands, and clapped the Marines on the back.

Through sheer superiority in numbers, wave after wave of Chinese, in their quilted cotton uniforms, rose upon the skyline, seeming to never cease. They grabbed our weapons, ammunition, food and any other valuables they could find.

I still remember (though wounded, bleeding and in a daze) that immediately after our capture, the Chinese, who were not familiar with the 75 mm recoilless rifle, while examining it, accidentally pulled the trigger. As I mentioned early, I had just reloaded the weapon and before I could fire it, I was shot in the forehead. About four of their officers who were standing to the rear of the weapon were completely disintegrated by the terrible back blast of the weapon, and though I was half conscious, I had the urge to smirk at my captors inexperience with modern weaponry.

At about 0300-0400 hours, on the morning of November 30th, 1950, what remained of our unit, a few Americans and British Marines, was sadly overrun by the Chinese Communists forces, during the bloody fighting at HELL'S FIRE VALLEY.

Though plainly outlined against the snow in the early morning hours, they were virtually unopposed and came in a never ending advance that climaxed in their overpowering of all the United Nations forces in this area.

Just prior to being shot in the head, Captain Peckham informed me, and what was left of my crew, that we were to be commended and cited for valor.

Despite my suffering and pain, I soon realized that I was lucky compared with several of my fellow men, who would probably die from their more serious wounds.

I remember one soldier lying on the ground next to me with half of his stomach blown away by a Japanese type mortar. He kept crying and screaming for help, only to be rolled off of the road to die by the Chinese Communists.

Immediately after our capture, the Chinese ordered the wounded to board the trucks which were undamaged (we thought that we were being returned to our lines). However, after a few minutes, we were ordered to dismount. The Chinese reneged on their promise to Major McLaughlin to permit the evacuation of the wounded to Koto-ri.

Soon most of us (approximately 143) were hastily herded into some farm houses which were hidden in a depression in the mountains some distance from the road. When I came to, we were in a small house, and I remember my head, arms and legs were hurting something awful. There was this terrible burning feeling, like a hot pin in my arms, legs and head. My arms, legs and head felt like they were on fire.

Not really understanding what had happened, one of the soldiers explained that we had been overrun at about 0300 hours (3 A.M.) and that only a small number of us had survived this ordeal. What I did not consider was the possibility that for the next thirty-three months I would be fighting just to survive.

I do not know, as I was half conscious from bleeding and shock, exactly how long we remained there in this house. I was told that we were kept there one day and a night. When we lay down to sleep, we would lie very close together for warmth. During the miserable cold morning, the Communists fed us a can of corn for each five men and they herded us outside for a miserable, unforgettable death march to our first Prisoner of War camp at Kanggye, North Korea.

Richard Rook

I was captured on May 19, 1951 at 5:45 AM. We were all taken prisoner about the same time, May 1951, during the Communist's big spring offensive. The 2nd Division was their main target because they wanted to punish us in particular for being the rear guard during the big retreat to the Pusan perimeter. After we were captured, they marched us back and forth across the peninsula to try and confuse us so we wouldn't attempt to escape. They always marched us at night to avoid air strikes from American planes.

During this time they didn't feed us very much to hinder any escape attempts. We were getting weaker and sicker by the day. We all had lice and dysentery and God knows what else because all the water we had to drink was from rice paddies which were fertilized with human waste.

During these nightly marches it was almost always raining, and it was so dark that we had to hold hands to keep from falling on the steep mountain trails. If anyone dropped out or lagged back, he was shot right in front of whoever was close by. They wanted the word to get around, and it sure did. Oh yes, to make matters worse, we were forced to carry the weapons they captured along with us. Each man had carry at least two M1s or maybe an A6 machine gun or a BAR or a Bazooka. Every man had to carry something. I can't remember how long this took place, but I think it only lasted for the first two weeks or so.

After about a month and a half, on July 3rd, 1951, we arrived at the place where I was to spend my 23rd birthday, the first of my three birthdays in captivity in North Korea. On my birthday,

July 24th, I was so close to death that it's very painful to think about it. We called this camp "The Mining Town" because somewhere, I can't remember now, we saw a couple of those little ore cars so that to this day that town is referred to as "The Mining Town." The next two-plus months, would become the worse period of not only my life as a POW, but of my entire life. By this time we were all pretty sick. We had lost several men along the trails to sickness not to mention those who were shot. We couldn't digest the "food" they were giving us, as little as it was. We all had dysentery so bad that we couldn't control ourselves.

The food, ah yes, the food. The food is easy to describe for the first three days because there wasn't any. When they finally figured out that if they didn't start feeding us, they were going to end up with a bunch dead GIs, they gave each of us a handful of something that was ground to the consistency of our baking flour. We had to use our helmets to collect this "stuff" and then try to figure out how we were suppose to eat it. It didn't come with eating instructions. We finally, after a couple of feedings, discovered that when mixed with some of that "good" rice paddy water, we could at least get it down. We very quickly named this stuff, "bug-dust."

Then we were introduced to another something that was unknown to most of us. This stuff at least had a name, sorghum. Sorghum is a grain that's quite popular over there; it's red and tasteless and cooked the same way rice is but doesn't taste near as good as rice does. The next strange food they gave us was millet. Millet is a very tiny seed that we found almost impossible to digest. Our group was not unlike any other general, run-of-the-mill group so naturally we had our share of farmers, and they informed us that in America, sorghum is fed to pigs and millet is sold as bird seed.

We were housed in what appeared to have been a school house. There were about 300 of us, and they crammed us into 3 or 4 of these big rooms. About 15 feet from the end of these buildings they had us dig a trench about 30 feet long, 6 feet wide and 5 feet deep. This was our latrine. It was out in the open without

57

any type of cover over it, and in few days it was crawling with maggots. We had no way of washing ourselves not to mention our eating utensils and the flies came directly from the latrine to our mouths. Speaking of eating utensils, mine were a rusty tin can that I had found somewhere and piece of wood that resembled a spoon.

We weren't there very long before men started dying. Every morning there would be four or five more. At first, we buried our own dead, but then after a while we were all too sick to carry the man or to dig his grave. All this time there was absolutely no medical care whatsoever.

This was one jam I didn't think I was going to get out of, and I wouldn't have if I hadn't made a pact with three other guys. We could always tell who was going to be the next to die, because he would refuse to eat and refuse to get up and try to get some exercise. The four of us promised each other that if one of us refused to eat or exercise, the remaining three would make sure that he didn't get by with it. Well, I was the first to go down.

I was so sick and so thin that I didn't even have enough strength to roll myself over. The other guys got me up and walked me up and down that big room until they were satisfied that I had enough before they let me rest. Every day for the next week or so they did the same thing until I got my appetite back and could move on my own.

We finally left that horrible place on September 21, 1951 and spent the next 22 days marching North to a little town by the name of Chung Song which is located about 12 miles south of the Yalu River. This march was also done under the cover of darkness. [For more information from Richard on this time period, see Chapter Four, Death Marches]

Harold Kaschko

By 20 August 1950, the entire 2nd Division had arrived in Korea. Our 38th FA Battalion entered combat on 20 August 1950 in defense of the Naktong River Line. We were in combat until 30 Nov. 1950 when the 2nd Infantry Division and other UN forces were caught in a Chinese roadblock 5 or 6 miles deep south of Kunu-ri, North Korea. About 2030 hours (8:30 p.m.) after the Battalion C.O. had been shot by the Chinese, and it was apparent that the battalion would never make it through the Chinese roadblock, the battalion Executive Officer directed the battalion to destroy all the 105mm Howitzers, to set the trucks on fire and destroy the radio equipment as best we could. The 38th FA Battalion traveled by foot over the hills heading south in hopes of joining other U.S. Forces.

I was to lead the column south over the hills, which I did, in total darkness and under terrible circumstances as the Chinese were also running over the hills shooting at us. Our trucks were burning, the ammunition was exploding and the enemy was on top of the hills shooting at us with rifles, machine guns, and mortars. Some soldiers made it back to the U.S. lines, but many did not. Many were killed at the roadblock area where our vehicles were parked. The 2nd Infantry Division Artillery had 1,461 casualties, and the entire 2nd Division had about 5,000.

I became a POW of the Chinese about 0430 hours (4:30 a.m.) on 1 December, 1950, and I was a POW for 33 months (1,011 days).

Edward Sheffield

The 14th day of July, 1950, after we had lost several of our big guns and some of our trucks plus a lot of men, we had pulled back six times and set up our seventh position. The enemy went over and around the mountains, closed in behind us, blew up the road and bridges. We didn't have much support from the Air

Force during this, so they had every advantage on us from four sides. We burned up some of the guns firing at them so fast. Their army was ill-equipped, too, with bolt action rifles and a few burp-guns, the automatic Russian type, but they had enough men to assign three to each weapon.

The country and people are several hundred years behind civilization and ignorant enough to charge a machine gun nest with a bolt action rifle.

About 2 o'clock that day they made their attack on our position —a day I'll never forget—bullets were hitting the ground just inches away on both sides of me. Four of my buddies were killed beside me, men were lying dead all up and down the irrigation ditch where we were taking cover.

I had emptied my carbine the second time and slid back down the ditch to put another clip in when I looked over my shoulder and six North Koreans had jumped in the ditch and had their rifles pointed at me. They stood there for about 30 seconds. I knew if I turned I'd be shot. Then more Koreans jumped in the ditch further down. One ran up to me and stuck the point of his bayonet in my back. I dropped my rifle to the ground. He motioned for me to get up. He knocked my helmet off with the butt of his rifle and a couple more of them hit me in the back. By this time, the firing had just about ceased.

They started marching me down the ditch. The water was red with blood. We stepped over several men lying dead. I looked up on the road and could see that they had six other men captured, two of them had been shot, one through the neck and the other through the stomach, but that made no difference to the Communist soldiers.

They tied our hands behind us with communication wire and rushed us back down the ditch. We were fired on again by troops who didn't know we were captured. That's when I got a bullet in the leg. It creased the knee but didn't seem to be so bad. The joint got stiff though, and with no medical care, it got worse before it got well about three months later.

They marched us back through their lines under close guard. There were thousands of Communist troops going south, destroying and confiscating everything the South Korean people had. They had no more regard for their own people than they had for us. They marched us through villages and towns that night that they were burning to the ground. The smell of flesh was sickening.

We could hear people moaning and children crying. Their parents had been killed or burned to death trying to save their home or what supplies they had stored for the winter.

The second day, my buddy who had been shot through the stomach died with his hands tied behind him. The wire that we were tied with didn't stretch any. Our hands had swollen so much the wire was cutting the skin. Three days and nights—our hands tied behind us with nothing to eat or drink.

They moved us north at night and kept us hid in a gully in the side of a mountain in the daytime to keep American planes from spotting us. The fourth day some old civilian women cooked up some rice with a little pork and brought it up to us. The guards untied our hands so we could eat. That was the best feeling I've ever had and the best rice I think I ever ate.

We finally reached Seoul where we joined other prisoners and were interrogated for the first time by young Communist leaders. They apparently enjoyed their first contact with American prisoners. They constantly warned us that if one man escaped, the rest would be shot.

The stench and filth increased with the hours. They had cut our rations in half and the men were getting weaker by the day.

After a few days in Seoul, we were loaded in box cars and on flat cars en route to Pyongyang, the North Korean capital. We traveled at night and stayed in the hills during the day. I can't remember now how many of us there were or how long it took to get there, but our train was bombed and strifed several times by British planes while we were in the hills. The railroads and railroad stations along the way were torn up by bombs and rockets.

When we reached Pyongyang, we were so hungry and weak we could hardly go. The guards herded us off the train and paraded us through the city to show the people what their army had done. The people laughed and spit at us and threw sticks and rocks at us. We were dirty and weak from starvation. I tried to brace myself as I thought of the day Christ carried his cross.

When they got through parading us, we were marched to a school building outside the town where we joined more prisoners who had been captured a few days before—the only remains of the infantry units—723 men out of a division of 26,000 fighting men, after the 24th Division had been annihilated.

Here in Pyongyang we had ringside seats at the early bombing of the city. The guards were so frightened that they would run and hide during the bombing, and we were free to see the effects of the attacks of the jets and bombers and witnessed the mass evacuation of the citizens.

Also while here, I had the horrible duty of helping to hold one of our men while the good Captain Bayson, who I admired so much, amputated his left leg with a homemade knife and no medicine of any sort. The man had been shot through both legs but didn't break the bone in the other. The man lived some few months after that, but this wasn't the cause of his death. Dysentery, severe conditions, malnutrition and the disease beriberi was the cause of the death of 475 men that winter. The doctor did all he could for everyone, but he had nothing to do anything with.

The military pressure upon the Northern Army was increased in September. We were loaded on flat cars and cattle cars again and hauled northward to within sight of the Yalu River. We were forced to travel by night in slow stages on a makeshift train. We were hidden in the daytime in the deep mountain valleys from the bombing and strafing American planes. Our train was strifed several times. With us on this journey were nearly 50 civilian internees, missionaries, war correspondents, diplomats, and some of them were women and children. They had been captured also. We weren't allowed to talk to them. I think they were treated a little better than us, and I was glad for the women and children anyway.

We arrived in Manpo September 11th. I liked this place better than any we stayed at. Out on the edge of town next to the river were three vacated houses close together. They were the typical Korean type stick and mud with straw roofs. Around these we made our compounds and were given enough lumber to build bunk type beds with rice straw for a mattress. This was better than we'd had so far. We were allowed to march down to the river under guard twice a week to bathe. We ate twice a day but our ration was still short with very little meat at all. They worked us up in the mountains on the other side of town building foundations for some type of military installations.

In mid-October as the United Nations troops began to push north and as the bombing increased, we were marched to another town, Kosangchin, 15 miles away. We stayed here a few days and were moved again two miles over the mountains to an abandoned mining camp at Choi-am Ni.

The United Nations troops came within 20 miles of us. We got all our news from straggling Communist soldiers coming off the front lines, but only a few would talk to us.

While we were here three men escaped but were brought back the next day, two of them dead, and the other one was tortured to death so we could see. The guards were more nervous and cruel than ever. They moved us back north within two or three miles of Manpo, leaving nine men behind who were unable to make the trip.

The roads and towns were crowded with soldiers and civilians who had been pushed back by U.S. troops. They marched us off the road and against the bank of the Yalu River in a cornfield. Here we stayed four days and had hardly anything to eat. I have eaten half green cornstalks and would take the chance of getting shot to steal an ear of corn from the fields to eat.

In that country it is very cold toward the end of October. I would dig a hole in the ground with my hands big enough to get in it, lie down, and pull some corn stalks over me at night. Some of the men huddled together and piled cornstalks around them to keep from freezing. We were not allowed even a small fire.

James H. Ransier

On March 1, 1951, the platoon I was in, the 3rd Platoon, "I" Company, 32nd Regiment, suffered heavy casualties while trying to take a hill. Our squad led the attack and ended the day with four men. We had no squad leader or assistant squad leader, so I was designated acting squad leader until such time as a replacement with more experience could be assigned.

Late in the afternoon, "I" Company moved into a defensive position along a ridge that was being held by a South Korean unit. They were spread out very thin. Our squad, the four of us, was placed between two Korean positions, and we began to dig in. Just before dark, the Koreans pulled out leaving "I" Company to defend the ridge. There was then so much distance between our positions we could not see anyone, not even the first position either side of us.

A field kitchen had been brought up to serve us a hot meal and was set up in the valley below. They started serving about midnight. It was the first such meal in a long time and was a good boost for morale. We had been eating C-Rations for many weeks. Half of the men went down from each position and when they returned, the other half went down. I went with the second group and played follow-the-leader as someone who knew the way in the dark led us down. As we approached the valley floor, through which a nice river flowed, the man in front of me made a turn as he followed the man in front of him. But I (and this would have made a good Abbot & Costello scene) did not see

64

him turn. I took about one or two steps and found myself in the river about up to my knees. Well, I ate my supper and returned to our position to try and keep warm. The temperature was below freezing that night, so I removed my boots and put them in my sleeping bag with me, hoping they would dry out, though I knew they wouldn't.

On the morning of March 2nd as the sky was just beginning to show signs of light, three of us were sitting up in our sleeping bags watching to the front. The fourth man who had been on guard was getting ready to have something to eat. What happened next was something that Don Faudskar and I have talked about many times. We were there, saw it, participated in it, but we both must have been in a state of shock as it did not seem as though we knew exactly what happened and yet we saw it all.

A small group of North Koreans (seven or so) came up either from the rear and/or one of the flanks. None of us spoke the other's language but it wasn't hard to figure out what they wanted us to do. We all stood up with our arms raised. One of them then stepped forward and fired an automatic weapon that shoots about a 45 or 38 slug. I was hit in both feet, although at the time, I thought it was only one. Don was hit in one foot and it was a bad one as it broke some of the bones in his foot. McLaughlin, a kid from Pennsylvania whom I liked but did not know too well as he had joined the squad the previous afternoon, was hit in the leg. Foreboard, a rough tough kid but a good man, was hit, I believe in the stomach.

The North Koreans immediately made it clear we were to start moving out. Don and myself along with McLaughlin did so, but Foreboard was doubled up on his knees and could not move. Without hesitation, one of the North Koreans stepped forward and shot him through the head with a pistol.

They tied our hands behind our backs and told us to move out on the double. We had not gone very far when it was apparent that McLaughlin was not going to be able to keep up. Once again, a North Korean stepped forward and put a pistol to McLaughlin's head. I turned away and did not watch, but I heard the shot and could see it in my mind.

We walked and ran at a very fast pace for about an hour or more. If we did not move as fast as they thought we should, they would hit us on the back with their rifle butts. They seemed to enjoy that, along with kicking us in the feet and jabbing us with bayonets.

When we finally stopped on one of the many hills we climbed that day, Don and I got a chance to look at our wounds. Don had his boots on and after removing one to look at his foot, he could not put it back on due to the swelling. I had not put my boots on that morning, so I was doing the walking, running and climbing in stocking feet. I was surprised to see my left foot was bleeding as I never realized it had been hit. It was not a bad wound, as the bullet had passed between the big toe and the toe next to it. Don wrapped his foot with his wool scarf and a few pieces of cloth and we continued on our way. My left foot was bleeding very much but it was my right which had been hit in the ankle that was giving me the most trouble.

We continued to walk all day, stopping once at a farm house to eat a raw turnip. We met our first North Korean officers at this stop. They let us inside where it was warm. Someone gave me some cloth to wrap around my left foot as it continued to bleed. One of the officers gave an order to a soldier who soon returned with a pair of American overshoes. Imagine, Goodyear rubber, fresh out of the original box, tissue paper and all. We did not stay too long as they were in a hurry to get us somewhere. We found out later that we were to be interrogated by North Korean officers.

We stopped walking about four in the afternoon and entered another farm house. The questioning started but did not go too well. We could not speak Korean, and they couldn't speak English. We were told we were going to spend the night in the farm house, but shortly after dark we were told to get up as we were going to be taken back to the front and released to the Americans. By this time our hands had been untied and we were guarded by only two soldiers as we started down the path that led to the valley and the river below. They did not have much to worry about as we were only able to move very slowly.

When we reached the river, we were told to stand at the water's edge facing the river. The North Koreans then stood some distance behind us and threw the bolts on their rifles as though to put a bullet in the chamber. We both thought this was our time and our place. Then they started to laugh. We turned to look and they motioned for us to again face the river. They then went through the whole routine again.

Although they did not shoot us, neither did we follow the river south toward the front. Instead, we turned north, and we knew that our return to the American lines was not to be.

At this point, one guard started back up the mountain. We continued to walk North following the river until about three or four in the morning with just one guard. Then we stopped at a farm house and spent the rest of the night. Early in the morning, we were given a bowl of rice and told we were going to see a doctor. I guess Korean doctors do not make house calls either as we were going to have to walk to wherever he was. So within a few hours, we were on our way again.

During the day, when U.S. Army spotter plans flew over, we were made to lie motionless in the snow so as not to attract attention. During these daylight moves, we seldom saw anyone, but when traveling at night the roads were packed with soldiers carrying ammunition, bags of rice, artillery shells and all sorts of supplies on their backs. The roads were so crowded it was very difficult to move. Late that afternoon we arrived at a farm house where the doctor was supposed to be. He, of course, was not there. We began to believe we would never see one, and we were right, we never did.

After our capture, and as soon as we had moved far enough from the front lines so the North Koreans were in no danger, we began to lose anything and everything that any of our captors might want or take a fancy to. Our wallets and watches were the first items to go. Then our warm clothing items like my wool scarf and fur-lined hat and gloves. By this time most of our warmest clothing was gone, but now one guy wanted my pants. I considered that the last straw and said, "No." He pulled a gun and I said, "OK, my pants for yours." We had struck a deal. As we were removing our pants, an officer came in and said we were moving again. So I pulled up my pants, smiled at my would-be trading partner, and we went our way, and he went his.

So here we were, at about 8 or 9 p.m. of the second day, and walking again. We were again told a doctor would be at the next house.

We had not been walking more than half an hour when Don became dizzy and couldn't move. He just dropped to the ground. With the shootings of Foreboard and McLaughlin in both our minds, I tried to lift him to his feet, but just did not have the strength. One of the North Koreans came over, helped Don to his feet and helped him walk for about an hour or so. His dizziness went away, and he walked without help for the rest of the night.

We reached our destination as the rays of the morning sun began to light the sky. As usual it was very cold, and the warmth of the two-room house felt good. We were each given a bowl of rice and told to rest. We slept for about 30 minutes when they woke us up and took us into the next room where we were questioned by two North Korean officers. One spoke no English. The other spoke excellent English, was a graduate of Chicago University and a Colonel in the North Korean Political Army. The other officer was in the regular army. The Colonel apologized for the food we would be eating as he knew we were accustomed to a different diet. He assured us we would be eating the same as they, one bowl of rice in the morning and one at night.

The questioning lasted well into the afternoon. It started with the army officer asking questions and the Colonel translating for him. He started by asking our name, rank and serial numbers. The easy part did not last very long. He then got into questions such as, "How many trucks in the 7th Division? How many tanks? How many 105's?"

We told them we didn't know, and, of course, we really didn't know. They thought we were lying, and we thought they must be kidding. The army officer pounded the table and spoke very loud in Korean and had fire in his eyes. The Colonel said, "No one is kidding" and advised us to tell or we would be shot. The Colonel then suggested we take some time to think it over, and they would return in a few minutes. We couldn't believe they really thought we would know the answers to such questions but decided we had best play the game to stay alive.

When they returned and again asked these types of questions, we picked figures out of the air and answered each question asked. I can't remember all the questions nor any of the answers, but some must have been way out. At some of our answers, the officer would look up at us in disbelief. He would then turn to the Colonel, and they would converse in Korean. The Colonel would then ask us how do you know there were three hundred tanks in the 7th Division? We replied that on several occasions we were given the job of counting them.

When the army officer had finished, the Colonel interrogated us. His questions were more along political lines. He asked if we liked Truman; we said, "No." "MacArthur?" "No." Would we like to become Communists? We said, "No." We discussed the Communist system briefly but no effort was made to brainwash us or change our minds in any way. We seemed to get along well with the Colonel. Although we talked on only a few occasions after the questioning, there seemed to be an understanding, or perhaps it was a mutual feeling of respect. Perhaps it was only that he spoke English. Whatever it was, I will always believe that Don and I are alive today because of him.

The next few days were spent sitting on the floor of a room about 8 feet by 10 feet. At night, ten North Korean soldiers slept in the same room with us, and that made it very crowded and uncomfortable. The days were spent looking for and killing the lice and other friends found on our bodies and in our clothing.

69

A soldier came in one day and said he was an aide man. He carried a bag in his hand and said he would take care of our wounds. He took out what looked like a knitting needle. Just as big and just as long. He took the old bandages off our wounds and then proceeded to try to poke some gauze bandage, which had been soaked in a red liquid, through the wound on my right foot. He wanted to push that needle in where the bullet entered and right on through to where the bullet came out. I made him understand that I did not want that done. He then tried the same with Don, who also refused. He then rewrapped our wounds, not with the dirty old bandages he took off, but with dirty old bandages he took from his bag. (Later, in an American Field Hospital, a doctor told us that frostbite had helped to keep our wounds from becoming infected.)

One night they woke us up and told us we were being moved to a near-by house. They had just brought in five South Korean prisoners, and we were to be kept together. By this time, I couldn't walk and wondered what they would do. Two South Koreans helped me, and another possible crisis passed. We moved about three hundred yards or so to another two-room house. A total of seven prisoners and five guards slept in our room each night.

Several of the South Koreans were wounded. One of them with a stomach wound which was a bad one. It was giving him a great deal of pain. He would scream and yell very loudly. I was convinced the guards would not put up with this disturbing noise very long and would take the poor guy outside and shoot him. So I quietly prayed, "God, please ease this soldiers pain to the point where he will be able to fall asleep. This will save the solder's life and, Dear God, Don and I will benefit from knowing of your presence, Amen."

As I said "Amen," the wounded man made no sound whatsoever. I believed him to be dead. Then I could hear the North Korean guards talking back and forth very softly. Then I could hear the South Koreans also talking in a whisper. I stayed awake the rest of the night trying to determine what had happened. As sufficient light finally came in through the paper windows, I could see a big smile on the face of the wounded soldier who had been screaming and yelling. He still had his stomach wound, but most of the pain must have left him. I quietly prayed again to God to give thanks for his help by relieving the South Korean of most of his pain and for God's presence with us in the house.

We lived in this room until March 11th. About noon that day, the Colonel came in and said we would be going to Pyongyang to a prison camp. They had hoped to have a truck but none was available, so we would have to walk. We told him, we couldn't walk and waited to see what he would say. He said nothing and turned and walked away. He returned later and handed us a white piece of paper with writing in Korean on it. He said the Americans were advancing, and they were being forced to retreat. The paper, he said, was a safe conduct pass that would be shown to any North Koreans who might try to take us as prisoners again. He felt it wouldn't be too long before American units arrived.

We sat there and watched them leave and take the South Koreans with them. Once out of sight, we started crawling south. We tried various forms of crude crutches from limbs and items found along the way. We never did come up with anything that really worked and stuck to just crawling. The pass was used several times that day as we met up with small groups of North Koreans on their way North. As it began to get dark, a group of solders stopped us and took the pass. It seemed to make no difference to them. We did not know what to expect as they made us leave the road and crawl (much to their amusement) up the mountainside to a farm house with a number of North Korean officers in it. They gave the pass to the officers, and we were then told to sleep. We did not do much sleeping.

During the night the officers and soldiers left. In the morning the pass was on the floor and the only ones there besides us were the farmer and his wife. The woman cooked us a breakfast of rice and dog meat. We ate the rice and left the meat, hoping we had not offended our hosts.

We got back to the road again and continued on our way south under a bright sun. Some of the snow and ice was melting because of the sun, but the day remained cold. We were not making good time, but had high hopes of reaching the American forces soon.

We had been moving south for several hours when someone opened fire with a machine gun. We made for the ditch by the road. Each time we raised our heads to see who was firing and from where, they would fire again. By this time of day, the ditch was filling up with run off water from the melting ice and snow. We were getting numb with cold and decided to continue south by staying in the ditch.

It wasn't long before we came to an abandoned house on the same side of the road. We knew we couldn't remain in the ditch and decided to make it into the house. The house was surrounded by a wood fence, but with enough holes in it to let us get through. As we left the ditch, a mortar round hit on the hillside across the road. We made it through the fence and were heading toward the house, when a second round landed closer but still on the other side of the road. We assumed we were nearing the front for anyone to be using a machine gun and mortar on two very obvious wounded soldiers. We also knew the house made an excellent target to zero in on and fully expected a few more rounds of mortar fire. No further shells were fired, and we set about trying to keep from freezing. We huddled together and covered ourselves with straw mats.

During our efforts to make it to the house, we had noticed another house across the road but higher up the mountain side. We assumed this was also an abandoned farm house. At dusk, however, we noticed a small amount of smoke coming from a chimney and decided that's where we wanted to be. By now, movement of any kind was a very painful effort. But the thought of a warm room kept us moving until we reached the house and knocked on the door.

At the time of our capture, we were in South Korea. During our captivity we were taken into North Korea. As we waited for the door to open, we did not know if a North or South Korean family would be inside. Of course, it did not matter much. Due to the close proximity of North Korean troops, no one would want to be found sheltering American soldiers.

It took a while, but the door eventually opened just a crack. It was then shut very fast. We knocked again and could hear a whispered but intense Korean conversation inside. We knocked again, determined to be inside where it was warm. The door opened a second time and an elderly Korean man invited us in but asked that we move quickly.

It was warm and dark except for the pot of charcoal sitting in the middle of the room and one candle burning at one end of the room. As far as we could tell, it was a Korean family, and we assumed some may have lived in the abandoned house we just left. There was fear written on all their faces, and we did our best to put them at ease. They told us we must leave after they fed us. We agreed, but after finishing a bowl of rice, we had no intention of leaving. We were still wet and cold but feeling much better than we had. Once that issue was settled, we all went to sleep except for the elderly gentleman. He sat up all night guarding the door.

In the morning, we each had a bowl of rice. The man then led us further into the hills to a bunker he had built. He said we could stay in it to hide from the North Koreans. Before he could leave, our Air Force made two air strikes on that hill. The first by jets and the second by Mustangs. It's easy to understand why the North Koreans were so fearful of our Air Force. We were safe in the bunker to just about everything but a direct hit. The firepower, when you are on the receiving end, is just devastating. We were hoping the family in the house below was safe.

We had been in the bunker several hours when two Koreans came to the bunker. One spoke some English and said he was a South Korean agent for the U.S. Army. He had been keeping track of us for several days. We did not know if we should believe him or not, but decided we had no choice. They had come to take us down to the road in the valley and said an American column was advancing along the road and would soon be there.

He carried me down the mountain and the other man helped Don. They sat down with us and said they would remain with us until the Americans showed up. We only had to wait about ten minutes when the point man of the column came around the curve in the road and stopped. We were about 60 or 70 yards from him and he raised his rifle. After looking at our group, he lowered the rifle and motioned for some backup to come forward. He then came toward us and realized we were Americans with two Koreans.

He called for three more men to come down where we were sitting. They were from "L" Company, 32nd RCT. The pointman then carried Don and the Korean who said he was a spy for the 7th Division carried me. The farmer turned and headed back up the mountainside to his home. We were carried to the head of the column and given C-Rations to eat as we sat on the ground waiting for a jeep equipped to carry two stretchers to take us to a helicopter landing sight.

When we arrived at the landing area, we were strapped into wire mesh baskets located on each side of the landing struts. We were then flown to a field hospital for examination and treatment by doctors. We were told that our frostbite had helped to keep our wounds from becoming infected. The date was March 13, 1951. On March 17, 1951, we were taken to an airfield and put aboard a hospital plane with other wounded men and flown to the 55th Army Hospital in Yokohama.

While in the hospital, we talked with some guys from other Company's in the 32nd who said that on the morning of March 2nd, "I" Company was attacked by a large force of North Koreans. Their positions were overrun and the entire company was killed, wounded, or missing. In just a few short hours the company just ceased to exist.

Richard Makua

When I got captured, it was the most frightening day of my life. Our company was to move up forward about a mile ahead of the main line on a hill. I was a forward observer for our company. At midnight, the Koreans and Chinese attacked us and overran the hill. They shot half the company, and the rest got away.

It was dark, and all hell broke loose. I ran out of ammo, and all I know that I was by myself and surrounded. The next thing I knew, I was knocked on the head and hit in the body, and all over. My hands were tied behind me, and I was dragged to the bottom of the hill. I guess I was passed out all this time. This is what I remember the most about the war.

Joseph Wilson

I was online about one week, but a POW for 27 months. I was captured April 22, 1951. We were 10 miles below the 38th Parallel when we were taken prisoner. I was wounded in the right shoulder and the left hand. I healed very good. The layer of clothes helped the shoulder gun shot. The hand healed OK. I never saw a doctor until June 22, but I had healed OK. I was held in Camp 1 and Camp 5.

Theo Baudoin, Jr.

Thanksgiving Day we were retreating from the Tockchon River located about 20 mites north of Sunchon. We moved into a pass below Kunu-ri, about 5 miles north of Sunchon. It was here we were surrounded by, it seemed, thousands of Chinese soldiers. Although outnumbered, we held out for three days. At night the bugles blared. The shrill sound of shepherd horns, and the clash of cymbals announced each charge.

It was here at Kunu-ri, on December 1, 1950, I was taken prisoner by Chinese Communist soldiers. We were marched at night. We averaged about 22 kilometers each night. The North Korean winters are very severe, with 20, 30, and sometimes 40 below freezing weather. We started walking about 5:00 in the evening, and walked until day light. They always kept us out of sight of our planes.

They put us up in whatever buildings were available, usually straw roofed, mud walled buildings, with dirt floors. Rooms about 10 feet by 10 feet. They packed us in 20 to 25 men per room. You just sat down, and pulled your knees up. No heat in the buildings. Our body heat kept us from freezing. In the morning about 9 to 10 AM they would put a sack of whole field corn in a pot of water and boil it. They then put it in a wood trough, like a pig trough. They would come by each hut and ask how many men. With a split gourd used as a ladle they would give one scoop per man. You extended your cupped hands out to get your one serving of about 12 ounces.

The day I got my first corn, it had been 5 days since I had eaten. Our hardship had only begun, for now we all had dysentery, and in our weakened condition we were made to carry bundles of rifles like pack mules. Later I was to find out the Chinese had tried to cut off the retreating American Marines who were on the east side of country.

When we arrived at a place called Koto-ri, the Chinese were very upset. They collected the rifles we'd been carrying and threw them in a pile. Later, I was to find out the Marines had made their escape in a snow storm.

CHAPTER FOUR

DEATH MARCHES

Jack Chapman

The first ordeal the prisoners had to suffer—and often the worst — was the march to one of the POW camps. The North Koreans frequently tied a prisoner's hands behind his back or bound his arms with wire. Wounded prisoners were jammed into trucks that jolted, dripping blood, along broken roads. Many of the wounded received no medical attention, but some received treatment upon reaching the camp. The marching prisoners were liable to be beaten or kicked to their feet if they fell. A number of the North Korean officers were bullwhip barbarians, products of a semi-primitive environment. Probably they had never heard of the Geneva Conventions or any other code of war. The worst of this breed were responsible for the murder of men who staggered out of line or collapsed along the roadside or trails. They were particularly brutal to South Korean captives. Many South Korean Army personnel were forced to dig their own graves before they were shot. Some Americans, with their hands tied behind their backs, were shot by the enemy. The journeys to the prison camps were "Death Marches." Especially in the winter of 1950-51 when the trails were knee-deep in snow and polar winds flogged the toiling column. On one of these marches, 700 men were headed north. Before the camp was reached, 500 men had perished...

Death March to Camp Kanggye

On the morning we were captured, November 30, 1950, my group marched back down the mountain to the road where we had fought. Many of the wounded were still there, and some of the prisoners took blankets from the trucks and covered them. The dead still lay on the road and in the ditch where they had fallen, rigid with death and cold. As we passed the trucks, some of the prisoners snatched up bedrolls from where the Chinese had tossed them onto the road, and stuffed their pockets with C-rations, but most of us were still too numb and dazed to think.

Then in single file, with the Chinese guards beside us, we left the road and began climbing into the hills that lay to the north and west. We were herded together under the instigation of the guns of the Chinese Communists who needed no coaxing to shoot down any prisoner bold enough to attempt an escape. We were marched off towards the Pyongyang-Manojin railroad.

We were then marched north through the most rugged terrain that I ever saw in Korea, to a point between Kanggye and the Manchurian border. On this march we witnessed quite a few deaths due to wounds, frozen feet, exposure, and killing by the guards. There was no medical care whatever, and we were fed boiled sorghum and on one occasion a rice ball. By the time we arrived at our destination, dysentery was prevalent throughout the group.

On this march the officers and Frank Noel, the Associated Press photographer, and many of the men who were in better condition (minor wounds or no wounds) were separated from the rest of us, and we did not see them again until we arrived in the north around Christmas, 1950.

We continued to march for hours, and finally we stopped at a Korean farm house deep in the mountains of North Korea, where our captors stripped us of all personal items, which were constantly used later for harassment. These were personal items such as pictures, wallets, identification cards, and some men had their field jackets and overcoats taken away. The only things that I managed to keep were my dog tags which were around my neck, taped together. The Chinese took my wallet, driver's license, Social Security card and military identification card.

Two of the Chinese interrogators had been raised near the international settlement in Shanghai, the pre-World War II home of the 4th U.S. Marine Regiment. As a consequence, they were familiar with American customs and slang.

For the next nineteen days, we marched either under Chinese or North Korean guards; tattered, torn, cold, and suffering. Many of the prisoners died from their wounds, some were beaten or shot to death when they could no longer walk or refused to continue.

The Communist guards were provided by the sector through which we passed. When the Koreans provided the guards, the treatment was noticeably rougher than the Chinese. They marched us by day when the clouds protected us from our planes, and by night, when the days were clear.

Those of us whose feet had been frostbitten the night of our battle in the ditch were the worst off, for the flesh began to break down into sores, and scabs formed on the sores during a long rest period, and when we started to walk again, we cried out in agony as the scabs began to tear loose. During the day, when we halted, those of us whose feet were causing us agony got up and walked about, causing the Chinese guards to be alarmed, as they feared our aircraft would spot us. However, we would not lie down even when the Chinese threatened us. The worst was the mountain climbs, on icy trails at night.

The first few days after capture, our only food was a few cans of C-rations which some of the prisoners had managed to slip into their parka pockets when we crossed the road after being captured. We all shared these. Once on the march we were given a boiled potato, and we also ate something that looked like sorghum seed and tasted like sand. Sometimes when we slept in barns, we would find ears of dried corn which we chewed on during the march. Our captors carried only enough food for themselves in a small bag, and when they were eating, they harassed and tormented us by flaunting the food in our faces.

We walked on painfully frozen feet, wincing each time the purplish flesh touched the frozen ground, staring blankly ahead, not knowing where we were or where we were going. There was one older Marine, Gus, who was about 50 years old. When he could go no longer, he just suddenly sat down in the middle of the trail, scooping up snow and rubbing it on his throbbing head, saying over and over, "Shoot me, shoot me."

About the eighth or ninth day out, I saw a North Korean guard throw his burp gun in one of the prisoner's face and shoot him. One US Marine who was shot in the leg refused to move; that was the last we saw of him.

Those too weak to continue or who did not have the will power to continue were left behind with a guard. Subsequently, shots were heard and the guard or guards who had been left behind with the prisoners returned to our group.

For nineteen days this death march continued, first north, then west, then north again, along narrow trails, in single file, until daybreak or dusk. We marched up high ice-covered mountain trails in the dark and bitter cold. The wind cut through our clothing like a knife, bitter and cold. We managed to keep going, by now we understood that to fall out of line was a sure way to get a bullet in the back from the Chinese or North Korean guards.

The march to Kanggye was characterized by the lack of food and shelter, forced marches, and exposure to the elements. We were forced to march through snow storms without adequate clothing or foot wear. The only water available for drinking was melted snow, the Chinese were deathiy afraid of the Korean water and would not drink it, or let us drink it.

Some of the men whose feet had been frozen began to die of gangrene, and when they pleaded for medicine the Chinese would say they were sorry there was none. They said, "Tonight we reach a place where there is much medicine. Tonight we will sleep in warm houses. There will be good food." But there was never warmth or food or medicine.

With few exceptions, we got to Kanggye by marching and the wounded being carried on improvised litters or helped by the stronger ones. One Marine, Hayton, was father and doctor to many of us. He would take a man on his back and carry him or, with a bull-like rush, grab two around the waist and help them the last few bitter feet to the top of a hill.

Many of us had only a field jacket, which proved to be inadequate for the bitter North Korean cold winter. Our back packs containing additional clothing were left behind in the vehicles. When we stopped, we all huddled together for any warmth we could generate, our bodies trembled violently throughout the long day. We slept pitifully, with no shelter or bedding for protection from the snow and ice.

When the Chinese did bring us food, it would be about an hour before they started us marching again. The march would resume at dusk, or at dawn with many of us being feverish from our wounds, trying doggedly to keep pace with the man in front.

I was very fortunate in that I was helped during the march by an American Marine (Hayton) and a British Marine. I had been wounded seven times, in both arms and both legs, my hip, and my forehead. They carried and dragged me over some of the most dangerous mountain trails of North Korea for nearly three weeks, in knee high snow and over ice covered trails from the Chosin Reservoir. I realize now that I would have died if not for these valiant men. The American Marine was released in May 1951. I learned in 1955 when we met at Fort Bragg, N.C. I never knew what became of the Englishman. (There were others who did everything you can imagine to keep me alive, for nearly nine months of my first year as a prisoner. Their names I shall never forget!)

I recall, most vividly, my own half-conscious dilemma, the brutality we suffered, prisoners being shoved from the snow covered mountain trails, being kicked to our feet and beaten with rifle butts when we fell and could no longer get to our feet, some being shot when they refused or would not continue to march.

The Chinese and North Koreans provided no special considerations for the wounded. All of us who were wounded were half carried and/or dragged along by the other prisoners, or we just limped along as best we could. Chinese or North Korean guards walked alongside, ahead and behind us and made no attempt to help in any way. Many of us died and/or were killed on this march north to Kanggye.

During this march, one thing that stayed in our minds was the scene where the United Nations forces were discovered in a railroad tunnel during the advance into North Korea, and hundreds of American prisoners had been massacred by the retreating North Korean Army (prior to our capture.) Every one of us retained a keen sense of imminent death.

The Communists would march us for hours without stopping, then give us a short break and then continue the march until daybreak before stopping. We just dragged along in the darkness. Like the others, my muscles were stiff and sore from the prolonged exposure and exertion, and I had to have help to get on my feet. The first few steps were agonizing ones, I had to force myself to get going and to walk endless hours.

One thing for sure, I had no desire to be left all alone there on a mountain trail. By morning, or dusk, we could hardly walk any more, and when we halted, we fell exhausted to the snow covered ground and laid there until the call came to start again.

During the daylight hours, we all huddled in or under any available cover we could find. During this forced march, we received one ration per day if we were lucky. Frequently, there was no food for two or three days. Many times during the march, I could imagine candy bars, hamburgers, French fries, along with all the other good American food just in front of me, but always just out of my reach.

Our meal usually consisted of watery soup, made from barley, and or sorghum seed, that was always served cold and consequently was no source of protection against the bitter cold. We gagged on the stuff, but managed somehow to get it down. We simply did our best to force the so called food down. There was virtually no opportunity for escape. Freezing weather, lack of food, and numerous Communist troops in the vicinity in addition to the adequate guard discouraged any attempts to escape. At least three Marines and several soldiers died on this march.

Finally, after about 19 days on the trail, and when one of the Marines was about ready to lie down and die because his tortured feet, swollen monstrously in his shoes, were hurting him so, we finally reached our stopping place. It was near the little town of Kanggye, far north, and just south of the Yalu River and the Chinese border. Kanggye at least offered some shelter from the icy winds, and it meant also the end of the terrible march northward. Kanggye was used primarily as an interrogation center. From this camp prisoners were shipped to the camps on the Yalu River.

During this time, our wounds went unattended and stuck to our clothing and each time we moved, our wounds would break open and start bleeding. We had no material for bandages and no way to clean them. The extreme cold weather helped save our lives, since the freezing weather slowed the flow of blood. Otherwise many of us could have bled to death. Medical supplies were non-existent, and treatment was limited entirely to first aid provided by our own people using improvised splints and rag dressings. Further injuries resulted from prolonged marches and exposure to the cold, especially on the trails which were knee-deep in snow.

The North Koreans who had been guarding us the last few days talked of exchanging us for medicine and other badly needed supplies. However, when the Chinese got word of this, they immediately assumed control of us and moved us to the northern part of Kanggye.

Morning Report for December 27, 1950, showed the following members of Dog Company, 31st Infantry (members attached to Baker Company, 31st Infantry) as Missing in Action as of December 1, 1950, in the vicinity of the Chosin Reservoir:

MSG Richard Nolen, SFC William H. Olson, Sgt. Charles W. Gregory, Sgt. Oliver Haney, Sgt. Sheldon L. Harriman, Sgt. Daniel Marinez, Cpl. James A. Nielson, PFC Clifton Arnold, PFC

Bobbie G. Brown, PFC William L. Bryant, PFC Johnny L. McAlpine, PFC James Talbert, PFC John R. Figgins, PFC William Gabou, and PFC Franklin (Jack) Chapman.

Wounded in action:

Pvt. Klmer C. Frazier, John D. Agostini, Cosma P. Cazakoglou who were taken to Army Hospital in Japan.

In 1951, the following men were declared as possible prisoners of war: Olson, Haney, Martinez, Nielson, Arnold, Talbert, Chapman and Figgins.

The March South

After several weeks at Camp Kanggye, we were again to set off on another of these marches. About March 3rd, 1951, we were abruptly shoved outside and marched from the camp to the town of Kanggye. The camp was abandoned, and some 290 men began the long trip south.

In the town of Kanggye we were loaded onto boxcars for a two day train ride to a place near Somidong, a point somewhere northwest of Pyongyang. We traveled only at night and hid in tunnels during the day to escape detection by our aircraft.

Three days after our arrival, we were all gathered in a schoolhouse and were informed that we were going to be divided into two groups. The Chinese announced that all but 60 of us (which included 24 Marines), would be returned to the north, with no explanation given for this sudden change of plans. The second group of about 230 prisoners, including Major McLaughlin, were to be taken back north.

Our group of 60 men (which included Lieutenants George Snipan of Baker Company, 31st RCT and George Shedd of the 3rd Infantry Division, and a Marine Lieutenant) left the larger group, and for about 5 weeks, we marched across Korea covering about 300 air miles, headed southeast to a point in the vicinity of Wonsan, based on information we received from Korean civilians.

84

On this march two Marines became sick, one was a Negro named Roebuck, who died from what appeared to be peritonitis. We buried him there in the middle of nowhere, using our hands to dig his grave. I believe that this was sometime around the March 10th, 1951. The second Marine had been carried for several days by Andy (Chief) Aguirre. He became too sick even to be carried, and the Chinese finally left him behind with the Koreans. He was never seen again and is presumed to have died shortly after being left behind. Being on the march with shoes held together with rags and whatever material I could use to hold my boots together and frost-bitten feet, I was given Roebuck's shoes.

After we left Kanggye, and the main group, Lt. George Snipan and George Shedd were the officers in charge of our group, which consisted now of 58 men, (US Marines and U.S. Army personnel from both the 3rd and 7th Infantry Divisions.) During the time that most of the prisoners from Kanggye marched to Changsong and Pyoktong, our smaller group undertook a march of an entirely different nature. We were led southward through the rugged mountains of north central Korea by the way of Tokchon, Yangkok, and Majon-ni.

We all froze from the lack of suitable clothing, as the temperature in North Korea at this time of the year fluctuates between 20 degrees above zero in the daytime to way below zero at night. Most of this time we slept outside, without any bedding. One older Marine, Gus, had barely survived the brutal march to Kanggye, and on at least one occasion during the march, sat down in the snow and dared the Chinese to shoot him. During our march across Korea in the spring of 1951, to amuse himself, he would charge the guards and the Koreans we passed. For a handful of cigarettes and/or pieces of yud (a kind of molasses candy), he would let them see him take out his false teeth and put them back in again.

The countryside of North Korea is made up of bare hills and mountains as the United States aircraft had reduced any concentration of industry or township to complete rubble. On April 5th,

1951, after leaving Majon-ni, we arrived at a temporary camp, in a village deep in a valley, in a very beautiful and rugged section that could be reached only on foot. We were called together and informed that our group was being further reduced, to thirty men. Every day, they would call us together and ask our opinion of this latest event. They wanted our opinion and answers in writing. After about seven days we were split again into two groups, one group consisting of twenty-eight men and the other group consisting of thirty men and each group moved south by different routes.

The group that Harrison and the other Marines were in was told that they were to meet some newly liberated friends, and that they were to help the Chinese in introducing them to their new life. This they did, explaining to the newly captured prisoners that the Chinese would not hurt them and would feed them as best as they could, and that the food supply was very low now, consisting of sorghum seed. They also helped the newly captured prisoners fill out the interrogators' questionnaires. (When I saw Harrison in 1955, he brought me up to date on their activities after we were separated.)

Out of this group of thirty, the Chinese picked eighteen Marines and one Army soldier to be released. They marched this group of eighteen Marines and one Army soldier a few miles to the south. There they stopped them, fed them well and loaded them down with pamphlets on the peaceful aims of the Chinese. They also gave them surrender leaflets which they were to pass out to their fighting comrades when they met them. On May 25th, 1951, they were picked up by three tanks of the Seventh Division.

The rest of the group which consisted of six Army soldiers and four Marines was taken back north and joined our group of twenty-nine men. The four Marines were Sergeant Mathis and Roberts, Corporal Aguirre and PFC Daniel Yesko.

It was during this period that many of us began to suffer more physically, more than at any other time during our captivity. Up to this time, we had not suffered very much from dysentery on this march and had managed to avoid other illness. My wounds bothered me and now I started getting excruciating pains in my legs from the knees down. My bones throbbed in pain like a toothache. The pain was much more intense at night, and I got very little sleep. As long as I was walking, the pain was not so bad, but, when I stopped, I had to sit down.

In April of 1951, after our group was split, the second group (which consisted of mostly Marines) departed. Nineteen of these men we did not see again until after the Police Action in Korea ended. Many of us met at a Military Court Martial (Trial) in 1955. That's when I found out that the nineteen Marines and one Army soldier had been released around May 25, 1951, in the vicinity of Chunchon.

After several days of moving from one place to another, dodging planes, we arrived in a deserted village. The Chinese took Olson and Cothperson from our group, which was no big loss as ever since our capture both had been suspected of ratting to the Chinese, and both were their favorites. Both always seemed to have cigarettes and received other favored treatment. No one trusted them, and we never discussed anything in their presence.

Around the end of May, 1951, we met approximately 200 American soldiers who had been captured late in April, 1951, in the vicinity of Seoul, near the 38th parallel. Most of them were from the 24th and 25th Divisions.

After about ten days, the Chinese moved our group away from the other prisoners, and we were marched toward the Hwachon Reservoir. We kept marching until around August, 1951, at which time we were taken to a village and stayed there about a month. Then the Chinese moved us out, going back north. We stopped at another place for a while, and they took Ray Hikida from our group, and we never saw him again until after the war ended. We stayed here about two or three weeks before being moved to the Mining Camp.

At the Mining Camp, which is about twenty miles northeast of Pyongyang, we met some Puerto Ricans, some British and some more American soldiers, about fifteen or twenty altogether.

Because of our planes, the supply situation was very serious. Our rations now consisted of a course brown flour, which we mixed with water to make a mush. It was almost inedible and gave no nourishment. About twice a week we had to form a working parties and travel at night, walking about twenty-five miles to obtain food. This meant marching night after night, wading small streams and rivers, and resting under any available cover from the aircraft overhead during the day. Sometimes these marches lasted two or three days, depending on how far we had to go to get supplies.

We were forced to carry 50 pound sacks of grain on our shoulders back to our camp. Some of the prisoners who were able to work feigned illness, thus placing an even greater burden on the rest of us, as the work had to be done or we all suffered. At every temporary camp that we stayed at more then three days, the Chinese singled out about ten or fifteen of us for the supply runs.

Many of us came down with beriberi that summer, which is the result of starvation and malnutrition, and most of us suffered from dysentery which sapped the strength out of us. This was brought on by the flies, mosquitoes, and unclean conditions. There was vitamin deficiency, and psychological depression was severe.

Following our separation from the thirty men, our group consisted of two officers and twenty-seven enlisted men and about fifty Chinese soldiers. We started a series of marches, first north, then southwest and west for nearly six months, before being taken to Changsong, North Korea, to Camp One. During this march, the Chinese guards tried to talk with us, however, since neither spoke the other's language, it was difficult to communicate. We were joined by the ten men who were separated from the eighteen Marines and one Army soldier. Our group now consisted of about thirty-nine men.

One of our temporary camps was at a North Korean farm located in a small valley, about 100 miles or so south of Kanggye, and away from all concentration of activities. This farm was occupied by a family of four; husband, wife, son and daughter-in-law. Their house was an average Korean home, with three rooms, of which the Chinese guards took two, one for their officers and one for the prisoners who were seriously ill and our two officers. The rest of us slept outside on the ground in the cattle stalls, which in itself was not really bad, outside of the bugs, lice, and the smell (or else it wasn't very noticeable to us because of our weakened and exhausted physical condition).

The untreated drinking water and outdoor toilets were the greatest cause of dysentery along with the fact that our diet consisted only of the thin, watery mush. During this time, several of us came down with hepatitis, typhoid, malaria, and plain diarrhea. The Chinese promised that they would get medicine and better food for us if we would only cooperate and write an open letter to the United Nations denouncing the war. However, our food ration was cut, and no medicine or medical help was brought in. Some of us who were ill pulled through, thanks to our fellow prisoners and this Korean family who was very helpful and decent to us. James Barber, who was from the 3rd Division and with us at Kanggye became very ill. We had to force the mush down his throat. At least he pulled through and made it back home. Several years after our return home, I made contact with James, and he said he was doing great, thanks to us.

Several years ago, when Roy Farley and I got together for the first time since our days in Korea, he mentioned how they had almost lost me during the summer of 1951. He said that I was very ill because of my wounds and lack of medical care. I had forgotten about this close call. At this temporary camp, with the Korean family, I remember they gave us tobacco and small amounts of food when they could without the Chinese knowing it. They also supplied us with some improvised bedding (straw mats) and helped several of us patch our shoes and clothing.

We welcomed the coming of summer, because it was comparable to a Midwestern U.S. summer. But it had more flies and mosquitoes then one could imagine. The mosquitoes, the snakes, and other factors kept us from getting any rest. So, with each day's labor, we continued to drift closer and closer to death, sometimes reaching the point of blacking out.

Of our guards, there was one English speaking Chinese guard named Pan, and there was Leo, who spoke a few broken words of English. Pan always took prisoners out on work details at night. We had Pan with our group until we arrived at a place near Pyongyang. One day the Chinese herded us together, and we started marching again. We were probably somewhere in the vicinity of Hamhung, as we could hear the United States Navy's battleship, the USS Missouri, with her 16 inch guns off the coast, bombarding the surrounding area. This continued for several days. Every day we could see the Communists retreating further and further north away from our position.

During this time, we were not allowed to leave our hiding place, for the fear of our planes, except during darkness to relieve ourselves, and then only for a few minutes at the most, with only three or four men allowed out at a time. We sat there, hungry, tired and thirsty, waiting for darkness to come so we could get out of the hole in the ground for a few minutes. We gasped for air, as none was coming into the hole.

After a few days at this miserable place, we too, were hurriedly herded together and moved farther north. The last couple of days in the vicinity of the caves, we had noticed small observation planes overhead and could hear gun fire off in the distance behind us.

The desire for food was building up. I would be marching along with my eyes closed and think about it. My mouth watered, then I would start thinking about all kinds of food that I'd eaten, and what I'd eat if and when I got released. I had visions of ice cream, candy bars and all the wonderful food back home and how I would pig out, if and when I returned. Whenever we crossed a stream or a river, we looked for dead fish lying about on the bank and ate them raw. Most of the fish we found crawling with maggots, but as we were starving, this didn't matter, and we ate whatever we could get our hands on. The millet and barley gave us awful cramps. Our indigestion was terrible. There would be little worms in our barley. If it was cooked dry we didn't notice them and ate them. But if the stuff was soupy, we could see the little things. Throughout this time the Communists discontinued their attempts to brainwash us with their indoctrination lectures. In order to stop us from making any attempts to escape or resisting in any way, they literally marched and worked the hell out of us, even though we were all starving, and half of us were either sick or half crazy.

On our march north during September 1951, we saw hundreds of Chinese Communist soldiers moving toward the rear. We never saw more than a handful of North Korean soldiers in a formation that I can recall. At nights we saw large search lights in the distance to the south, moving toward us, but never close enough for us to attempt an escape. We later learned that the United Nations forces were using large spotlights for artificial moonlight.

As we moved further north, we saw Chinese soldiers pulling, and/or pushing by hand, United Nations artillery pieces, trucks and other equipment that had either been left behind or overrun. Finally, after several days of marching, we halted in a large valley, several miles north of the front lines. After many days here, we named the valley AWOL Valley, meaning 'absent without leave,' for it was here that nine of us attempted an escape only to be recaptured, beaten and bound for long periods of time. This was near Suan, North Korea. Here we met and saw other United Nations soldiers who had been taken prisoner only a short time before. Many were Turks and South Koreans. Also, I recall that this place was crawling with fleas.

During the trip to Pyongyang, we stopped in a small town about forty or so miles north of the 38th parallel. At this time we saw two women who had been captured. One appeared to be Korean, and the other one we believed to be French. The one lady could have been one of the French Nuns or the lone German lady who had been with the French who were taken prisoner during the summer or fall of 1950. These women were dressed only in their slips and looked as if they had gone through hell.

One of our biggest problems here was dysentery, and if one developed dysentery and did not get up and walk around, he would likely die within two or three days. It did not take much to lose control, and there was no means to clean up afterward. Once a person got sick, it was very hard to get him to eat, and many times we had to sit on our friends and push the food down their throats. The worst thing was seeing a friend give up and die.

Several American prisoners who had been captured during the late spring or early summer of 1951, joined us at AWOL Valley. These prisoners had also been doing some type of forced labor for the Chinks. It was here that we lost our two officers and about twelve others from our group. We later met at Changsong. Our group now consisted of about twenty-five men. Here we witnessed fellow prisoners being mistreated, hands being tied behind their backs, prisoners being tied by their wrists and left hanging from poles or whatever was available to hang one from.

The March North

In September 1951, our group was herded together once more and then started to march farther north, this time toward the city of Pyongyang, and to one of the most miserable and unforgettable prisoner of war camps in all of North Korea. The day that we arrived at the city, everything in the area was a complete wreck. Our aircraft had done a damn good job of reducing all concentration of industry to complete rubble. The city smelled of death, you could feel it in the air, on your skin, like something crawling on you, and you could see hundreds and hundreds of graves on the mountain side. Death seemed to be everywhere. Americans and other United Nations troops were buried here in graves so shallow that arms and legs extended from the earth.

There were several other United Nations prisoners "alive" still. I say "alive" because most of them were so bad off that they knew neither their names or whereabouts. Most were half alive, just sitting or lying about, without the strength to move or care for themselves. They were too sick to care for the dead and dying.

Several of the dead had not been buried and remained where they had died; in cells, outside of their cells, with nothing to cover them and no one to look after them.

We had heard rumors of torture such as hanging prisoners by their fingers or forcing them to stand on their toes until they became unconscious, and beating the prisoners to death for small or imagined infraction of their camp rules. Evidence of such treatment was visible all around the compound. The guards here showed no signs of the so called "Lenient Policy."

The filth of this place was indescribable, the smell of the huts and the cells was out of this world. Everywhere you looked, there were horrible things, making any normal person sick to his stomach, and the stench of death was everywhere.

We stayed here until around October 12, 1951, I was never so glad to leave a place in all my life. I vividly recall my anxiety and anguish at having to leave behind all of the poor suffering soldiers who could do nothing for themselves and/or were beyond help.

One of our English speaking Chinese (Wong), wore a black arm-band on his sleeve. We called him the "Black Arm Bandit." During the death march, Wong pushed a number of prisoners off of the trails. He was Lin's assistant at Changsong, Camp One, and did all the punishing of prisoners. He claimed that he had studied at a University in the United States.

Malnutrition had begun to take its toll. We all suffered from a series of painful muscle deteriorations where the muscle would stiffen up, causing first mild, then extreme pain from the tip of one's toes to the top of one's head. The food ration was very small, mainly millet, and we were down to one meal a day.

We were put on a train and rode a few miles. We stopped in a tunnel, and the Chinese claimed that an American aircraft had sighted the train and that we had just made it to the tunnel. We almost suffocated from the smoke of the train. This ended our ride north to Changsong, Camp One. We were forced to march the rest of the way, and during this trip, we were strafed numerous times by our own aircraft.

As we moved further north, we saw many Russian trucks, and near the end of our march, the Chinese marched us right into the City of Sinuiju, North Korea. (I believed that was the name of the city.) The North Korean people lined the road to see us, and they spit on us, threw rocks at us, and tried to strike and kick us. At least the Chinese guards did their best to protect us from the North Korean people.

At the outskirts of the city, we walked right by some big ack-ack batteries, which were manned by Russian soldiers, and I recall that the Russian soldiers gave us some bread.

Our trip north to Camp One, took about 13 days. We arrived at Camp One on or about October 25, 1951. Camp One was located in the town of Changsong, which is about 30 miles or so northeast of the Korean border city of Sinuiju.

Looking Back

Today, I have to say that the hardest things for me during my captivity were the death marches and the caves and the death camp at Pyongyang, North Korea, the most miserable unforgettable prisoner of war camp in all of North Korea. Here there were Americans and other United Nations troops buried in graves so shallow that arms and legs, and even heads, were extended from the earth. It was here that we saw many U.S. and UN prisoners too sick to care for, as they were only about half alive, just sitting or lying about, without strength even to move or care for themselves. I know now that what kept me going through my captivity was the constant thought that I did not want to die over there.

Richard Rook

I mentioned earlier that the Chinese wouldn't march us during the daylight hours for fear of air strikes from American planes.

I don't know if it was for fear of our lives or theirs. I rather believe it was for theirs because they hadn't been concerned for our welfare in other areas. Anyway, we still had several close calls in spite of not marching during the day. On one occasion in particular, I was scared as hell. We were on our long march up to Chung Song, our final destination. It was about the middle of the day, and we were trying to get some sleep in preparation for the long night's march. This particular day we were housed in Korean mud huts instead of the usual creek beds, barns, or mountain sides. About 15 feet in front of the hut that I was in, there was ditch about 8 feet across with a plank that served as a bridge.

The Chinese set up their headquarters on the other on the other side of this ditch. Like I said, we were trying to sleep when all of a sudden we heard jets diving on what we thought was us. It was especially frightening because we had never seen a jet this close before. The F-80 Shooting Star had just been introduced about the time we were captured, so our experience with jets was minimal. The Chinese opened up with small arms (which was not unusual), and the jets countered with 50 caliber machine gun fire. Of course we couldn't see anything because the Koreans don't believe in building windows in their houses. All we could do was listen and try to imagine what was happening outside. All of a sudden, several big explosions rocked the mud hut that I was in. Big chunks of the mud and straw roof came falling down on us. I suppose you can guess what I was doing. You got that right—I was praying as hard as I knew how.

After the planes were obviously gone, and after we mustered up enough courage to venture outside, we discovered what had taken place. The pilots of those F-80s knew exactly who was where. They almost leveled the Chinese billets on the other side of the ditch. Not one round landed inside our compound. You talk about a surgical raid, they certainly knew what they wanted to hit. There was a huge crater on the far side of the ditch bank which meant that the rocket that caused that hole couldn't have missed the top of our hut by more than a couple feet. I kid my brother about being a fly-boy himself, but those guys have my respect and eternal gratitude.

I think that the South Koreans liked us. It's hard to tell with those people, but I know for sure that the North Koreans hated us. As we were marched through the tiny villages, they seem to come out of the woodwork to throw stones at us, and when they could get close enough, they would spit at us. Our guards would do nothing to discourage these people from doing anything they thought they could get away with.

Edward Sheffield

The Chinese troops had crossed the river and were going to the front lines with combat equipment. Column after column—we watched them go by for four days. Then the worst thing happened to us on October 31. This was the day the "Tiger" took over our command, and this was the beginning of the infamous Death March or one of the major Death Marches.

He and his company of guards were men with hatred and revenge in their hearts. After all, our United Nations, and especially the American troops had deprived these men of rich war loot and victory over South Korea. They were determined for us not to fall into the hands of the fast advancing UN troops, even if it meant death for us.

Leaving 16 more men in this cornfield too weak to walk from dysentery—some of us had built a wind break around them, but the Tiger wouldn't let us move them.

Before we got on the road, we heard a machine gun rip the place apart.

Tiger was commander of the North Korean people's police force with a company of guards with automatic weapons. We learned later that he and his guards had killed around 300 prisoners on a train that was about to be liberated.

The civilians and Communist troops were all in a state of confusion and unrest. Before we reached the town of Manpo, again we were rushed off the road and against a big mountain cliff. They huddled us together and set up three machine guns out in front of us.

The Tiger was giving some commands we couldn't understand until the group of civilians following behind broke loose from their guards and came running, crying and pleading with the Tiger. They could speak and understand the Korean language and knew we were about to be shot. He suddenly left and went into town. In about 20 minutes he came back, hurried us on the road and marched us through the town.

It was dark, and they had no electric lights. A few houses were still burning from the bombing late that afternoon. The streets were crowded with people, military and civilian, and none had any love for us. Three men were grabbed from the column as we went through town.

We never saw them again.

About two miles the other side of town we spent the night in another cornfield. There must have been two inches of snow that night. We were not glad for such weather. At dawn the next morning, we found 10 men frozen to death, and they wouldn't even let us bury them.

The news came when the Tiger walked down and told us we were going on a hundred mile march with only six days to reach our destination.

Any man who fell behind would be executed. Lt. Thorten jumped up and told him he was crazy, called him a mad man. The Tiger pulled his pistol, walked Lt. Thorten over to a high cliff, and shot him in the head.

By forced marches, we were taken up through the rugged mountain country of far Northern Korea. This march would have been rough for an able-bodied man. We were sick, tired, and starved.

The narrow roads up through these mountains often had ice on the road which made it more difficult to walk. The best of us were in no shape to help carry the ones who fell behind, but we would try to brace the men and help them along until the column would get ahead.

The Tiger was walking at the rear of the column, and when we couldn't keep up, he would motion for us to put the man down and catch up to the column.

Trying to crawl, our buddies would beg us not to leave them, but there was nothing we could do. Then the Tiger would shoot them and roll them down the side of the mountain.

I saw men fall to the side who I thought would make it for sure. This made me wonder if I would be next; 125 men died on this march by a bullet in the head from this Tiger's pistol.

CHAPTER FIVE

LIFE... AND DEATH... IN THE CAMPS

Jack Chapman

Camp Kanggye

The first camp I was at was referred to as Camp Kanggye, and was located about eight miles north of the village of Kanggye. I recall that when some of the prisoners removed their boots for the first time after reaching Kanggye, skin from their feet came off with their boots. The cold was so intense that our feet froze to the bottom of our boots, and the skin just peeled off when we removed our socks and boots. Skinner, from Baker Company, lost the toes from both of his feet.

Here we were divided into squads and billeted in Korean houses, about twenty plus men to a room, which was approximately eight feet by eight feet in size, in mud houses, with no heat, and some of the rooms had the windows and doors broken out, zero degrees and below temperatures. Housing for the most part consisted of typical small buildings, constructed of mud with thatched straw roofs, and were in a poor state of repair.

For the first few days we were so tired and beaten that we did not move. We lay in the houses, huddled on the floor, and would merely reach from beneath our jackets to take the food the Chinese poured into our ration cans. Some men, though, had no cans, and ate the boiled sorghum, and the bean curd, from their caps.

We slept on the earth floor with our heads to the wall and our feet to the center of the room and there wasn't any room for any passage between us. We were so crowded that about half of us had to sit with our knees under our chins while the other half of the guys laid down.

The huts that were supposed to give us shelter were so flimsy that the cold wind blew straight through them. We had no blankets and we slept in what clothing we had on, which was not much. We stayed here for a few days, and then we were moved to the north end of the town. We were organized into two companies and billeted in houses with Korean civilians, spread out down a valley along a river and what appeared to be the main road to the border. My squad consisted of eight to ten Army personnel, and in the room next to ours, there was about six or so Marines and one Navy corpsman.

When the organizing and billeting were completed, we were informed that we were to be put through a period of schooling to enlighten us regarding the true political situation existing in the world, and when we learned these facts to their satisfaction, we would be released to return to our homes.

Every man was fully interrogated several times, and a record was kept of each man, including an identification photograph. These interrogations were more economic than military. They appeared more interested in family and economic backgrounds than any military information we might be able to give. Such things as salaries, prices and the availability of different commodities before, during and after World War II, if we had money in the bank, owned a radio, automobile, television, etc., what kind of work we did before entering the service, why we entered the service, etc. They also wanted to know any political connections we might have had in the states, and our opinions of the various leaders in the United States, both military and political.

They asked a lot of personal questions. They wanted to know how much money we made as civilians, how much did our fathers make and did we own any land, etc. When one prisoner was asked if he was wealthy enough to take his wife to a restaurant once a month, he told the Chinese officer that he could take his wife out four times a week if he felt like it. That seemed to make the officer angry. Many times we and the interrogators got into sharp arguments. They told one prisoner that he was op-pressed by the capitalists. His reply to them was, "The hell I am." He told them that he had a wife, two children, a car, a place to live, plenty to eat, and that they were crazy.

From the very start it became apparent that the Chinese inter-rogation techniques were an integral part of their indoctrination program. Instead of soliciting truthful answers to their questions, the interrogators were satisfied only with answers that suited their purpose. We found ourselves arguing with the Chinese over such matters as to the amount of income or social status of our families

As we revised our status and income statistics downward, the Communist seemed more pleased and less prone to argue. Soon we began to see that these were the wrong responses. As the questioning continued along the same lines, we began to down play our estimates of our family income, the beauty of the family home. We began to fabricate stories of hungry childhood, a family income so small that after food was bought there was no money left to buy clothes. This seemed to please the Chinese.

I first met my good friends Andrew (Chief) Aguirre, Jim De-Long, Roy Farley, Ray Hikida, James Petty, Daniel Yesko, and Daniel Martinez and James Talbert (who were from my Dog Company) to mention a few here at Kanggye, and we were to-gether throughout our period as guest of the Chinese Communists, except for Martinez, Petty, and Hikida, who were taken to Camp Five, sometime in 1952. I was 18 years old when I was taken prisoner. (With my POW friends today, I am known as the baby.) For my twentieth birthday, my roommates stole some food from the North Koreans and made a special dish for me. That was very special. It was only a small bowl of food, but very special. This was at my first permanent camp, Changsong, North Korea.

We were allowed to write a letter, which was supposed to be sent to our parents and families. Contents of the letter, "We are in the hands of the Chinese Peoples Army. They have been very nice to us. They gave us a very good Christmas dinner, and we will be home after the war."

The letters were received by a Sharon Maffioli from her husband (Leonard J. Maffioli, who was also captured at the reservoir.) My parents received the above mentioned letter during the spring of 1951. That was the last news that they had from me until some time during 1953.

Here, we discovered that our captors recognized neither the Geneva Convention nor the humane treatment of prisoners of war that had been developed over the years. The fact that these principles meant nothing to our captors immediately placed us in fearful dilemma. I don't think the Chinese had any compassion for life, especially American lives.

Their favorite excuse for poor food, lack of medical care and clothing was that the United States aircraft was constantly bombing their supply lines, preventing necessary supplies from getting through. We were told that we were being fed because the Chinese were good and were concerned about our well being. We never received any Red Cross packages, until July 1953 as the Chinese regarded the International Red Cross as a "Running Dog" of the American imperialist.

Not all of the prisoners captured during the Chosin Reservoir battles shared the same problems or experiences. According to some of the Marines, a Chinese doctor provided medications of a far lower standard than would be found in a normal field first-aid station. Aspirin or APC pills were a common remedy; the next most common service seems to have been removing black, frozen toes without sedation. Some of the sickest prisoners disappeared from camp; we were told that they were being taken to a hospital.

During January 1951, a sergeant and a corporal were among those taken from Kanggye to the so-called Chinese Hospital. One had been wounded, and the other was suffering, among other ailments, from frozen feet. Two others were also taken at about this same time. One was suffering from wounds and the other had acute dysentery. Of the four, only one survived. He stated that the Chinese Hospital seems to have been a primitive collection of mud and wattle huts in a nearby valley.

However, I do not recall any medical care being offered as the Chinese soldiers had no medical personnel in their ranks. The Chinese never medically attended my wounds. My wounds took nine months to heal.

Shortly after Christmas, we were allowed to clean up. We heated water in an old 55 gallon drum, and I think everyone from our hut (which consisted of about 30 men) washed in this water. This was the first opportunity that we had to clean up since being captured. According to some of the Marines, they arose at 7:00 a.m. and either took a short walk or performed light calisthenics. They also stated that they were allowed to wash their faces and hands. The only time that I can recalled being able to clean up was when we washed up in the 55 gallon drum.

As I mentioned before, just prior to being wounded in the forehead, I was firing a 75 mm recoilless rifle and had just reloaded the last round when I was hit in the head. After capture, a curious Chinese soldier, while examining the weapon, pulled the trigger. The back blast from the weapon killed or wounded several of their Officers. Sergeant Olson said that I should tell them that I was the gunner.

Two or three days later, I was called up to the Chinese Headquarters for questioning. They asked me over and over, time after time what was my job on the front lines and I replied that I had only been a jeep driver and that was all, because of my age (eighteen years old), I had not been trained in any special field. They said, "You are lying, we know different." I maintained that my job was only a jeep driver and that was all. They insisted that I was lying and that I had the innocent blood of the Korean and Chinese People on my hands.

We had to perform daily chores which consisted of several hours of wood chopping, gathering dead wood from the surrounding hillsides, hauling water from the river, which was about 3/4 of a mile away, and keeping the snow cleared from the court yard of our quarters. During these daily work periods, the Chinese herded us into the hills to gather fire wood for the camp. These work details would leave camp and walk two or more miles to gather dead wood which was covered with snow. We had to carry the wood back to camp on our backs.

There was little chance to escape; we could not blend in with the Korean people, and we had no food, and we were at least a couple of hundred air miles from our front lines. Our chances were about a thousand to one of succeeding. Still recovering from wounds like so many others, I did not give damn, as I was hurting, hungry and cold, and when the guards pushed me around, I got angry and threw a large chunk of wood at one of the guards. I was knocked down by another guard with a rifle butt against the small of my back. Another time I was hit against the right ear.

We were forced to do work that called for men in top physical condition instead of the weakened condition that we were in. The Chinese on many occasions claimed that I was not doing my share of the work and that I was too slow and lazy. Any organization or preplanning on the part of the Chinese when were herded into the hills to gather fire wood was lacking. Most of the time we did not have any tools to cut the wood with.

They remind us daily that they were peace-loving people who had come to the aid of their North Korean allies. They told us on many occasions that they did not want to keep prisoners, but, were forced to keep us temporarily as they were unable to negotiate with the United States and the United Nations, and that they would be as lenient as possible with us. They continuously reminded us that we would be released as soon as possible, if we would cooperate during interrogations, classes, and work details, and if we did not impede their efforts by being rebellious or attempting to escape.

One of the prisoners who had walked for two days and nights in the snow without shoes made a speech for the Chinese, because he understood that "we would make it home if we acted like we were studying." He wrote two or three articles for the camp newspaper. When he was asked to write more, he refused. He finally told the Chinese that he was through and that he was going to depend on God to get him out of there.

This soldier, on the march to Kanggye had after several days of marching, removed his boots one day, and a Chinese guard took them, leaving this poor man without any shoes. We saw each other after the Police Action ended in 1955 at a Military Court Martial of one of the sergeants who collaborated with the Chinese.

As I had mentioned before, one form of early POW collaboration was giving speeches denouncing the United States and its policies, democracies, etc. These prisoners received compensation for their articles and speeches. Each of these was constantly rubbed in our faces by the Chinese Communists as we withstood the misery of subzero weather, inadequate clothing, food, medical attention, shelter, and any other misery these sadistic masters of cruelly could dream up.

Seven weeks now and my wounds still had not been treated, and they kept breaking open every time I moved. There was no doctor in camp to care for the sick and wounded. American corpsmen (medical personnel) were allowed to assist, but no medication or medical supplies was provided. At no time did the Chinese provide any help. I and others used our undershirts for bandages.

During the first three months of captivity, approximately 35 or more of the prisoners here died, and these deaths were not accidental, but caused by deprivation and dehumanization and on top of all this came severe illness without any medical care. Later, probably in February, several sick prisoners were loaded on oxcarts ostensibly for movement to a hospital.

(One of the prisoners, a sergeant, related that the sick prisoners were told they were being taken to a place where there was a large hospital with beds, doctors and nurses. The small caravan of ox-carts departed from Kanggye at midnight, but instead of taking the prisoners to a hospital the Chinese turned them over to North Korean Police. According to the sergeant, the sick died like flies. The Chinese took control over the group for about two weeks, but then they were turned back over to the Korean Police again. Finally in May 1951, the survivors were turned over to the Chinese at Camp One, Changsong.)

We, like the Chinese guards, were infected with body lice, our skin was infected and we were constantly scratching lice from our clothing and hair. Our thumbs turned black with ingrained blood from killing the lice between our nails.

Camp One, Company Seven

After the march north from AWOL Valley, we arrived at Camp about October 25, 1951. It was in the town of Changsong, about 30 miles northeast of the border city of Sinuiju. There were more than one thousand United Nations prisoners in this camp. This was the most western camp along the Yalu River. It was near a railroad junction which we could not see, but which American aircraft bombed just about every night. We could hear the bombing and see the search lights, searching the night sky for the bombers and fighters.

Upon our arrival, I remember seeing American GIs locked in the dark stinking cells of solitary confinement. They had been placed there after pain and infection from wounds had driven them insane and/or for some infraction of camp rules. Our captors had cruelly (without proper medical knowledge or equipment) removed bullets, amputated infected limbs, and then placed these suffering animal-like creatures in solitary confinement for months, to live or die, as they would, to get them out of the way so that moans and screams could not be heard.

As we straggled in, the GIs (POWs) there saw us coming and gathered around, hoping for some news, and they were surprised to hear that we had been captured nearly a year before. Some of these prisoners had been here for six months or more, some taken during the Chosin Reservoir and some captured during the early spring of 1951.

It was a cold freezing day, and the Chinese kept us standing around for hours waiting to be assigned to one of the several huts in the compound and to be given some food. The next day, we were registered at the Guard Headquarters and assigned to squads and huts in the seventh compound (Company Seven) with anywhere from ten to twenty men to a room. This of course, was much better then what we had been used to living in. The housing arrangements were similar to the average Korean home, with straw roofs, mud walls, paper windows (in the doors only), and an earthen-floored kitchen, consisting of an old kettle, used for cooking and heating water.

There were approximately two hundred or more starving American soldiers and Marines in this compound, suffering from wounds and other illness. The first week here, we were given one blanket for every two men (our first since being captured.)

There was one other compound to the south of us, which was separated from us by a barbed wire fence. It also had about the same number of prisoners in the same physical condition as ourselves.

The main road (Main Supply Route) ran right through the center of our camp. Several times our planes strafed and bombed the Chinese trucks using this road. During one of these strafing and bombings, several of our men were wounded. One was Roy Farley, who got a piece of shrapnel in his foot. Our Air Force had no way of knowing that we were being held here. There were no identifying markers to indicate that this town was being used as a prisoner of war camp. It was approximately six months or so later that we finally got the Chinese to put up a camp marker.

We were all housed in three rows of thatched huts with under the floor heating, contrived centuries before. The system, called, "Ondal" consists of a kind of furnace from which hot air and smoke flow through the passages under the floor. Our huts were on the right side of the supply route, with the last row being approximately one hundred yards from the main road and with a fence enclosing three sides. The Chinese guards occupied the housing on the opposite side of the road.

Our food—which consisted of barley and millet—was brought to us in a bucket twice a day and served to us like pigs. The morning meal was usually a barley or millet soup, and occasionally we would get a bowl of white rice for our evening meal.

One day we found a dead chicken and we cooked it, not caring how rotten or diseased it might be, and every one in my squad tried to get a bit of the cooked meat. We had experienced near-starvation from the time we were captured and during our isolation over the past ten months. Here at least, we were getting two small meals a day.

Near the end of 1951, the Chinese separated all of the officers from the enlisted men and moved them to Camp Two. Around March 1952, the Non-Commissioned Officers were moved to Camp Four. I never saw any of them again during the so called "Police Action."

During the day, we could see American and Chinese Communists planes firing at each other overhead. The U.S. planes were always out numbered two-to-one. One thing that cheered us up was the air fights between our planes and the Chinese. Our camp was right under Mig Alley, and we could see the Migs and our planes going after each other almost every day. We had a hard time identifying who was who, until one day when they brought in a captured pilot, and he told us to listen to the rate of fire. The Mig's had a slower rate of fire than our planes. After that we cheered every time a Chinese plane got shot down.

We had a good group of men here (with the exception of a very few), blacks and whites working together, helping each other and sharing without complaining. A friend, Barnes from Missouri, made up crazy country stories, jokes and songs, which we would all join in and sing. Farley (captured same time as me and from Baker Company, 31st Infantry) told us about his life as a boy growing up in West Virginia before joining the Army. Farley and I both were eighteen at the time of capture. After this, we all took part in relating something that we did as a youngster and why we joined the service. One of our friends, Harbour, also from Baker Company, knew how to hypnotize, and he tried to teach us.

As soon as the sun went down, the Chinese herded us back into our dark cells, where we sat in the dark until we fell asleep, which wasn't too long afterwards. Soon after, the Chinese came

108

around to each room, took a headcount, and positioned a guard at each hut, with a couple or so patrolling between the huts and a dozen or so posted around the back of our compound. If we had to step out to go to the outhouse (latrine) which was located approximately ten feet directly behind the huts, we would be challenged by the guards in front and rear of our huts, and they would remain near us until we returned to our room.

Little did we know or realize that their eyes were also as bad as ours at night (from night blindness). The blindness was caused from a lack of food nutrients. We all suffered from night blindness, the condition varies from a simple small dot to total darkness. I could not see anything at night. When we went out at night, we had to be led by the hand. What a sight, a line of grown men holding hands going to the toilet.

I remember my 20th birthday. My friends surprised me with a small dish of food that they had prepared, after smuggling different ingredients in after the day's labor in the hills. This was small bits that they had stolen from the local Korean farms; this I shall never forget.

I believe that it was early 1952, that the Chinese moved the black prisoners to another location. The treatment and status of these prisoners was and still is unknown to me. I am sure that they were treated better than we, as the Chinese claimed that we were all prejudiced and that we treated the blacks like slaves. One of the Chinese officers made the statement, that he had been to the United States and saw how the Negroes were the scum of the land, how they are raped, beaten, and hanged. He went on to say, 'We the Chinese people feel sorry for you, the American Negro. We want to be your friend. We, the free people of the world, welcome you like a brother, with you as our equal.' One of the black prisoners (Turner from Michigan) refused to be moved and told the Chinese that he was an American and that he wanted to stay with us.

After the separation of the Officers, non-commissioned officers and blacks, we settled down to a more routine camp life, working in the hills, cutting trees, hauling the cut trees from the mountains three to five miles to the town center on our shoulders and backs. Many times, these logs would require three to four men to carry them. The logs were used to build outdoor toilets, repair the bridges around Changsong and for fire wood.

One time the Chinese asked an American Indian, Hatch, "What is your nationality?" and Hatch replied, "F.B.I." The Chinese immediately became very interested in him and started asking him a lot of questions. They wanted to know what was he doing in Korea, and why would the FBI have an agent in Korea and the U.S. Army. Hatch was with the 31st Infantry Medical Company, captured at Chosin Reservoir. Finally, after several days of questions, Hatch told them that he was a full blooded American Indian, "F.B.I." for short.

Here at Camp One, the Chinese cruelly performed operations for removing bullets and amputating infected limbs and toes, and the incisions and drainage of abscesses. All were carried out without anesthetic and by using improvised instruments. Surgical problems were handled in a haphazard manner. It was necessary to wait several weeks to obtain a few surgical instruments and the barest minimum of anesthetic materials.

I recall that during the winter of 1951-52, one of our fellow prisoner's feet were frozen so bad that he could not walk. The Chinese proceeded to amputate the toes on both of his feet with an old pair of scissors. They did not use any medication to prepare him or later to avoid infection or to kill the pain. His name was Red Campbell. The Chinese then turned him loose in the compound, where he ran around, screaming with pain, on his swollen, bloody, blackened feet. He eventually went out of his mind, and at nights, you could hear him screaming from his cell across the way from us. We tried our best to comfort him and looked after his feet as best as we could, but as we had no medication, there was nothing that we could do for him. After the operation, he could no longer recognize anyone from the compound. Finally, after weeks of agony, the Chinese moved him to some other location. We never saw him again after that.

Another close friend and squad member, Kaver, had been wounded in the throat with the bullet still lodged there. He could only eat soup because of the infection, and we stole anything that we could get our hands on to keep him alive. He was exchanged during Operation Little Switch, in the spring of 1953. (During Operation Little Switch, many of the sick and seriously wounded prisoners were exchanged through an agreement worked out between the United Nations and the Chinese Communists and North Koreans.) Kaver's weight went from approximately 180 pounds when he was first captured to about 90 pounds of skin and bones when he was released. In 1954, I received an invitation to his wedding. I am sorry to say, he died a couple of years later.

The Chinese doctors were not properly trained for their jobs. On the average, their medical training consisted of anything from no formal training whatsoever to approximately six months in a hurry up aid course designed for bandaging, which is somewhat similar to the First Aid course provided us.

Camp Rules which were posted and/or made known to us at Camp Number One were:

Kinds of punishment set for violations of discipline and system
Hard labor (at least three days)
Lock-up (at least seven days)
Imprisonment and hard labor for not reforming oneself
(at least three months)
Life imprisonment
Students committing the following misbehavior, will be
considered as violators and disciplined:
Reactionary elements (Imperialist elements) who adopt a
hostile attitude toward the Chinese People's Volunteers,
swear at the Chinese personnel, refuse to go for work details and continue to be stubborn after being questioned,
organize and take command of an escape and cross the
wire fence at random, throw away or burn one's clothing, shoes, bedding or blankets (such as those who defe-

III

cate in the pants and with lice on them, or adopt
any other method to destroy them), rob the Korean
People's personal belongings, urinate or defecate at
any place other than the latrine, leave the compound
without asking for leave, damage any book or magazine for no reason, or use them as toilet or cigarette
paper. All captured officers and men must correctly
understand the Lenient Policy of the Chinese People's Army, observe the directions, and strictly ad-
here to the disciplinary rules.
Every Sunday each squad shall hold a daily life criticism meeting to review in focal points, the carrying
out of life and study disciplinary rules and regulations of the past week. While attending classes, everyone must be serious and in an orderly manner
should line up to report the number of men present;
pay full attention to lectures and taking notes; ask
permission from the instructor before leaving for the
latrine. The bad behaviors of disobedience, such action, as making noises, joking and dozing are
strictly forbidden.

Camp One, Company Four

Company Seven was broken up during the month of August,
1952. Several of us were moved to Company Four, which was
located at the north end of Changsong. Many others, including
Daniel Yesko, Bill Carter, and Bobby Gene Rains were moved
to another camp further north. It was here at Camp One that I
first met Richard (Dick) Rook and Norman Deatherage, who was
with Baker Company, 38th Regiment of the 2nd Infantry Division.

At one point in the summer 1952, the Chinese had made us
catch and kill flies. We each had to kill at least 20 flies each
day and then tell them. A couple of friends decided that we would
go down to the latrine (outdoor house) and get our catch. We

caught our flies and let them suffocate. We counted the same flies for three or four days, before they got wise to our little game. The Chinese stated that we had to have sanitation and that each of us had to catch at least 20 flies each day.

About this time, the Chinese put up a loudspeaker throughout the camp, and every day we heard the Chinese news report in English, for our benefit, that described how they were beating the United States and the United Nations forces in Korea. Come rain or snow, winter or spring, we had to go outside and sit on our little stools and listen to the lectures for hours, sitting there freezing and aching from not being able to move.

One of the worst things about the location of our compound, was that we could see the British Soldiers, and they would be playing ball, smoking cigarettes, going for walks and so forth, while we were allowed none of these privileges.

Here, every one suffered from dysentery and beriberi. All around were cases of malaria, jaundice, and bone fever illness. Many of the men merely lay down, staring empty into space, refusing to eat, until one morning they were found dead. It was easier to die then it was to live. One of our friends refused to eat and we told him, "Go ahead and die, we will help your young wife spend your insurance money when we get out of here." This helped him make it back.

Friday, who was from Massachusetts, took sick one night, and the next day, he was dead. Kilpatrick disappeared one day, and the Chinese said that he had gotten himself killed.

The Chinese finally made a so called camp hospital around fall of 1952. Just about everyone tried to get into the hospital for better food. The hospital compound was frequently as cold as our own huts, however, there were some sleeping cots, and better food was provided.

The average Chinese doctor, who conducted sick call, elicited only the chief complaints and prescribed medicine for that symptom. It was a general rule that only one symptom would be treated at a time. Many prisoners who went on sick call complaining of pain in any part of their bodies were treated by the so-called "needle doctor". This treatment consisted of a short blunt needle connected to a spring device and a handle which was placed on the skin in various parts of the shoulder of the patient. After the needles were in place, the needle doctor thumped the handle of the needle so that the spring would cause a vibration. Another practice was the administration of chicken liver, where a small piece of chicken liver was implanted in the prisoner under the arm, in the skin on the right side of the chest.

It was here at Company Four that I met Howard Evans from Binger, Oklahoma. Howard said one day shortly after my arrival at the fourth company that I came over to his squad room and stated, "I understand that there is a soldier here from Oklahoma!" From that time on we became close friends. After mails stated arriving, Howard received several letters from his young bride (Loretta). Loretta managed to put a cigarette or a stick of gum in each of her letters. Howard either read or let me read Loretta's letters. Howard had been drafted into the Army on January 8, 1951. After basic training, and prior to being shipped to Japan, he and Loretta were married. They enjoyed one week together before Howard had to report for shipment to Japan. Howard joined the 1st Cavalry Division in Korea during October 1951 and was captured on November 2, 1951. He was wounded on the right side of his head. After being captured, his trip to Chang-song (also known as Camp Three and later known as Camp One) involved a truck ride and on foot. He and Ben Comeau and a few others made the trip to Changsong. He and Ben arrived at Changsong on or around November 19, 1951. Howard was assigned to the 8th squad of the Fourth Company.

After our arrival at Company Four, and until we were released, a few of us paraded around the compound pretending to be playing imaginary music instruments or taking our imaginary dogs for walks around the compound.

With the coming of winter, 1952, the Chinese issued us a blue cotton padded jacket, pants, overcoat and a pair of padded tennis shoes. They were warm, but we wore them throughout the winter,

114

and by the time spring came, they were so stinking and filthy, you could hardly stand them.

During our wood cutting details, we met some Koreans and traded our small sugar ration (we were given a small ration of sugar, starting around the end of 1952) for whatever vegetables mostly turnips we could get from the Koreans.

For Christmas of 1952, we got a small treat, a whole dried fish and some white rice. We had not seen this much food since being captured. We ate the head, eyes and all.

We lost many good men because many just refused to eat the stuff that they called food. If you didn't eat for three or four days, you would die. We had many who just stayed in their huts, lying down and refusing to get up. We told them to get up. We had to harass them so badly that they would occasionally get up and say "If I could get my hands on you, I'll kill you." If you got them angry enough, they would get up and have a chance to survive. There were at least 500 who died in Camp One.

Very few North Koreans lived in Changsong or around our compound. Most of them had moved into the hills, away from the MSR (Main Supply Route) which ran right through Changsong. When the Chinese Communists took over the town, they ran the rest of the Korean families into the hills so that they could use the town as a POW Camp. Many of the Korean families that lived near the camp were quite friendly with us, giving us tobacco and other things that we could use without the Chinese knowing about it. I think that most of the North Korean people that I came in contact with hated us and perhaps hated the war just as much. There were several North Korean families that helped us, and there were others that really hated us.

Near the end of 1952, our food supply did improve a bit; we were given some soy beans, soy bean milk, and a little meat every once in a while. We were allowed to boil our drinking water and to take a bath in the river which was located a couple hundred yards to the rear of our camp. This river (Ch'ong Ch'on) was a part of the Yalu River.

115

December 1952, a fellow prisoner from West Virginia went to the hospital and was operated on for a rupture. Just as he was about to be released, he suddenly came down with a pain in the testicles and a Chinese doctor operated on that. As a result of this operation, they removed one of his testicles, claiming that it had become gangrenous. He was returned to the compound after this operation. The doctor informed him that he was better. However, sometime in January 1953, he was back in the hospital complaining that he still had pains in the same area. They kept feeding him shots to cure the pain each day, but the shots only provided temporary relief. He was in constant pain for about two months. The Chinese doctor informed two other prisoners that they each had the same problem as the young man from West Virginia, and that their problem was caused from V.D., and that they would give them special shots to cure the problem.

The young man from West Virginia started acting crazy at times, say crazy things and having fits. He said that the Chinese who gave him the shots always had to stick the needle in four or five times before he finally got the needle in the right spot. One day three Chinese soldiers went to his room and beat him over the head with a metal pipe. They stated that he had attacked one of their guards. The Chinese then put him in a cell, that was the last time we saw him.

As I mentioned before, better than half of our compound had night blindness. The winter of 1952-53 was really bad. It was comical in a way, but also pathetic. Every night, just before bed-time, there would be a long line of men holding onto each other going to the latrine. We ran into fence posts, huts, etc.

Several of our fellow prisoners were losing their eye sight, both during the day and night and had to be led everywhere. One friend, (Austin) lost the center vision of both eyes, and he was still required to work in the hills cutting and carrying the logs back to camp.

While at Camp One, I recall one prisoner whose legs were so infected that the Chinese attempted to amputate them with an old pair of scissors. During the first operation, the skin was not peeled back to cover up the amputation and further infection set in. Several weeks later, his legs had to be amputated again. This operation was performed by a Chinese doctor, who had been educated in the United States. The soldier suffered agonizing pain and had to be carried everywhere until finally, he learned to walk on his stumps. This young man was very remarkable, considering that after losing both legs and suffering the most horrible pain, he still maintained a high morale and returned home after the Police Action ended.

During the winter of 1952/53, we talked the Chinese into letting us build bunkbeds, so that we wouldn't have to sleep on the earthen floor. To this date, I still can't figure out how we built these beds. We didn't have any tools, and the only material available was logs that we gathered from the hills.

In the spring of 1953, the Chinese brought in rice flour with which we made rice bread once a day, this being our only meal in the evening, with our usual barley soup in the mornings. We steam-cooked the bread, something we learned from our friends Richard Makua and Joe Young from Hawaii. I recall that one time we received some baked bread from China. It was during the winter, and it took about two weeks to reach our camp. The temperature was about 38 degrees below zero which helped to keep the bread from spoiling. The bread was frozen solid, like a rock. There was no way we could eat the bread.

The Chinese were very skillful in their form of torture. A favorite one was making a prisoner stand at attention, holding his arms straight out from his body for hours, and if he dropped them, they would strike his arms. We were also made to sit for hours at attention on our damn little stools, and it was very miserable after a while. Throughout the period of captivity, there were many instances of individual brutality, solitary confinement, beatings, witholding of food and water, and exposure to cold weather were common punishment.

Special confinement consisted of restriction from freedom of the compound either in a small area with other prisoners or individual cells measuring approximately two and one half feet by

117

five feet, with an earthen floor, no bedding, only the clothing you had on and the friendly rats. Solitary confinement was always accomplished by restrictions on the quantity of food and water, time spent out of doors and other activities.

Prior to being placed in solitary confinement, you were tried by a so-called "Kangaroo Court" for alleged crimes against the Chinese and/or Korean People, resistance or being a reactionary and the punishment would vary for each offense. After being confined for a couple of months, you would resemble someone from the caveman days, with long coarse masses of hair and shaggy beards, unsteady walk, scratched skin from digging for lice and the other types of bugs crawling over your skin and through your clothing and the horrible filth from not being able to wash.

Occasionally at nights, the men in solitary confinement could be heard screaming from pain or the anguish of being in solitary confinement. Sometime the Chinese would give you a glass of water and a few peanuts for your meal. The peanuts played havoc with your bowels. You couldn't talk to anyone, and no one was allowed to come near your cell. You were allowed to sleep, but you were continuously roused by the guards to make sure that you were still there.

The Communists frequently tied up prisoners, hand to feet, with rope or whatever material that was available, so tightly that the circulation was cut off or the rope cut our arms and legs and caused us to lapse into unconsciousness. They never beat us in camp, but as soon as they got us away from the compound, they would beat us.

One prisoner refused to give the Chinese Communists the information that they wanted. He was taken out one evening and beaten by two Chinese guards until the early hours of the morning. At one point another guard came and took him to the river and gave him a personal beating. Winter months provided the Communists with opportunities for increased torture.

Prisoners were known to have been marched barefoot onto the frozen river and water poured over their feet, with temperatures well below 20 degrees. The Chinese guards in charge of the prisoners in solitary confinement were adept at this sort of brutality and seem to have been given full rein to stand prisoners at attention, spit on them, kick them and wake them at odd hours throughout the night and humiliate them at will.

Ten of us had to report to the guard headquarters three times a week for four weeks. We were made to stand at attention for hours, holding our arms straight out in front of us. One day, I was pulled from the morning formation and had to stand at attention in front of the compound until late in the afternoon without eating or water to drink. When one of my friends brought me some food and water, the guard took the food and water and threw it on the ground.

They were good at tying prisoners up for long periods of time, standing us at attention for unbearable periods or until we dropped. These and other forms of treatment forced many a prisoner to assume a less defiant attitude and became less resistant. The Communists had no rules about the treatment of prisoners of war. They used browbeating, mental pressures, and varied physical tortures that they had learned over thousands of years. Goodburlet, a friend was subject to continuously inhumane treatment because he refused to pay attention during the lectures and discussions. He spent many hours in solitary confinement.

Lively, Bittner, Patton, and Fulk, all were placed in solitary confinement because someone had informed on their activities. Benton, refused to sign any confessions and was put in solitary confinement in January 1953.

Many times I was gotten up during the night or early morning hours and taken to the guard headquarters to be lectured to and stood at attention for some infraction of their damn rules. Austin, upon his release, during an interrogation made the statement to the Military Intelligence Processing Board, that I openly made statements against Communists.

During the winter of 1952/53, the Chinese singled out many of us for intensive individualized pressure and torture. One or more nights each week, they came our huts and got us up after midnight, and we were taken to the guard headquarters, stood at attention, listening to the guard commander lecture us on being reactionary.

One night during the winter of 1952/53, Douglas, myself and several others risked severe punishment by breaking a fellow prisoner out of solitary confinement, where he had nearly frozen to death and was suffering from malnutrition and cold. When we got to him, he had turned blue, almost purple, from the cold, and he was unable to move.

The Chinese guard discovered our act and tried to herd us back to our huts, but by now our group had grown, and we had the prisoner mixed in our group, long enough to get him some food and some warm clothing.

From that night on, once again we were pulled from our huts between midnight and two a.m., and taken to the guard headquarters, where we were made to stand at attention in low ceiling rooms, for hours, arms held straight out in front of us, while the guard commander lectured and interrogated us for participating in the break out and about being reactionaries. During these interrogations, they read statements which they had allegedly obtained from other prisoners, with the names of each one of us who had participated and who had been named as reactionaries.

They kept us there for hours, with threats that if we didn't cooperate, we would be sentenced to hard labor and not returned to our loved ones. This harassment went on for about three weeks. Several nights later, two fellow prisoners were taken from our compound to some other camp or place.

Richard Rook

I had been captured on May 19, 1951 at 5:45 AM. We had been surrounded for three days before, and as you can imagine, we were all very hungry and dirty. I personally hadn't shaven for 8 or 10 days. Of course, we had no idea that we were in as much trouble as we were, and it wouldn't have made any difference anyway. On the front line a person can't keep as clean as he should. I believe that all the time I spent on line before being captured, I had had only two showers and changes of clothes. We took sponge baths, using our helmets as wash basins, whenever time and situation allowed.

We thought that was bad enough, not knowing how our lives were about to change. And change they did because it would be the middle of the following December before we were given soap, shave and haircut. That's approximately 7½ months for lice and dirt to have their way with us. And have their way with us they did. The lice had a picnic in our extremely long hair and in the seams of our clothes without the threat of being accosted by their number one enemy, soap and water. I don't know this to be fact, but I feel that some of the men that died had succumbed to thousands of lice bites. During the day, when we were resting from the previous night's march, we would all sit around and "snap" lice between our thumb nails. Having no soap, this wasn't very sanitary but it was the only way we had to try to keep up with their ever increasing numbers. We would rinse our hands every chance we got in rice paddies (with that good old human waste water) or in mountain streams. The adage about the "cure being worst then the disease" probably held true here.

When we finally arrived at our final destination, which was October 13, 1951, we were really "crawling," if you get my drift. We were assigned 10 men to an 8 foot by 10 foot room. At this point we still hadn't had a haircut or been issued soap. In these close quarters, it became almost unbearable. It's hard for anyone to imagine what it's like to have thousands of little bugs feeding on you and not be able to do anything about it. We were not allowed outside of our rooms after dark, so we all had to just lie there and let the lice eat away at us. We hated for the sun to go down because there wasn't any electricity in the rooms, and all we could do was lie down and try to sleep, that's when we came under attack.

When we were finally given haircuts and soap we had a fighting chance. They used the old styled, hand-operated hair clippers to give us both a shave and a haircut. They used those clippers all over our faces, including our eyebrows. We were sure strange looking guys until our eyebrows grew back. I was appointed a squad leader by the Chinese, so I told my squad members that there was going to be some changes in our life styles. We all agreed that one SOP (standard operating procedure) would be adopted and rigorously enforced. That SOP went something like this: Every man in the squad, regardless of weather conditions, would strip down, completely naked, and bathe. He would, at this time, put on fresh clothes which had been previously boiled for not less than 15 minutes. In just a few short weeks we were lice-free. Of course, we had to maintain our vigil for the duration of our incarceration, and it wasn't easy. It was difficult to find the wood needed and also the opportunity to accomplish what had to be accomplished. It wasn't long before other squads saw the success we had had and followed suit.

Do you remember what I said earlier about the "latrines" being close to our living quarters and without covers? We thought that would change after we became settled into our permanent quarters. When we arrived in Chung Song, North Korea on 13 October 51, they put us to work digging the typical hole, 30 feet long, 6 feet wide and 5 feet deep. The only difference with this one was that it had a roof, no sides, just a roof. I started to complain immediately, only to deaf ears. I told them that we would make extra trips into the mountains to get the wood we would need to build a proper latrine—still no response.

The next spring, when the weather warmed up enough for the flies to breed, I renewed my efforts to get us a fly-tight latrine. Again, it was to no avail. It was then that we noticed strange goings on. The off-duty Chinese guards were running around swatting flies and collecting them in, what appeared to be, match boxes. It wasn't long after we saw the guards doing their "thing," that the powers-to-be called us together. They told us that in order to control the fly population, we would each be required to kill and collect 10 flies each day and each squad leader would be held responsible for their squad. This was so ridiculous that it wasn't even funny. I couldn't convince those stupid guards that during the time it took to swat one fly, about a million were hatching just a few feet behind our living quarters.

We went along with this stupid order for about a week or so. They collected the dead flies every evening and one night when they called me to turn in the flies for my squad, I told them again how dumb it was and that my squad would not be turning any more flies in. The other squad leaders agreed with me and that was that—no more fly-killing. In the spring of 1953 we finally got the materials we needed to build a fly-tight latrine. It was a real beauty too, everything was tight and clean. It was at least a "24-holer" with tight lids, and a urinal to accommodate from 10 to 15 men. I don't think one man ever abused this facility by not closing the lids or leaving the doors open. We even had lime to control odors—like I said it was a real beauty, and I'm sure the Chinese learned something about controlling fly populations.

After we were in Chung Song only a short while, no more than a month, we were bombed. It happened about 10:30 p.m. At that time we were still totally integrated. They had us all together, British, Turks and African-Americans. They even had the officers, not living with us, but closeby in the same town. The only reason we knew this was they told us that an American officer was killed as a result. The next morning, after the bombing, the "Chinks" didn't waste any time in drafting and circulating a letter of protest against the bombing, addressed to none other than President Truman. I would have died before signing that protest until Jock, a British soldier, convinced me that this would be a great way to get our names out. He was at least 10 years older than me and a WW II veteran, so I decided to sign. I knew that my family had no idea of whether I was dead or alive. As it turned out, a month or so later, they reached an agreement in Panmunjom to exchange names and to mark the camps clearly. I don't know why, all of a sudden, they reached agreement so soon after we were bombed. Maybe it was because of the letter we signed, but I rather believe it was because the UN scared the hell out of them.

Everything in Korea was, and probably still is, very primitive. The only source of energy available for cooking and heating was wood. As soon as weather permitted, we were forced to go into the surrounding mountains to cut and haul wood back to camp, which in many cases was as far as 8 to 10 miles. The Chinese call their measure of weight a kaddie, which is equivalent to the metric measure for a kilogram, 2.2 pounds. Each man was required to bring in 1000 kaddies of wood each year. In addition to carrying the wood in, we had to fall and cut up the trees into logs of approximately 50 kaddies in size. The only tools supplied for this task were 2-man cross-cut saws and dull axes. We would spend several days cutting the wood, and then we would spend several more hauling it in. If I remember correctly, it took five or six sessions of first cutting and then hauling, to get our quota in.

I know that 110 pounds (50 kaddies) doesn't sound like too much weight for a grown man to carry but when you compare our weight to that of the log, it's a lot—a whole lot. Most of us weighed less than 100 pounds and were weak from dysentery and malnutrition. To make matters worse, the Chinese didn't haul their own wood—we did. They told us that the wood was used only to cook "our" meals, and they not only cooked their meals, they also heated their buildings with OUR wood. They were so afraid that we wouldn't carry a full 50 kaddies that they had a guard at the bottom of the mountain with a scale mounted on a tripod to weigh each log. Many men were injured during these episodes in the mountains of North Korea. I'm still suffering from a back injury from one of those details.

When a person's diet changes drastically and very rapidly the way ours did, you can't imagine what a situation like that can do to the human body. We all took for granted such things as meat and vegetables. We didn't know or could care less about the vitamins that we obtained from the various foods that we ate on a daily basis. I could detail all of the vitamins necessary to keep us healthy but there are far too many (almost two dozen). I'll hit on the most important and most commonly missing from even our diets of today, especially our young adults' diets:

Vitamin A is obtained from fish oils, milk and dark green vegetables. The lack of which causes night blindness, beriberi and cracking at the corners of the mouth. Vitamin B complex obtained from yeast, meat and bran from grains and without it one's metabolism is upset. Vitamin K is obtained from green vegetables. Without vitamin K, blood won't coagulate.

I could go on and on, but I'm sure the picture is quite clear. We were all on the same diet, so naturally we all suffered the same types of ills. Beriberi was the one I suffered from the most. I remember the pain was so bad at night, that it was impossible to sleep. I would lie on my back with my knees pulled up under my chin and just rock back and forth, back and forth.

As soon as the sun started to go down, we all went blind. It was quite a sight, for those of us who didn't get it as bad as others, to see the half-blind leading the blind down to the latrine before bedtime. It was total confusion, believe me. There were many, many other problems suffered because of our poor diet, but these will give you an idea of what it was like.

In the camps, the cheapness of life was very difficult to handle. The way men were dying all around us made us feel that life didn't mean much which made it seem easier to accept the possibility that maybe, "I might be next."

I didn't spend a Christmas "on line" (in combat) but did spend two as a POW. As you no doubt know, the Communists do not believe in God so naturally they didn't want us to worship a God that they didn't believe in. So, that meant only one thing; that we would just have to sneak around. We were not allowed to gather in groups of more than two, which made the situation even worse. We lived in 8' by 10' rooms (10 men to a room) so we couldn't gather too many at one time. But we managed to have several services so that everyone who wanted to, could attend. We had to place look-outs in front of the hut to warn us to keep our voices down when a guard was near. We also had Sunday services and believe it or not, we were only caught a few times.

In those days everyone smoked, and this was one of the hardest things to adjust to. Of course the Chinese didn't care if we had cigarettes or not, so it didn't take long before we were smoking anything that could be rolled up in paper and smoked. Some of the stuff we smoked consisted of leaves, pine needles, rice straw, weeds and, like I said, anything that would burn. God only knows all the crap that we smoked. There was an unwritten rule that if a guy was smoking and another guy asked for "snipes" or "butts" the guy who was smoking had to save at least a "drag" or two for the second guy.

The Koreans grow marijuana as a crop to be used in the weaving of their clothing. It seems that after it matures, they stack it in bunches in the fields to dry. After it dries they strip the strings (hemp) from the stalks and weave it into clothing. Then they either dye the garments white or black.

During the very few hours that we were marched in daylight, the fellows that were knowledgeable in this area spotted this stuff almost immediately. Of course, we were guarded too closely for anyone to get their hands on any, at that time anyway. I had heard about marijuana but had never smoked any, and had no desire to try it.

Several weeks after this grand discovery, in the "mining town camp," I asked a guy by the nickname of Frenchie for snipes on whatever it was that he was smoking, so, according to our unwritten rule, he handed me the "snipe." It was no surprise when I didn't recognize the peculiar taste or smell because of what we had been smoking the past two months or so. Frenchie just stood there, waiting for my reaction. He didn't have to wait long. When he started laughing, I knew what I had just smoked.

After we got situated in Chung Song, North Korea, and after the camps were marked to protect us from American air strikes, we were forced to go into the local mountains to cut and carry wood back to camp. This detail had to be accomplished during daylight hours which gave those who knew what to look for the opportunity to steal all the marijuana they could without getting caught. You would think that with men in our situation would go overboard with something like this, but you'd be surprised. Sure, there were some guys that would be "high" every chance they could, but for the most part, I think we handled it quiet well.

I myself was afraid of it. After my initial encounter, I think I only smoked it three or four times because every time I did, I thought of my wife and daughter, and I certainly didn't want to go home an addict.

In my squad of 10 men, 5 of them were Mexican Americans who came from the barrios of cities like L.A., Phoenix and Dallas. (This was one reason we were able get rid of the lice so fast. Every one of them liked to be clean, unlike some of the others we had with us.) All but one of them had had some contact with marijuana before coming to Korea. Every time we went out on wood details, each one of these guys would see who could steal the biggest bunch of marijuana. Remember, I mentioned earlier that the Koreans would arrange it in shucks to dry. After they managed to get it back to camp without being detected, which in itself was no easy accomplishment, it would have to be cleaned (all of the seeds taken out it.)

Can you imagine what our little 8 by 10 room smelled and looked like? How we ever got away without being caught, I'll never know. The Chinese would have surely punished us for a serious crime against the Korean people. It wasn't too long before the whole company (about 120 men) were "hanging" around our squadroom. We were not allowed to gather in groups over two, but our room was very popular anyway.

As I indicated earlier, I didn't smoke very much of that stuff because I was afraid I'd become addicted. Every night almost everyone else in the squad would smoke until the wee hours. They would laugh and laugh and speak in Spanish and then laugh some more. It was some time before they let me in on the joke

—I was the joke. They always tried to get me to smoke with them, and when I would refuse, they would start speaking Spanish and laughing. Finally, they told me what they laughed at when they would smoke in the room most of the night. They were laughing at me because I was getting almost as "high" as they were by just being in the same room with them. That's how stupid I was when it came to marijuana.

There was a small tree in front of our squad and somehow, someone planted some marijuana seeds around the tree in a cute little flower-bed. I was worried about what the Chinese would do to us for growing drugs in camp because I thought they would recognize the plants immediately. When the plants were about three feet high, the Chinese came over to our squad one day and actually complimented us on our efforts to beautify our living quarters.

I don't know how I could ever forget "Cyclops." Cyclops came to us one extremely cold morning. It must have been 25 to 30 below zero, and this poor chicken was caught outside overnight and was close to death. His comb and feet were black from frostbite. We brought him inside and wrapped him in extra clothes, hoping that would be enough to bring him around. We kept him wrapped up all day and finally he showed signs of survival. He was hungry, we fed him, he was thirsty, we gave him a drink.

He stayed indoors, completely wrapped up overnight, and the next morning he appeared to have recovered except for his comb and his feet. They were even worse than they had been the day before. One of his feet was much worse than the other, and his comb was completely black. I can't remember who decided that if we didn't perform surgery, and soon, that he wouldn't make it. Again, I can't remember who did the surgery but I think it was me because I was the only one in the squad who had ever butchered a chicken and knew its particular anatomy. To make a short story shorter, we amputated one leg at the bottom end of the "drumstick" and almost all of his comb. He bled surprisingly little and after a week or so of recuperation, he was as good as new.

One of the guys made a little boot out of some thin leather and tied it on him—it worked perfectly. He was such a weird looking chicken that he should have a weird name. He was called several names but the one that fit him best was Cyclops, so Cyclops it was. I can still see that crazy chicken running across the compound. He became everyone's friend. I can't remember just how long we were able to keep him hid from the Chinese but it was quite a long time before they finally got him, just before he was to be fitted for his hand-carved peg leg. Cyclops will always have a place in my heart.

We had another pet; it was short lived, but we had him long enough to become attached. One day a medium sized, black and white dog ran into our compound. He ran directly into an open squad room. It was obvious that this was one frightened dog. Of course we knew that Koreans eat dogs, and without a word of discussion, we were going to protect our newfound friend. It wasn't long after the dog came into our compound before a Korean Papa-san and two guards came in looking for him. He had been hidden well enough to send the Korean and the guards away empty handed. The guards didn't speak any English, but it didn't take much imagination to figure out that they were mad and were using every nasty word they could think of.

That night, at roll call, the company commander got into the act. He was equally as mad as the guards and promised severe punishment if we didn't produce the dog. It was only a matter of time before they found the dog, and after we hadn't turned our friend in by noon the next day, they called a surprise roll call. While we were standing in formation, they sent several guards to search our squad rooms. They found the dog. About 30 minutes after the formation was dismissed, we got one last look at our short lived friend. Our compound was bordered on the north side by civilian Korean's houses. There, just outside our compound, I suppose for all to see, they hanged the dog and were hitting him on the head with a shovel. That was the last pet we had.

Edward Sheffield

When we reached our destination it was colder than ever for we were about as high in the mountains in North Korea as you can go. The temperature gets 30 and 40 degrees below zero. The largest building was a little school house with three rooms with one wood burner heater in each room. They put 50 men in each of these rooms. The rest were put in shacks close by — the North Korean type mud shacks with 25 men in each room.

The only heat we would get was when we cooked our corn or millet in the kitchen. The fire and smoke went through tunnels in the floor and out through a stack at he other end of the house. They gave us just enough wood to cook with, and the wood was green bushes and twigs cut and tied in bundles from the side of the mountain. The crowded conditions was all that kept us from freezing to death, but some froze to death anyway. There wasn't enough room to lie down and stretch out. Everyone had to lie the same way and turn over at the same time. If the man next to you didn't turn over at the same time, you knew he was dead.

Usually two or three died every night.

I would volunteer to help take them out and bury them so that I might get his pants or shirt or shoes. It took four of us to carry one body that probably wouldn't have weighed 70 pounds. We didn't need a stretcher for he was froze stiff. We took him up the side of a mountain accompanied by a couple of guards, found a gully and raked the snow back, put him down and piled snow over him. It was impossible to dig a hole. The ground was frozen as hard as concrete.

Starvation, cold weather, filthy conditions, body lice, dysentery and beriberi was what we faced; 425 didn't survive. More men died of dysentery but the most dreaded disease was beriberi. If you get this disease in the feet and legs, you had a chance of survival, but if it got you in the head or stomach, you would live from four to ten days.

I can never forget the look on those men's faces, there was no one to shed a tear for them or hold their hands. It wasn't the thought of dying that mattered so much as having to leave your body in a shallow grave in this God forsaken country. I don't like to mention dying so much, but death is what we faced 37 months. The winter was so cold you couldn't get outside, especially with no more clothes than we had.

I decided that I had to forget about home and all the good things and try to adjust myself to this sort of condition. I tried to stay as active as possible in order to divert the temptation of giving up.

Christmas, 1950, the Koreans brought fifteen already skinned and frozen dogs. They hauled them in on sleds pulled by bulls from China and distributed the dogs among our shacks. This was the first meat we had had to eat since August. It wasn't so good, but no one turned it down.

The punishment for stealing was severe, usually three ways: the rubber hose, standing in the cold with no shoes on, or squatting on the pole behind your legs. Knowing the punishment, men would still take the chance to steal a little something to eat. Myself and the rest have caught frogs and snakes and roasted them over a fire, with no salt. They were not so good, but it was something more to eat.

We went for six and eight months without a haircut, shave, or a bath. There was not even enough water to drink. The floor we slept on was hard as concrete.

I still have the sign on my wrists where my hands were tied, the scar on my knee and the one on my back from a 3-corner bayonet, but worst of all, a sad memory of 475 young American men and the cruel way the rest of us had been treated.

Spring finally came in 1951 and ice and snow melted; the creeks and rivers began to run. The farmers started to work in the fields and rice paddies. They hitched us to bull carts, four men to each cart. We hauled rocks and built dams so the farmers could irrigate their fields.

We never were given the chance to write home or read up on news around the world. Finally in October they told us we were leaving but didn't say where we were going, but moving was simple. The only belongings we had were our bowls and spoons.

They marched us down to the Yalu River where the remains of us were loaded on two boats, about 40 feet long. We floated downstream for four days and three nights.

We didn't know that our little group wasn't the only prisoners until we reached our destination. The sight of the other men, their physical condition and morale gave us inspiration. This was a great day.

Andrew (Chief) Aguirre

I spent two years and nine months as a prisoner of war of the Chinese Communist forces. I saw many things that I did not think I would ever see while a prisoner. I saw the chain of command break down where an officer had as much authority and command as a buck private. I saw where even chaplains, who are supposed to be men of God and spiritual leaders, convert to rat-holing (storing food) for survival, knowing and not caring that many other prisoners had not yet eaten. I saw the daring, who would take a chance to obtain whatever it was that would enhance survival be ostracized and made to feel bad by those cowardly ones who would not have the courage to take a risk, yet were willing to share his prize. I saw officers whose conduct invited a smack in the nose, but would have resulted in a court martial for the smacker when the prisoners would return to U.S. control.

It is amazing how quickly people forget they are still soldiers and military men, who have an obligation and are still responsible to the U.S. armed forces. These individuals have the attitude that they have been set free of military control and their conduct is not important and have only to answer to themselves.

It is a sad situation to be in. One day you are a mighty American warrior, you are part of a great fighting force which includes a Navy, and an Air Force. You are superior to any Northern or Southern Korean or any coolie chink. You have the capacity to kill enemy Asian Orientals who oppose you, and think differently politically, and believe in an ideology different from your own.

Then one day, without warning, under circumstances that are unexplainable and it seems like over night, you are captured and stripped of all you have enjoyed all your life. And most important, you are stripped of your liberty. You have no recourse when it comes time to defend yourself. You have nobody to complain to or anybody to help you keep living. You must do it on your own. You have nobody to rely on but yourself. Your buddies can only help so much as they themselves are going through the transition from a U.S. armed forces member to a Prisoner of War.

I have heard many men say they have a guilt feeling because they were prisoners of war. Why shouldn't the individual feel guilty? Like it or not, he must humiliate himself and become complacent to slant-eyed slope-headed gooks, who under different circumstances a few days before, would have been dead meat and fallen dead in front of the sights of an M1 Garand or other weapon at one's disposal. Now one seeks comfort with the minimum of food, inadequate housing, minimal medical attention, and the separation from all that he once was. It is like being taken from one world where one had everything to a world where one has nothing.

Remembering Christmases I had at war, the first one was 1944, when I was in Pauuvu in the Russell Island group in the South Pacific Ocean. I celebrated with church services in the company of my fellow Marines who were given an extra ration of beer. In 1945, I was in Tientsin, China, and I celebrated in the company of the Chinese girl friends and my fellow Marines. In 1950, I was prisoner of war of the Chinese troops in Korea and spent Christmas in a small storage room with three of my tank crewmen who had also been captured. That night we were bombarded by the big naval ships who were covering the evacuation of the 1st Marine Division and Tenth Corps at Hamhung. In 1951, I spent Christmas at Camp One in Changsong, North Korea, still as a POW. We were living in native huts without any heating, and the weather was about -30 degrees. Most of the prisoners were infested with body lice, intestinal worms, and uncontrollable dysentery and diarrhea. Many prisoners died that winter. In 1952, I was still in Camp One in Changsong, North Korea. Conditions had improved to where we had a little candy, bread, adequate heating, and the brainwashing process had been discontinued.

My birthdays were like any other day. There was nothing different about them and the days passed like any other day. I was 18 and 19 during WW II and 25, 26, and 27 years old in Korea.

My worst and most frightening experiences were not inflicted by the enemy, but by our own American forces. Two stand out the most. One was when, as a prisoner, I was bombarded by naval forces. It was very frightening hearing those tremendous loud explosions that would make the ground tremble, followed with blinding flashes of light. The bombardment was all around us while we were down in a culvert that was under a railroad embankment. The Chinese had forced the Korean civilians to get out so they and us could get in the culvert. The civilians ran out of the culvert into the bombardment, and many were blown away. The other incident was one of many where we were attacked by our own aircraft who thought we were enemy, as we were being forced marched in large groups to the prison camps.

While I was held POW in the prison camps by the Yalu river in Korea, marijuana was introduced into the camps by some guys who had used in the United States and knew all about it. Marijuana was planted by the locals. They planted it in large fields to make cloth and clothes and rope out of it. We used to go on wood runs during the summer months to bring wood for usage in winter, and since we were not watched too closely, we were able to get it by trading with the locals or by finding it growing in the creek beds. Marijuana is supposed to be addictive, but many guys used it for months and when they were released and back to civilian life, they had nothing to do with it. Marijuana helped many of the sick and ill, as it alleviated their pain and made them hungry, and they would eat the food which normally they would reject. I do not think it was a problem there as every body that used it knew his limitations, just as that of alcohol.

I bear no animosity toward the Japanese, Korean or Chinese people. On the contrary, I have a warm feeling for them and feel an attachment because they were part of my life, even if at the time they were the enemy. I have a lot of respect for my former Chinese adversaries. I respect their courage. Their stringent self-discipline which enables them to walk all night while living on two small bowls of millet, or ground corn, or sorghum, or rice a day. They did not have the luxury of enjoying the many privileges that the average mm enjoyed, and that was a variety of food, mail, usually a sleeping bag to sleep in, superior clothing and footwear, artillery and air support, packages from home, and cigarettes.

Their military discipline was such that if a Chinese soldier ever got separated from his unit, no other unit would feed him. Once while being held as a prisoner of war and being taken to a camp, I was with a Chinese unit, and we stopped to rest while the cooks cooked some sorghum. When the sorghum was ready, they sent me to fetch the food. I came back and Paul Gray (another prisoner), myself, and the interpreter started to eat. There was a Chinese soldier talking to the interpreter, and when we three were eating, I asked the interpreter if the Chinese soldier was not going to eat.

"No, he is not, because he got lost from his unit last night and therefore will not eat until he finds it," the interpreter said. There was a period when only Paul Gray and I were with this Chinese unit as prisoners of war, but we had been so long with them they were treating us like one of them. Many mornings at dawn, after marching all night since sunset, the unit would gather around in small bands and drink hot water in a circle. The hot water was the only thing they had which was used much as we use coffee. After the hot water, they would eat the powdered millet, corn or sorghum and retire to some cave, dugout, hut, or when there was nothing else, sleep under the trees. They would sleep all day and be ready for another all night march in the late afternoon.

One must admire the way they endured the cold during the Chosin Reservoir, where temperatures got as low as 30 degrees below zero. We, when still with our American units, were sleeping in a tent with a red hot stove for heating, and we were still cold. The Chinese coolie soldier was sleeping in the mountains with only token blankets for warmth. In the day time they could not build any fires, as this would bring down on them the fury and devastation of our airplanes. The thing I admire the most about the Chinese was the self-control they practiced to drive themselves to the limit and to endure the hardships without any complaining. No, I cannot say I hate my former enemy.

Richard Makua

Living conditions in the POW camp were horrible. Rotting, bad. What was the hardest thing to deal with? Just being there was hard enough. The food was crap. Yes, sleeping and eating came hard to me, but if you wanted to stay alive, you better start to eat, sleep, and crap at the same time, or you'll never see home again. You ask what did I rely on the most to keep sane? Eat crap and stay alive. Yes, I was scared. It felt like hell to see my friends die.

After getting into the main camp, Camp One, it took awhile to know anyone real close because I found I could not trust anyone. Later, there was friendship among us. I remember Harry Fulks and a few others who were close and I could talk to.

I think if I would have to do it again, I would rather be shot or dead. There's no fun in war.

My Christmas there was terrible and horrible. You can only think and wish because you didn't know what will happen to you from minute to minute, or day to day, whether you'll live or die. My birthday was the same thing. Things were just bad!

Joseph Wilson

I was held in Camp One and Camp Five. We had to sleep on the cold floor. The conditions were not good. If we did have wood, to keep warm, we had to go on wood detail and find it. So I had to walk on the frozen Yalu River, so that I had both my feet frostbitten.

The food was not bad, sometimes we had three meals a day. Mostly rice, beans, fish, pork, and steamed bread. We got a sugar ration of three tablespoons. We had better food than the Chinese people. We had games of basketball and track. We were treated all the same, the American vets. But for the other vets from England, it was different. I felt the Chinese were better than the others. They were nice to us.

We had a really nice Christmas. A Chinese girl gave us some extra rations of meat, pork, and rice and beans. My birthdays were not good. I was on a death march the first year. The second year was OK. The third year I was happy because we were about to go home.

I did have some problems with the enemy. On the march, in May of 1951 some Chinese there had never seen a black American with hair on his face, so they wanted to make fun of me. So I said, "You'd look like this too if you had hair on your face." They didn't like that. Also, in Camp Five, we were to build a brick wall around the whole camp. They wanted Co. 1, all black vets, to work. I thought the whole camp should do the work. So we had to do it. I had to write a letter and let them know that we were all the same.

In the sick room, in the camps, if you were really sick and not doing too good, they put you in a "house." You would die if you went there. I lost my pal; he died in such a house. It was like a place if the sick stayed they would die. So I had to keep them well, so I had homemade cures. I tried to help them to stay well.

The hardest thing to deal with personally for me was trying to help my fellow POWs get well who were sick. I had cold meal and mud to put on their faces and their legs for them. For dysentery we would cook beans and rice for them also.

Some of the people who I best remember were Big Tom and Poor Joe and many others. I did not see a lot of prejudice among the Americans I was with. We had to stick together. We still are close after. (Some of our Americans these days should try to be close now; we would have more love towards each other.)

There were many experiences that I would say were my worst or most frightening. When we had to walk on the frozen Yalu River in December, when we went to get wood about one mile away. And then when the jets would sometimes fly over the camp. And again when they flew over when we were on the death march of 1951, from April 1951 until June 22, 1951.

What kept me going when I was so far away from home? God, and the hope to get home, as well as thoughts of my wife and my infant son. I did get three letters from my family. It was very hard being away from home for such a long time.

Being a POW for 27 months is what I remember the most about the Korean War. It seemed to me that our government did not care about us POWs. When we became POWs, they forgot about us.

Theo Baudoin, Jr.

We were then headed north and arrived at the first camp on December 23, my 19th birthday. That day we were made to walk all night and all day. We were far into North Korea. No American planes were seen overhead. I didn't think I could have walked another mile when the lead guard, whom I was following, pointed downhill to a mining camp. We left the mountain road and started down hill into the snow, grabbing onto pine trees to slow our decent. I remember crying all the way down that hill. Later, I wondered why. Maybe it was because I had made it to the camp.

A few days after arriving at the mining camp, our officers arrived. My Battalion Commander, Major Fry, was there. Later, he played a big part in my survival.

The men started dying. Two or three men per room per night. We stacked the bodies in an ox shed at the end of the buildings. We all had dysentery, and some came down with pneumonia. We had no medicine, and now we were infested with blood sucking body lice.

After two weeks in this mining camp we were again marched to our next camp. We walked on the frozen Yalu River to open the west end of Camp Five, known as Pyucktong. It was a bombed- out town.

By the spring of 1951, more than 1,800 Americans died here at Pyucktong. I saw the dog tags of more than 1,600 Americans held up on a POWs arm, from wrist to elbow. Many of us did not have tags, for the enemy soldiers had taken them at the time of our capture.

Here, while the PA system played the Blue Danube, Strauss' Waltz, and Tales of the Vienna Woods, they tried their political indoctrinating program, later called "brainwashing."

Around Thanksgiving of 1951, some of us classified as reactionary elements were put on a boat and sent down the Yalu River to open Camp Three, known as Changsong.

In 1953, the peace negotiations brought some improved conditions. It was my will to live, my belief in God, and a desire to go home that helped me survive my ordeal as a prisoner of war.

CHAPTER SIX

COMMUNIST INDOCTRINATION

Jack Chapman

In December of 1950, our schooling started one night when the Chinese herded us out into the bitter cold and marched us about two or three miles to a large, centrally located, huge barn (which later they called the Big House) where we were all herded together and sat on the earth floor. By this time there were approximately 325 men in this camp, all suffering from wounds, extreme cold, malnutrition and barely conscious of their surroundings. This group consisted of some 41st Independent Commandos, British Royal Marines, some Puerto Ricans from the 65th Regiment, 3rd Infantry Division, but most of then came from the First Marine Division and the Seventh Infantry Division. Some of these prisoners had been captured a few days before we were hit.

Three days after this get-acquainted meeting, the Chinese began their campaign to capture our minds. On Christmas Eve, the Chinese decorated the barn with wreaths, candles, two Christmas trees, and a sign bearing the cheerful inscription, "Merry Christmas." Two huge placards also decorated the barn. They read, "If it were not for all the Wall Street Imperialists you would be home with your wives and families on this Christmas night." Communist slogans and posters stating, "Who is responsible for your being away from your wives and families at this Christmas time?" and "We, too, want to be with our families."

Examples of other posters: "Why are you freezing and dying here in Korea, 5000 miles from home, on this Christmas Eve, while your money-mad bosses, the Capitalist Warmongers of Wall Street, are enjoying Christmas dinner in their warm homes?" We were each given a handful of peanuts, six or seven small pieces of hard candy, and six Chinese cigarettes.

The speaker on this festive occasion was a wheel of some importance and great lung power. He wished us a Merry Christmas, denounced MacArthur and Truman, stating that Americans had launched the war in Korea. They showed a photograph of John Foster "Doolus" Dulles, peering across the 38th parallel toward North Korea.

A British soldier who had been told to lead the singing got up, paused a moment and then launched into God Save the King. Before the Chinese had the time to grasp the words, his own Marines shouted a warning, and he quickly swung into "Roll Out the Barrel."

After that we sat through a five hour lecture on the subject of, "Who is the real aggressor in Korea?" The gloating, smiling, Chinese high camp official informed us of their victory over the retreating United Nations forces and told us how they were going to drive the United Nation forces into the Sea and of the impossibility of escape and that our lines were daily being driven fArther and farther southward away from our position.

The North Koreans treated their prisoners cruelly, but their brutality was physical. The Chinese introduced a more insidious form of cruelty. With them physical violence was less general but more purposeful, and it was liberally spiced with mental pressure.

The North Koreans made token efforts to extract Military information from their prisoners, taking more pleasure in maltreating than in exploiting them. The Chinese Communists were more effective in their intelligence activities. In addition they made an intensive effort to indoctrinate their prisoners of war or to gain a propaganda advantage. The prisoner of war camp system was designed to support the Chinese aims for control and use of POWs, and they called it the "Lenient Policy."

We were made aware of their so-called "Lenient Policy." We who were captured in the Chosin Reservoir campaign and those taken in the northwestern Korea were the first to encounter this "Lenient Policy." (Simply stated, this meant calculated leniency in return for cooperation, harassment in return for neutrality, and brutality in return for resistance.) We would not be treated as prisoners of war, but as friends in need of help. Here we stood and or sitting on the earth floor, freezing, miserable, and (myself along with others) crying from aching feet, pain from wounds that had not being cared for and from starvation, for five long hours, listening to this gloating, smiling Chinese officer. Finally, we were pushed outside and taken back to our cold huts with no heat, to sleep on the earthen floor, covered with straw mats that were crawling with lice.

The Chinese high camp official made it known that they planned a party for us on Christmas. Christmas Day, we were given a pork stew and white rice, the first meat since our capture. It was very good, but as we thought of the annual holiday meal being served to the U.S. forces in South Korea, ours became not so enjoyable as it might have been.

After Christmas we were marched to the barn two or three nights a week for lectures, and we took these opportunists to get together with our officers and discuss any problems that had come up and ask their opinion on what our attitude and behavior should be in those matters.

Major McLaughlin was the senior officer, and in direct opposition to the Chinese, he began the task of establishing communications between our scattered groups. By doing so, he sought to maintain effective control of our group and to present a united front against the enemy. Because we were scattered throughout several farm-houses, it was extremely difficult to create any effective organization. Every few days, however, we were taken to this large barn where we had to listen to the damn lectures.

It was at these meetings that McLaughlin was able to issue instructions, advice and encouragement to the enlisted men, and his advice was always followed and undoubtedly saved us from many hardships that we might otherwise have had to endure.

We learned to tell how long a Chinese officer would speak by the way he was dressed. If he wore a fur cap with a leather bill, he was just a little wheel and wouldn't talk very long. If he wore a fur cap with a leather bill and had a wrist watch and a fountain pen, he was a medium-sized wheel and might speak for an hour or two. If he wore a fur cap with a leather bill, had a wrist watch, a fountain pen and a leather jacket, and if he smoked tailor-made cigarettes and had a small boy bring him hot tea as he talked, he was a big wheel, probably straight out of Peking, and we would have to huddle there in the cold the better part of a day or night.

The first meeting in the Barn, was in the nature of a welcoming session. The Chinese officer was a moderate size wheel, who told us that we were not to think or speak of ourselves as prisoners. We were newly liberated friends and should refer to ourselves as such. The Officer said that the Chinese were not angry at us for been in Korea, for they realized that it was not our fault. We had been duped by our aggressive, capitalists warmongering leaders. We therefore would be treated with kindness. But if we disobeyed the rules laid down for newly liberated friends, we would be severely punished. We would be made to stand at attention or we would be rebuked in front of our fellow prisoners.

The Chinese stressed the virtues of communism at every opportunity, in lectures, in discussions, and in casual and informal conversations. They continually exhorted their charges to progress more rapidly in our studies, and their promise of release for the more progressive of their newly liberated friends.

Lectures were held on alternating days and, on the in between, the squads were supposed to hold group discussions at which the interpreters would sit in, taking notes on what each man said.

Reading material was passed out—copies of the *Peking Daily News*, *People's China* and the *China Review* and *Shanghai News.* Often these newspaper were only a week old. The Chinese officers, who spoke English, marked certain articles which we were to study and discuss.

Many of the newspaper articles dealt with the courage of the Chinese soldiers who were awarded membership in the Communist Party (rather than medals) for great acts of heroism. One article which fascinated the Army and Marine tankers was the account of a group of Chinese Soldiers who had leaped onto the backs of U.S. tanks and "ripped open the hatches with bayonets" in order to throw in grenades to kill the crews!

If we did not have much to say, the interpreters, known variously as Egg Head, B.B. Eyes, Stupid, the Snake, Pluto, Ace and Little Caesar, would take us aside and lecture us personally at great length, trying to clear our mind of any "misconceptions." Soon the word got around that the men who showed themselves the most "progressive" would be released, and many prisoners began to show great interest in the discussions. Since the Chinese wanted everyone to be released (according to them), the brighter men would coach the duller, less-imaginative ones in what to say to please Egg Head and his friends. As the indoctrination program continued, many of the progressive POWs gave lectures on the same subjects the Chinese had covered. Group discussions were encouraged, and with the help of the progressive prisoners, the Chinese exerted influence on the "unprogressive" prisoners to quiet their opposition and to bring them in line.

Throughout the entire indoctrination program, the Communists denounced religion as a superstition and a device for controlling people's minds. The Chinese attempted to teach us the Darwin's theory of evolution, but when they encountered strong resistance to that proposal, the Chinese dropped the idea. Some prisoners were permitted to keep whatever religious articles they had on their person at the time of capture. As a result several testaments, rosaries and other religious articles were available in Camp Kang-gye. One older man stated bluntly, "These people are no good. They don't like God."

B.B. Eyes, Egg Head and their friends encouraged us to argue with them and to ask questions, and for a while we did. But we soon found that to do this meant that one of the Wheels would call a special lecture session at the ice box (Big House) to answer those questions, and after a while we dread the long cramped hours of sitting in the cold. We would tell Egg Head, "You have made everything very clear, there is no reason to ask questions."

One of the best speakers in our group was Major McLaughlin, (also known as the Major of Kanggye) whose speeches, though always brief, had meanings both to the Chinese and to us. He would say "The Chinese have told us why we are in Korea. So now, of course, we know why we are here. When we return to our homes we will have our work cut out for us. There we must continue our fight for peace."

Each day an interpreter came to our huts and we had discussions on the last lecture in which we were to ask questions and air any doubts we might have as to the "truths" they were expounding. Squad leaders were held responsible for proper discussions by their squads of assigned topics in Marxian dialectical materialism. There was little opportunity for opposition to the indoctrination for the study periods were mandatory, and we did not have the option of refusing to attend or to participate in lectures and discussions. Saturdays and Sundays passed like any other day. It was evident that the Chinese wanted all of us to concentrate on the enforced studies.

The curriculum was more intensive than most college courses. This leniency was coldly calculated to neutralize possible resisters and to convert those who could be bent to the Chinese Communists' will. We argued with them and asked questions that obviously angered and embarrassed them. Such questions went unanswered. It was made clear to us that we were expected to believe anything we were told simply because they said it was true and that our doubts and foolish questions would only prolong our period of instruction, therefore, prolonging the day we would be released. We were told that the more progressive we were and the faster we learned, the quicker we would be released.

This was discussed with our officers and the Major of Kanggye, and it was decided that cooperative attitude would be best. It was decided that no useful purpose would be served by antagonizing our captors, and the promise of early freedom was most appealing.

The Major of Kanggye directed us to listen to their lectures, answer their questions the way they wanted them answered, ask a few simple questions ourselves and accept their answers without argument. I believe that this led to improved living conditions, averted many deaths due to slightly improved food ration (cooked barley and some white rice) which tasted much better than that horrible, indescribable, watery mush which we had received during the march and the first few days here at Kanggye.

We were exposed to a series of propaganda lectures, that were designed to make us believe that the United States was the aggressors in Korea and to publicize and make us to accept the rest of the Communist propaganda. It was intimated to us that the sooner we learned and cooperated, the sooner we would be released. Some half dozen brainwashed prisoners, made speeches denouncing the United States, its policies, interventions, leadership, and etc. One of the American POWs during his speech asserted that the Korean War was a "Millionaire's War" and that we, the prisoners, had innocent Korean blood on our hands. Another (Olson) recounted his experience as a prisoner of the Germans during WW II. He said that the Germans treated their prisoners badly when compared to the Chinese. Another American (Dusty) sang a song for the Chinese.

The articles written by the Marines and U.S. Army prisoners were of a similar tenor, and our leaders came under heavy attack in several of the articles. Peace was the basic theme demanded by the Communists, and it served as a front to hide their true motives.

The Soviets had set the stage at the close of World War II when, through fraud, coercion, deception and the use of German collaborators, they complied large numbers of signatures on various peace petitions which then received wide circulation.

A U.S. Senate Subcommittee investigating Communists exploitation of American prisoners concluded that the Chinese made extensive use of Soviet methods after adding a few refinements of their own.

The lectures (schooling) continued seven days a week, either at the Barn or in our squad rooms. The lectures at the barn were normally conducted by a suave, high-booted Chinese Communist Big Wheel, who spoke in Chinese, and was translated by another Chinese officer who spoke better English then many of us. These infernal lectures consisted of talks on how the Communist Party began (The Doctrines of Marx and Lenin) encompassed about four to five hours.

We were lectured on the Chinese-Japanese War and on when the Communist Party was founded. We were told that they followed the leadership of Mao Tse-Tung and Mao accepts the interpretations of the Communist philosophy as put forth by Stalin. We were lectured on how the People's Republic of China had overthrown Chiang Kai-Shek's government and that Taiwan (Formosa) rightly belong to the People's Republic of China. They tried to teach us the People's Republic of China's National Anthem, "Dong Fong Ho" and the song of "Mao Tse-Tung." However, none of us wanted to participate and that made them mad.

They constantly reminded us that the United States had nothing to do with winning the Second World War against the Japanese. They questioned us as to who started the war in Korea, why we were in Korea, and what were we fighting for! They kept telling us that the blood of innocent North Korean people was on our hands.

We were reminded daily that we would be home with our loved ones if our capitalist leaders had not sent us to war upon the peace loving people of North Korea. We responded by stating that if North Korea had not attacked South Korea, none of us would have been here including you the Chinese People's Army. Most of us during these discussions would only talk about how good an American meal would taste and that most of us had asked to be sent to Korea, that no one had forced us to fight in Korea. We stated that we came to Korea in response to the cry for help of the South Korean people.

The squad of Marines in our hut stood very high among the group, due mainly to the efforts of a staff sergeant and a technical sergeant who were very good with a pen. (19 Marines were later released during the spring of 1951).

Several of the brainwashed prisoners wrote a substantial number of articles which was published in the camp newspaper, called the "New Life" by the Chinese. These articles were distinctly anti-American and pro-Communist in nature, and consistently derogatory toward the cause of the United Nations in Korea. One prisoner drew cartoons which promoted communism and reflected adversely on the U.S.

This individual participated in the publication of the newspaper called the "New Life." He was one of the most active workers in the Chinese indoctrination program. The charges brought against this individual after the Police Action ended were:

Assisted the Communist propaganda program by:

(1) writing and circulating peace petitions promoting Communist causes,

(2) writing and publishing articles containing information adverse and inimical to the interest of the United States,

(3) drawing cartoons which promoted Communist and reflected adversely on the United States,

(4) participating in the preparation and dissemination of frontline surrender leaflets,

(5) attempting to influence prisoners of war to accept Communist,

(6) participating in the publication called *New Life*, and

(7) actively participating in a group called "Yen-so-yen" (meaning workers) whose apparent mission was to interrogate and indoctrinate newly captured prisoners of war.

The Chinese took phrases from some of these articles and used them in their every day conversations and lectures. The United States was accused of fighting an unjust war for the sake of capitalism and imperialism and was charged with being responsible for the death of innocent people.

Being the youngest member of our squad, the Chinese appointed me as squad leader, I don't know why to this day! My attitude and wounds prevented me from carrying out the duties in that capacity. Finally, they appointed Sergeant Olson from my company, Company "D," 31st Infantry on the front lines as squad leader. He wrote several articles for the camp newspaper and participated in the indoctrinate of newly captured prisoners.

Later in the course of lectures, which lasted about ten weeks, during a brainwashing lecture, the Chinese camp official decided that it would be a good thing for the prisoners to draw up a document similar to the Stockholm Peace Appeal, which all of us newly liberated friends would sign.

One Marine was chosen by the Chinese to draft the document, which he did with great care, for he knew it would probably be broadcast in the United States. Unfortunately, though he was one of the more progressive of the POWs, somehow he failed in this great task.

Finally Lieutenant Pan, the chief interpreter, rewrote it completely. Finally they demanded that all prisoners sign this appeal to the United Nations denouncing the war in Korea and that the United Nations should pull out of Korea and let the Korean people form their own government. We all refused to sign such an appeal. I recall the continuous threats and brutality because we would not sign such an appeal, and how they called us "War Mongers, War Criminals and Murders." After several days of demands for signatures, the Chinese instructors informed us that we were reactionaries, opposing the Chinese People, their plans for world peace, and all the things that they and the other peace-loving people were striving for.

We were again told that a few prisoners would soon be released. This prompted some cooperation and or collaboration by some of the prisoners who believed that by cooperating they would gain favoritism and possibly be among the first to be released. After several days of threats and harassment to get signatures, the Major of Kanggye passed the word to other prisoners via the grapevine to appear to cooperative, but not to do anything

149

that would hurt or harm a fellow prisoner or his country. He was always concerned about the men in his group. Finally, we all signed this "peace appeal" to be sent to the United Nations, which did get our names published in the outside world.

From this time on, things went fairly smooth. The schooling continued, and the discussions kept on. During one of the discussions, a Chinese Officer asked me, "Who had started the war in Korea?" I replied, "You damn people did" after which he informed me that I was very young and that I had a lot to learn. I replied that I didn't have a damn thing to learn from them. This caused them to leave the squad room very angry, but, they returned to lecture me about their policies and to tell me "they were my friends and were only trying to help me." I told them that I did not need their help.

Here at Kanggye we were subject to psychological and physical pressures. We were confronted daily with the demands for propaganda participation, such as signing peace appeals and petitions, and for information about one another.

Men were divided into small groups and indoctrinated by the Chinese instructors, normally one Chinese to every 10-15 prisoners. The squads were broken up and reorganized. The slow learners were put into squads with those considered to be good students. Many of the instructors had been educated in American Universities, spoken English better then most of us and were familiar with American idioms, attitudes, and value systems.

The Camp Command had a small staff of Chinese who worked directly for him and assisted in administering the two POW companies. The staff included about fifteen interpreters and fifteen administrative aids in addition to several cooks and more than 100 guards. The administrative aids were charged with the political instructions and indoctrination of the prisoners.

One of these instructors met with a squad of prisoners each day and gave us a warm, humble, sincere speech requesting our cooperation. During these periods of interrogation, the Chinese would abruptly shift from brutality to shining kindness, offering cigarettes, allowing one to sit down, etc. If this failed, then relentless punishment would continue.

The term "Menticide" was used with reference to this type of physical and psychological pressure. The Chinese Communist also use letters and pictures and other personal effects, during these periods. (The letters and pictures were the ones taken during the search which was made after we were first taken prisoner.) They constantly asked, "Wouldn't you like to be home with your loved ones? All you have to do is to cooperate and you will be returned to them."

If we didn't and replied or stated, "Go to hell" or something similar, they then told us that it would be a shame if we never returned to our loved ones. Those who were married, took more punishment then the single ones in regards to harassment over their family lives. The Chinese said that their wives were probably sleeping with their best friends, etc.

One day, the Chinese told us that they could help us if they knew more about us, and that by letting us write a statement of our personal history, they would know where to start improving our camp life. The personal history questionnaire had a lot of questions, such as, "Who is your commander? Who is your best friend? What did you do in the service?" and so on.

The question as to who was your commander, received many different answers, such as, "I do not know as I was new in the company and never met my commander," or "That's a military secret and I can not tell you." One man wrote, "The only friend I have wants to borrow money," another kid put on the form, "I filled out something like this before and I ended up in the Army," still another wrote, "This is too much for me, I request transportation to go back and have my lawyer fill it out."

It was all humorous comments, and it teed the Chinese off. All of these things were designed to weaken our resistance and I might add, can prove somewhat effective under some or a combination of the aforementioned torturous conditions.

Someone was always sick in our squad. Every one had dysentery in varying degrees. There were no facilities for bathing, no heat and temperatures as low as thirty-five degrees below zero. Food was very poor, but our captors were eating same thing that they were feeding us. The main diet consisted of boiled sorghum and a couple of spoons of boiled soy beans sometimes twice a day. The food was cooked by the Chinese, and on two occasions such as Christmas and Lunar New Years, we received a small portion of rice with boiled fatty pork. We were told over and over that we were being fed because the Chinese People were good!

The Korean civilians, with whom we were housed, were very sympathetic to us, when our guards were not around, and often at night, would slip corn to us through a side door. One Korean boy, about 15 years old kept us informed as to what was going on by whispering to a sergeant in Japanese through a side door. The sergeant was an ex-prisoner of war in WWII, in Japan, and knew the language.

During the summer of 1952, we were forced to attend movies about the Chinese and Russian People. Most of the films were about life in China and Russia. They were shown out under the open sky with prisoners from the entire camp herded into one big group or else one compound at a time attended these movies.

After these movies, they lectured us about Russia and how Russia had her revolution and how the workers lived, boasting about how many bricks a worker in Russia could lay in a minute —now who in the hell cared about how many bricks a worker in Russia could lay?

In the fall of 1952, the Chinese started what they called a "Peace Committee." This was a discussion and study group which several of the prisoners took part in. One prisoner who was chairman of this committee, refused to return to the States after the Police Action ended in 1953. This individual, also organized several theatrical performances in the camp. He recruited other prisoners as performers and stated that the purpose of these propagandized performances was to promote good morale among the POWs.

The Chinese took one of the buildings in our compound that had been used as a classroom and turned it into a club room. One night a couple of fellow prisoners got into an argument with the chairman of the so-called Peace Committee, and threats were made to burn the place down. The chairman of the Peace Committee said that he would have these two and/or any others who attempted to destroy the club house confined.

Several nights later, the building was set on fire. The two men who had the argument with the chairman were immediately singled out and placed in solitary confinement and a water diet and later removed from our compound, even though these two men were not the ones who set the building on fire.

To this date only a very few men knew who set the building on fire. For several weeks after the fire, myself and several others were harassed by the Chinese over this incident. We were taken from our huts about midnight on ten different occasions and taken to the guard headquarters for interrogation, where we stood for hours at attention.

On one of these interrogations, the Chinese shown me a signed statement from another prisoner with my name and several other names of fellow prisoners of our undesirable activities (what the Chinese considered undesirable anyway.) They told me that no harm would come to me if I would give them a written statement concerning my activities and that of other prisoners. After about three hours of denying any knowledge of activities within our compound. I was returned to my hut, only to be recalled several night later.

This time, the Chinese offered me cigarettes and informed me that they had more written statements from other prisoners of my activities and that they would forget this incident if I would give them a written statement concerning my activities. After about two hours of silence, I was taken back to my hut.

The next morning, I was pulled from the formation and made to stand at attention in the corner of a low ceiling building, where I stood all day. The hours dragged on as the day wore on, as I stood there, legs and back aching, I wanted to cry. However, I was not about to give in and let them see me in pain. I was relieved when I was allowed to return to my hut and to sit down.

One of the English speaking Chinese officers would make the rounds of each hut, bring with him newspapers from Shanghai and Peking that were printed in English especially for us. This officer would lecture us on the material contained in the newspapers, which was mainly on the Korean War and American Imperialism and how the United States and United Nations (which was controlled by the American Imperialism according to them) were at fault in Korea.

The interrogations were more or less constant, being intermingled with the lectures. Harassment, deception, repetition, and writing essays and personal history were some of the techniques used. We would be called for interviews at odd hours of the day and night, awakened from our sleep or summoned during meals.

All that they ever got from us during these lectures, was how good American food would taste, about how good some American ice cream would taste, and how every American family owned at least one car and that some families had two. After a period of time the Chinese officers would question us about our life in America and if we owned a car, home, etc., and they became interested in what we had to say about our American dream and soon they would forget about the lecture for a few minutes.

We were allowed to write a letter home around the spring of 1952, and some of the prisoners who had been there prior to our arrival received their first mail somewhere after the new year of 1953. I believe I received my first letter somewhere around June of 1953, which was a dream in itself. Most of the letters that were received were "Dear John" type letters or notices of illness or death in the family. If we include such phrases as, "I am in good health, being well treated," and "wish that the war was over" in our letters, it helped to get them out.

154

If you disobeyed an order, you would be ordered to write a self-criticism confession that you had done wrong. If you refused to self-criticism yourself in front of the compound, you would be interrogated and/or stood at attention for hours at night by the Chinese. One fellow prisoner was put in a dug-out for a month or longer for talking back to a Chinese Officer.

During some of the self-criticism, we would make statements such as, "I promise not to call 'Pam' or 'Lee' that 'No good son of a bitch,' or 'I am very sorry that my hostile attitude had to be pointed out to me,' or 'I promise that I will never again be caught stealing the property of the Chinese and/or the Korean people,' or 'I promise not to destroy the property of the Chinese and/or the Korean people.'

No matter how bad they had us down, as long as they were around, we never showed them that we were down; they never could understand how we could still laugh and joke in our condition.

Many of us expressed our opposition to communism within our compound, and we were punished by being jailed or by being stood at attention for hours. A fellow prisoner who, when was exposed to one of the lectures came back to his hut and mentioned to another prisoner that the lecture that he had just listened too, was not worth the paper that it was written on. A Chinese officer (interpreter) happened to be standing outside of the hut, overheard the statement, and took the prisoner out of the hut to the Headquarters where he was taken out and punished. He was required to stand there in front of the guard headquarters for a prolong period of time, until he completely collapsed.

Several men—Raymond Goodburlet, Thompson Lively, and Bill Carter (Bill was a leader of our group who harassed our captors)—were confined for 90 to 120 days in cells with no heat (during the winter months) sometimes with their hands tied behind them for not signing confessions or self-criticisms. Some of the cages were not large enough to stand up in, or sit down comfortably.

155

We hated the damn lectures and their discussions. Each day, we would be herded together for these lectures which lasted for hours. We would have to listen to the lectures in Chinese and then be translated into English. We were forced to participate in the damn lectures and discussions which lasted six to eight hours a day, and if we were unable to produce what they considered the right answers that they wanted during the discussions, they would continue far into the night.

Many times during these discussions, we talked about our home life and all the good things about home and what we would do if and when we returned home. Some of the men who were captured during the spring and summer of 1951 had managed to keep some of their pictures and would show them. The Chinese officers would take a look at them and comment to the other officers, "Look, Comrade, he says that he owns that house, a car and bicycles. But you and I know what Comrade Mao says about these imperialists." The other officer would reply, "Yes, he says that they lie and exploit the working class people."

A fellow prisoner who came from a farm (we called him the Pig Farmer) said, "When they see the pictures of our farm with our tractors and other machinery that my Dad owns, they will say that I am an imperialist, too." Another said, "Wait until they see the picture of my new car that's waiting for me when I get back home."

The Chinese commander at a lecture told us, "Study hard, Comrades, with open minds and you will get to go home soon, but if you don't, we will dig a ditch for you so deep that even your bourgeois body won't sink."

We had to write a damn autobiography, over and over. Each time we lied like hell. The questions that they asked was a big joke. We wrote down anything that came to our minds and sometimes we would get together and make up things. They called us "Capitalist Pigs," stating "You have refused to examine your conscience and confess so we must punish you."

156

After a nearly a month of negative results on these lectures and classes, they gave up and started to have study groups on a much smaller basis, consisting of volunteers from our ranks. (A couple of these men, Morris Wills and Richard Tenneson, from our compound, refused to return home after the Police Action was over in 1953.)

Richard Rook

This was the first time in the history of war that POWs were subjected to brainwashing and psychological torture. There has been a lot of criticism of the Korean POWs for collaboration with the enemy. Yes, there were some who collaborated, but they were very few considering the methods they used on us. They had interpreters who spoke our language better than most of us did. They had several who had graduated from UCLA and USC. They even knew the latest slang, and they were experts in the judgment of people. They picked only on the weak of character. They also went after the African-Americans and the other minorities. After only a few months of total integration, they moved all the African-Americans to a separate camp. They told us over and over that we were nothing but "cannon fodder" for the "Wall Street war mongers" and that our country was controlled by men like J.P. Morgan and J.D. Rockefeller. It was amazing how much they knew about our government.

For about six months to a year they marched us downtown, to an area large enough to hold six or eight hundred of us. There they would lecture us on the virtues of communism and the corruptness of capitalism. After each lecture, we would return to our squad rooms to discuss the tons of wisdom we were supposed to have gotten from our saviors. After about an hour of "discussing" the wonders of our newly acquired knowledge, it was test time. The only words (at least in my squad) that were turned in were, NO COMMENT, as large as the paper would permit.

They soon tired of our antics and discontinued both the lectures and the study time but not before they made us write an autobiography. You can't imagine the stories they got back. We compared stories for weeks after that and actually thanked the "Chinks" for giving us so much material to laugh about. I can't remember any of the stories now, not even my own, but there were some good ones. After they discontinued the lectures, they concentrated on the weak and confused and were rewarded for their efforts when 23 GIs refused repatriation.

When I returned home in September of 1953, I discovered that the Chinese had sent my wife this beautiful magazine, in full color, depicting our life as guests of the Communists in North Korea. I can't remember much of what was inside of that magazine because the cover was quite enough. On the cover, in beautiful color, was a mm standing with one foot up on the bottom rail of a split-rail fence. In the background was a beautiful mountain surrounded by a brilliant, cloudless, blue sky. The mm had his jacket off and draped over one arm while his other arm was leisurely resting on the top rail. He was smoking what appeared to be a nice pipe while he gazed off into nothing. Propaganda at its best.

Edward Sheffield

The Chinese quickly took charge of us, and we were glad to get away from the Korean guards. It had been raining, and we were all wet, frozen and starved. The Chinese moved us into a couple of long barrack-type buildings. They issued us cotton padded clothes and gave us a good meal of rice. In this shell of a barracks, we began to winterize for our home with what poor materials we could find or improvise.

Food, clothing and medicine wasn't for the asking, but I must admit we were much better treated after that date. We had bread and potatoes often, but rice most of the time. They let us go to the river which was only 200 yards away to bathe every day, and for the first time we had soap. With better food and housing, better health was a natural result. But there was the increasing strain of continued internment and the lack of definite hope for release.

They gave us the opportunity to write home once a month, but informed us that only certain things would be expected. Most of the mail never got through. I don't guess I wrote the things they wanted me to since my family only received two of my letters.

The Chinese were very nice to us at first, but we found out they had a purpose in mind—indoctrination. They held classes and we were forced to attend, but they couldn't force us to listen. The interrogations were usually individual and came at odd times.

Some of us were questioned and persuaded more than others because we were supposed to be more valuable or more dangerous to the cause for various reasons. Each of us argued the merits and demerits of communism in his own way. All attempts on their part to convert any of us were in vain for quite some time. We remained an inseparable group.

Their efforts increased after awhile, and they picked six men to attend a special school which lasted about 3 weeks. Upon their return, five of them admitted that they had been converted and really believed in communism. When we tried to talk to these men about the mistake they were making, we suffered for it. The collaborators would report us to the Communists.

For punishment we were put in solitary confinement and hard labor with half rations and handcuffs at night. The men who insisted o being faithful to their country had a hard time of it. The collaborators organized their own study group through which they tried to convert others and influence others with Communistic doctrines.

Myself and some others were brought to headquarters at a different time and tried before a court of Communist officers. I was not allowed to speak in my behalf. I think there were 14 charges they read to me—an imperialist warmonger, reactionary, trouble-maker, instigator, underminer of their studies, etc.

They put me on hard labor and half rations for an indefinite time. A man from another camp doing time also and I manned a cross-cut saw all day sawing wood for the Communists' use for the coming winter. At night, I slept on a little pile of straw about twelve feet underground in an air-raid shelter with a guard standing at the outlet.

CHAPTER SEVEN

PROTESTS, HARASSMENT, AND ESCAPE ATTEMPTS

Jack Chapman

During early spring 1952, several of us formed an organization that called itself the "True Americans," better known to the Chinese as the "Reactionaries." We made plans for escapes and organized other types of resistances. During this period, we were still located in the seventh compound at the south end of the Changsong. During the day, when we went out on work details, we carried what food we could spare into the hills, hiding it in hopes of an escape. We would assist any one who wanted to a make a break. We gathered whatever items we could for him, and when the time came to leave, we would attract the attention of the guards.

Not once did an escape from Camp One succeed. Nick Flores, a Marine who was captured at the Chosin Reservoir, managed to be gone the longest that I knew of. He was recaptured by a Soviet anti-aircraft artillery unit.

There were too many obstacles for us to overcome. The mountains offered one of the toughest problems, for their height would soon have you crawling, and the dogs from the Korean farm houses would chase you, revealing your location, and of course we certainly did not look like the Koreans or Chinese.

One of our protests was to refuse to stand in the freezing cold and be forced to listen to the Communists and their damn lectures. One cold morning, right after we were called out for roll call, several of us broke ranks and ran back to our huts and we refused to return to the formation. This action caused many of our inmates to break ranks and run for their huts.

In April 1952, we were informed by the Chinese that we would be marching in a May Day parade that was to travel through the center of town (Changsong). Our group passed the word around to those we could trust and told them not to march in the parade, and everyone agreed.

About a week before the May Day parade, the Chinese issued us new clothing, blue summer uniforms. This uniform consisted of a light-weight jacket shirt type and baggy trousers, as they did not want us to wear our old worn-out American field uniforms in the parade. This was the first issued clothing for us since we had been captured.

We were given a hair cut and shave. We somehow managed to write POW across the back of the jacket and kept them hidden until the day of the parade. We then began to put our plans for refusal to march into effect and told everyone not to move after being lined up. Before we could carry out our plans, a progressive ran to the Chinese and informed them about our plans of refusal to march in the parade. The Chinese herded us all together and once more lectured us about their lenient policy.

May 1st, 1952, the Chinese Communists herded us onto the main road for the parade. We were all dressed in our new DRESS BLUES that the Chinese had issued a short time before, and when they saw what we had done (painted POW across the back of the jackets), they became extremely upset and began lecturing us about the destruction of the clothing that the Chinese people had worked so hard to provide for us. They said that we deserved to be severely punished, and they accused us of being nothing but American War Mongers and that we were against the peace loving people of the world.

As they tried to assemble us into a parade formation on the main road, everyone in my squad, except for a couple of guys, sat down and refused to move. The Chinese began running around us, screaming about their lenient policy and that "if we did not cause any more trouble, they would forget about this incident."

Eventually, they did get us back into a formation on the main road, where we once more sat down and refused to comply with their commands. This time they forgot their so called "lenient treatment" and started pushing and threatening us about what they would do if we did not obey their orders, however, still no one moved. They began screaming and pulling individuals to their feet, however, whenever the guards succeeded in getting someone to his feet, others would sit back down, until finally the Chinese officer in charge called for more guards and brutally forced us to walk down the main street, with kicks and shoves from the guards.

That night in the public square, the men, emboldened by the open mocking of Mao Tse-tung by a British Marine, came close to rioting.

After the "parade" was over, we were herded together and lectured on their so called "lenient policy," and we were told once again that we would be severe punished if we continued to behave in such a reactionary manner as we had in the parade. We had to go through our "self-criticism" act once again. We promised that we would never again destroy the property of the Chinese people!

The progressive (Richard T.) who ratted on us was kept under guard at the Chinese headquarters for several days for his protection. When he was returned to our compound, he was badly beaten up by members of our group. After that, it was rumored that the Chinese had given him a knife to protect himself with against other prisoners. He was one of the twenty-one individuals who refused to return to the states after the Police Action ended in 1953. However, he did return to the United States in the late fifties or early sixties.

We labored in the mountains, cutting timber and carrying the logs down the mountains for miles, with two and sometimes three or four individuals per log. We needed the wood for fuel, for the Chinese and for the cooks.

Each morning the guards came around, screaming accomplished by kicking and pushing us as we laid on the earth floor. We worked and/or were lectured to from dawn to dusk, and froze during the cold North Korean winter months. Before we left on work details, the guards took a head count, and after the work detail was completed, and upon our return to camp, there would be another head count. The guards were always afraid that someone would escape; however, escape was only a dream. No one in his right mind would dare to try an escape during the cold winter months.

In August of 1952, after our arrival at Company Four, and until we were released, a few of us paraded around the compound pretending to be playing imaginary music instruments or taking our imaginary dogs for walks around the compound.

One day, a friend, Bob, complained to a guard that my imaginary dog bit him on the leg. The guard did not understand what Bob was complaining about, so he called for an English speaking officer. When the English speaking officer arrived, Bob explained that he had been bitten by my dog. The officer wanted to know what dog!

Bob, stated, "There he is, can't you see him?"

Before the officer could answer, Bob called out, "Jack, get your dog off of his leg, don't let your dog piss on him."

The officer jumped and grabbed his pant leg. We broke up laughing over the reaction of this officer. After this little incident, the Chinese informed us that we could no longer have dogs in our compound. The Chinese could not figure us out; they thought that we were all crazy.

By the fall of 1952, we knew that the Chinese guards also suffered from night blindness; and we knew that they were afraid of strange noise, eerie night sounds. After learning of this, we waited for the darkness and commenced making weird noises and sounds. The Chinese guards who were suffering from night blindness, ran into the fence poles and huts while crazily chasing and searching for the origin of the sounds. We were threatened and stood at attention constantly over this, and each night there-after the Chinese posted a guard at several of the huts, hoping to catch us making the weird sounds. They never found out who or from where the sounds came. The guards remained posted around our huts for some time to insure that we were under sur-veillance and to halt our harassment of them.

During one of our wood cutting details, my saw partner Tony, the guy on the other end of the saw, and I tried to fell a tree on one of the guards. (Tony was from Missouri and had a gift for telling stories and keeping one's attention.) One of the other pris-oners saw that the tree was going to fall on the guard, rushed and pushed the guard out of the path of the falling tree. Tony and I had a hard time trying to explain that the tree had fallen the wrong way.

As I mentioned before, we had wood cutting details which took us several miles from camp and each one of us had to carry a quota of wood back to camp. The amount that we carried back in turn had to be weighted by the Chinese guards and if we didn't bring down our share, we would be herded back to the hills for more. Each man's share was approximately 200 caddies. A caddie is a weight of measure in the Orient and one caddie equals about 36 ounces.

On one wood gathering detail, a couple of the men, Norman Deathrage and one other member from the room next to mind, came down fairly late and upon their arrival, dumped their log in the river, hoping to wait until the next day to weight it, thinking that the log would be wet and would weigh more. However, the Chinese guards didn't buy that little trick and made both of them return to the hills for more wood.

During the winter of 1952, several of the prisoners still had their U.S. Army combat boots, and when they wore out, we took the metal insteps and sharpened them with a stone until eventu-ally, they were razor sharp. We used these home-made knifes to shave with and as weapons, to swipe at the crueler guards during the night, trying to inflict jagged wounds upon them. After a couple of these instances, the Chinese tore up our thatched huts looking for these instruments.

During the evening hours we would parade around the compound, pretending to be out of our minds, harassing the guards until they chased us into our huts.

I remember during the winter of 1952/53, we had to remove snow from the straw roofs of our huts. One of our fellow prisoners got up on the roof and in an attempt to push the snow off, he came down with the snow, landing on top of one of the guards. Other times we would throw snow balls at the guards over the huts or from behind the buildings.

During 1952, the Chinese finally agreed to put up a camp marker and our aircraft stopped flying directly over our camp. At nights we had to be alert for the bombers, which flew over just about every night. We could hear the bombers flying north and then return a short time later.

The Chinese would come around to our huts and make us put something over our mouths, claiming that the United States was using germ warfare against the North Koreans and the Chinese People's Army. The subject of bacteriological warfare was not new in the Korean War; in 1952, the Chinese give it a new twist. They charged that the U.S. was waging a bacteriological warfare. They claimed that the flies, fleas, ticks, mosquitoes, and spiders had been spread by the U.S. Air Force to disseminate contagious diseases over North Korea.

There was very little humor to be found in the day-to-day routine of a POW camp, to be sure. That which did surface more than likely involved one of the ingenious schemes that we came up with from time to time, both to antagonize our captors and to help maintain our own sanity. One such story which certainly bears telling was the case of two American officers who, having tired of the Chinese falsely accusing the U.S. of germ warfare, fashioned a tiny parachute and drew an Air Force insignia on the canopy. Attaching a dead mouse to the "shroud" lines, they then hung their handiwork on a bush where it was certain to be

166

seen by the Chinese. The screams of the guard who found the abomination brought camp officials running, one of whom carefully lifted the mouse from the bush with a pair of tongs and placed it in a glass container.

The container was then placed on exhibit in a nearby school house, irrefutable evidence that the Americans were in fact engaging in bacteriological warfare. The dead-serious Chinese, so satisfied with having proved their case, never realized that they had been the butt of what the whole camp though was a hilarious practical joke.

They came out and said, "We have proof that your capitalistic Air Force dropped germ bombs loaded with sick insects. They are capitalist insects, we know that for a fact, we have proof."

Richard Rook

One night, I have no idea of what time it was, I found it necessary to visit the latrine. The Chinese word for bathroom or latrine is "banjo" or at least it sounded like banjo. Anyway, I yelled "banjo" when the guard on duty challenged me, and I went my merry way. The latrine was approximately 50 yards behind our living quarters and between our quarters and the latrine the Chinese kept about two dozen chickens. I had often dreamed about eating one of these chickens and I'm sure there were others who shared my dream. I don't know why I decided that this would be the night to fulfill my dream but I did. On my return trip from the latrine, I made a detour into the chicken coop. Of course, they were all roosting, and I knew that in this state they could be easily handled without making any noise.

I felt their legs and then their breasts to make sure I picked a fat one and then I put the chicken's head under its wing and returned to my room. Once in my room, I stuffed the chicken into the sleeve of my field jacket which I was using for a pillow. Naturally, I found it difficult to sleep, and the more I thought about it, the more I realized that one chicken wouldn't go too far among 10 men. So, I went and got another one. After being

167

disturbed, the chickens were, quite naturally, very restless and kept making little chicken noises. In an effort to keep them quiet, I started talking to them. The other guys in the squad heard me but didn't say anything because they thought I was "losing it." (About three weeks earlier, one of the squad members, Ed Campbell, came busting into the room shouting, "I am Jesus Christ, we're having an air drop in the morning and we're all having ham & eggs with chocolate shakes for breakfast." He was one of several who broke under the strain of being held prisoner.) Well, that was why the guys thought I had "flipped out" when they heard me talking to the chickens.

I was so proud of myself for stealing two chickens that I couldn't sleep the rest of the of the night. When the sun finally up came and I told the men what I had done, they were just as excited as I was and were more than willing to participate in the "preparations" for the upcoming feast. The guards walked just outside our door so we would have to be very quiet while we did the chickens in. I had one guy hold the chicken up-side-down by its legs over a steel helmet, and two more guys, each one held a wing while I did the deed. While this was taking place we were all singing, to cover the noise. I cut the chickens up and put the pieces in a helmet filled with snow and water to await "dinner."

As the day drew on, I decided to cook a little appetizer for the guys (and myself too). So, I got a little soybean oil, some garlic and some peppers from a buddy who worked in the cook shack and started cooking. One of guys came up with a little hibachi and a can—we were all set to go. It wasn't long before we had our little appetizer in the making. I had forgotten that one of the guys had gone to headquarters that morning with a very infected finger and was told to go back to his squad until they decided what to do. They decided to pay him a visit just about the time my chicken was done.

When they realized what was going on, they came "unglued" and ordered the squad leader to headquarters. Of course, that was me. They took me and the can of chicken to headquarters and after we got there they sent a guard back to the room to look for, I guessed, more chicken. This was a real big deal to these people. They even used their old threat, "maybe we shot you" if I didn't confess to stealing chicken from the Chinese People's Volunteers. I told them that I didn't steal the chicken but found a dead one behind our quarters. I had no idea what the guard they sent back to room found, but I stuck to my original story. It wasn't long before they started to get real rough, but I still stuck to my story. By this time it was getting dark, and they were getting tired of pushing me around so they took me across the street and locked me in a little room, about the size of a closet, to "consider my crime against the Chinese people."

Over the next three days they brought at least five different confessions for me to sign. Each time I refused, they would get a little rougher so finally I decided to sign but not until the confession said what I wanted it to say. It ended up a very simple:

"I, Richard C. Rook, had stolen a chicken from the Chinese People's Volunteers, and I am sorry."

I had to be careful of what I signed because the Chinese were masters at propaganda.

The guys were happy to see me when I got back to the squad and told me that they had hidden the rest of the chicken before the guard came to search the room. Of course, they had eaten all of the chicken—so after all my trouble, I ended up with nothing. It was fun anyway, and I would have done it all over again.

For the next year and a half or so, we would see our Air Force in action many, many times. After the camp was marked, on many occasions, our planes would give us the old "fly-by" on their return trip from a raid on the hydroelectric plants on the Yalu River, which was only 12 miles north of our camp. (Camp One). On more than one occasion, a lone F-80 came in quite low to wave at us, and there just happened to be a man on his way to or from the latrine. The latrine was out away from the billets about 75 yards, and this mm had his hat turned inside-out, with the lining showing. The lining was white so

NATURALLY, the guard thought he was trying to signal the pilot, for what reason no one knew. The guard cranked a round into the chamber and took a shot in the direction of the GI.

Of course, quite a large crowd gathered, both GIs and Chinese. I never have known when to keep my big mouth shut, and this case would be no different. In jest I said, "Maybe we shot you" —a phrase they always used on us when they were mad or wanted to exert their authority over us. One of the Chinese interpreters overheard me and immediately called a guard. At bayonet point, off to headquarters I went. I had no idea why I had been taken to headquarters but I didn't have to wait long to find out. They accused me of threatening to shoot a Chinese People's Volunteer. When I informed them that I didn't have a weapon, they said, "You have a rifle in your mind." My immediate reaction was to laugh, but a rifle butt smashed into my back made me realize that they were serious. How does one defend himself against such stupidity? Of course, I couldn't and as a result, spent almost a week in a box made from 1 X 4s that was approximately 4 feet long, 4 feet high and 2½ feet wide. After that little ordeal, needless to say, I was very careful where I was when I said, "Maybe we shot you," which incidentally became quite a popular saying.

Our camp was directly under "Mig Alley." Every clear day we were able to watch the Mig-15s and the F-80s dog-fight right above us. Early in 1952 the F-80 was replaced by the F-86 Sabre which gave our guys a better chance against the Mig-15 which was a superior "bird" to the F-80. (I picked up that "bird" stuff from my brother.) We were able to watch planes being shot down (we seldom knew whose they were), and the pilots parachuting down. Of course, we would always assume that only Migs were shot down, never one of ours. We would say to the Chinks, "Mig-wadie (Chinese) sleepo," and then we would make like an airplane crashing into the ground. This would really make them mad. (No sense of humor) The Migs were armed with 20mm canons as well as 50 caliber machine guns. The 20mm rounds had explosive heads, and on several occasions, rounds would explode in our compound. That had a way of getting and keeping our attention.

One more story about planes and then I'll go on to something else. As I said before, Camp One was only about 12 miles south of the Yalu River—the site of hydroelectric plants. During the last year or so, we started using B-29s to bomb the hydroelectric plants. These raids usually took place at night. It was quite a show, believe me.

One night, it had just gotten dark, and we were being herded into our billets when the B-29s started their raid. This was in the days when they still used search lights to spot planes in flight. Every time when the B-29s flew over us, we knew that we were in for a light show. This particular night we certainly were not disappointed. As the bombers flew over us, several lights locked in on a single B-29. I counted a total of 37 search lights in use that night, more than any time previous. I'm sure that the crew of that plane could have read the morning paper without any trouble. There were about 200 GIs watching the turn of events in silence. The guards were no doubt instructed not to force us to go to our billets because I'm sure that the powers-to-be wanted to make sure that we witnessed the "downing" of one of our planes. Those Chinese who could speak English kept saying, "the men in that plane will spend the night in China." After what seemed like an hour (actually, it was only about 10 minutes) a blue streak appeared from the right of the bomber, and all of a sudden the B-29 disappeared and the search lights started moving all over the area, trying to pick him up again. This was our chance to rub it in a little. We started with a loud cheer and that went into the National Anthem. Immediately the guards started to herd us towards our billets, and not too gently either. (No sense of humor.)

Naturally, our captors never told us their names. Even if they had, we probably wouldn't have been able to pronounce them anyway. The Chinese army was structured just like ours; squads, platoons, companies, battalions, etc. The only Chinese soldier we called by his name was my platoon leader, Sun Lee. He was by far the most humane of any of the Chinese people we came in contact with. I guess that's the only reason why we didn't hang a nickname on him. But, everyone else was subject to a nickname, and they were always descriptive names. Some of the names that I remember are: Rabbit, Johnny One-note, Sore Jaw and The Little General to name a few.

The Chinese were great on propaganda. They would sneak around with concealed cameras and when they would come upon a couple GIs telling jokes or just laughing in general, out came the camera to catch "happy GIs discussing the virtues of being fortunate enough to be captured by the Chinese Peoples Volunteers and getting the chance of their life to learn about Communism." This practice was so obvious that it wasn't even funny.

One day we had a roll-call, and they informed us that they were going to issue us new uniforms. In the next breath they said that we were all going to march downtown to perform in a parade for some high ranking Chinese officer. Sure enough, we were issued new uniforms and the plans were made for our "coming-out" party. About two hours before the scheduled happenings (photo session) someone started to pass the word around that everyone should wash their new uniforms just before we were to fall-in, so they would be wet, and we couldn't wear them. I think that Willi Ruff was the one who started that little deal because it wasn't long after that that he was pulled out of the company in the middle of the night, and I didn't see him again until 1991 in Denver, at a POW reunion. Ruff's little prank was a huge success, to say the least. Boy, the Chinks were sure mad. (No sense of humor) I can't remember what our punishment was, but whatever it was, it was worth it. I can still see the Chinks storming around, shouting and spitting all over themselves.

When I was captured, I wasn't wearing any stripes, so I figured what the Chinese didn't know wouldn't hurt them. When they asked me what my rank was, I told them I was a corporal. I wanted to stay with my men and I figured that they would separate the NCOs from the rest. Everything went well until they released our names, and we started to receive mail. One day,

172

after our first mail call, the Chinese called me to headquarters. I had no idea, this time, why I was being called in on the carpet. As usual, the CO was screaming at me in Chinese while the interpreter very calmly told me what he was saying.

On the table in front of them was a letter from my wife addressed to Sgt. Richard Rook. They accused me of being a CIA "plant" and a Black Dragon, whatever that was. In addition to the Sgt. thing, (now this is funny) they said that the letter contained a coded message because I was referred to as Richard on the envelope and Dick in the contents of the letter. I don't know why they didn't transfer me to the Sergeant's camp right then and there, but they didn't. It would have been much easier on me if they had, because every time something went wrong, I was called to headquarters. This took place in Camp Three, and my reputation went with me when we were all moved to the other end of town and became Camp One.

CHAPTER EIGHT

OPERATIONS LITTLE SWITCH AND BIG SWITCH ... "FREEDOM AT LAST!"

Jack Chapman

Operation Little Switch

During March 1953, the Peace Talks were going along fairly well, and the Chinese started giving us better food, and around April 1953, the sick prisoners were removed from our compound. We were informed that they were to be repatriated (this was Operation Little Switch). In April 1953, three months before the end of the hostilities, Operation Little Switch, the exchange of prisoners of war, took place. About 6,000 Communist Chinese and North Koreans were returned in exchange for approximately 600 Allied Personnel. The Allied Personnel included 149 Americans. Among those released during Operation Little Switch that I knew were, David W. Ludlum, James J. Coogan, and Virgil A. Kaver.

During Big Switch many prisoners indicated that in most instances there were less than half the sick and wounded returned and that a substantial number of those sent back were considered to be progressives and had no obvious physical impairment. Furthermore, upon our return during Big Switch, we indicated that most of the sick and wounded who were not returned had not been examined by the Chinese physicians prior to Little Switch.

The following is a list of physical conditions suffered by those prisoners who were not repatriated during Little Switch: chronic chest conditions, amputation of portions of lower extremities, digestive disturbances, multiple cysts of skin, chronic amebiasis, mental illness, back injuries, severe malnutrition, cold injury, and malaria.

However the exchange of prisoners during Operation Little Switch was great news, for we had been living for the day when we would hear these words, and our hopes grew knowing that maybe one day soon we too would be released. When this group of prisoners was released, the Chinese brought in cigarettes and a few other items such as new clothing, tooth brushes (our first) and soap, this was about June or July 1953.

On July 27, 1953, we were assembled in the compound and told of the news that at Panmunjom an armistice had been signed. We all shouted, hollered and cried, for now we knew that we would soon be going home.

We received our first Red Cross packages about a week before the exchange of prisoners started in July 1953, tooth brushes, cigarettes, soap and etc. The International Red Cross issued each prisoner a cartoon of cigarettes, a razor, a comb and soap. Good old American cigarettes. We would sit around smoking one after another, enjoying them like we had never enjoyed a cigarette before.

Our appearance really changed, after a clean shave, etc. A totally different group of men. We were not permitted to see or talk with any members of the Red Cross. All items were turned over to the Chinese, and they in turn passed them on to us.

After being told of this good news, the Chinese allowed us to visit other compounds within our camp and we were able to meet and visit with old friends for the first time since our arrival at this camp.

Operation Big Switch

On August 3rd, Operation Big Switch began, and with the exchange in progress, we saw trucks with prisoners from other camps further north from us, passing through our camp each day. Daily we watched these trucks heading south and waved to the men on the trucks. Finally, they got around to our camp, and each day we waited as names were called off. Every day, I saw friends of mine leave, and I began to wonder when would my name be called. Every day, the Chinese read off the list of names, and these men would board trucks for the trip south and freedom. With each passing day, I would say good-bye to friends and watched as the trucks pulled away.

Camp One was becoming deserted, and still my name had not been called. We had been told that some of us would never return home, that we would remain in Korea. Those of us left in Camp One were beginning to fear that maybe we were not going to be released.

On or about August 15th, 1953, the exchange had been going on for about two weeks, when a member of the International Red Cross asked to see some American Prisoners still being held in Camp One. The International Red Cross apparently had been informed by a British Soldier that there were some American prisoners still being held.

On the morning of August 18th, 1953, myself and the remaining prisoners of Camp One (about three truck loads) were told that we were leaving for Panmunjan. We boarded trucks for the trip south and to freedom. We were very very happy to know that the International Red Cross had intervened, or who knows when we would have been released.

We traveled from Camp One to Freedom Village by trucks, arriving there the morning of August 20th, 1953, and 65 of us were hurriedly exchanged. Prior to leaving Camp One, the Chinese took away our personal belongings and addresses of other POWs and our personal notes.

On our trip south, we passed many trucks going the opposed direction with Koreans and Chinese prisoners who had been released by the United Nations. They were standing up in the back of the trucks and were fatter than hell. They were all rosy cheeked and hog jawed. Glancing at the guards in the back of our truck, and then at my skinny arms and legs, I knew none of us was more than a walking skeleton.

One of the guards in our truck could speak English, and he told us that the Chinese prisoners would all have to be re-educated before they returned to China. Their minds had been twisted and warped by the United States, and now they in reality had to be re-brainwashed before they could see or talk with their friends or families.

We were stopped a short distance north of Freedom Village, this being the release point, where our guards jumped from the trucks and tried to shake our hands. We told them to go to hell. Our own troops arrived and opened the tail gates and said, "WEL-COME HOME."

We started removing our prison clothing as we were heading for the exchange point. An American military policeman told us to keep our pants on as there were women present. We were then loaded into ambulances for our trip to freedom village. As we sighted Freedom Village, we had tears in our eyes and lumps in our throats. We were met by a Chaplain and had prayer.

I was met by an American Lieutenant Colonel and his first words were, "Here comes the Reactionaries."

He then asked me, "What would you like to have?"

My first reply was, "A dish of ice cream, please!

We were then taken over to the Red Cross for refreshments, which consisted of cigars, coffee, ice cream and milk. This was about all we could have, for we weren't used to rich food, and they said a meal would be waiting.

We then went to the showers, and as we came out, we were sprayed with DDT, given clean pajamas and a chance to relax. A short time later, food was brought to us, and I looked at my first decent meal in thirty-three months—roast beef, peas, mashed potatoes and a lettuce salad. We weren't allowed to eat very much, as our stomachs weren't used to eating food such as this. After eating we were permitted to visit with newspapermen. We were informed that we weren't compelled to meet them, it would be strictly up to us.

Right after our meeting with the press we were issued clean clothing and new boots. It was comical walking in hard soled shoes for we had to learn to walk all over again. We had been wearing tennis shoes for about two years during captivity. We then were taken over to the helicopter pad which took us to Inchon.

Inchon, the golden gate, our last stop before boarding a ship for the good old USA. As the helicopter landed we were greeted warmly and fed a good supper and assigned a clean bunk for the night. We spent the night at Inchon, and the next day we were given some back pay, allowed to do some shopping at the Post Exchange.

Head lines in the newspaper on Thursday, August 20th, 1953 read:

'REDS HAND OVER mm PROBLEM CHILDREN: FREEDOM VILLAGE, THURSDAY, AUGUST 20, 1953 (AP)

The first batch of "problem children" from North Korean prison camps—Americans who bedeviled their Communist guards and beat up turncoat comrades — came back yesterday. Filled with contempt and hate for their captors, they were firm in their belief that the Communists would be holding them yet had it not been for intervention by UN Red Cross Teams. These men, who stood steadfast against Red propaganda despite intimidation and actual torture, and were labeled "problem children" by their captors, told of their own secret organization.

On the morning of August 21st, 1953 we were loaded on buses and taken to the pier and put aboard ship for our trip home.

Richard Rook

On July 13, 1953, just two weeks before the war was over, I was pulled out of my group and taken to a building in the center of town. At first there were only a few of us there. After the group began to grow and we started to compare notes, we realized that we were not being gathered together to received merit badges. We finally reached 23 in number, and then the "defecation hit the twirling blades." The camp commander came in and after "chewing" us out for 10 or 15 minutes, he said that we were "bad elements" and had to be "removed."

178

We were loaded unto a truck and with a truck in front and in the rear with machine guns trained on us, we were taken out of town. Try to envision this if you can. It was just getting dark, it was raining, we had two machine guns trained on us, we were being taken to a place unknown, and we had just been told that we were "bad elements" and had to "removed." Naturally, we all thought that this was the end of the line. Well, it turned out that all they wanted to do was isolate us so they could beat us on a regular basis. They also tried us as spies and gave us each ten years at hard labor. The war was over July 27, 1953, so we were saved by the bell.

When the "Chinks" took my watch off my wrist back on May 19, 1951, it was 5:45 AM. As I walked across the exchange point at Panmunjom, North Korea (Freedom Village) on August 26, 1953, there was a clock (on the American side, naturally) that read 10:50 AM. The time I had spent as a POW was exactly 27 months, 7 days, 5 hours and 5 minutes.

After we came through the exchange point at Panmunjom, our lives changed immediately, to say the least. Everything was suddenly right. The air seemed fresher, the sun brighter, even our MPs looked good, but most of all, our flag was so beautiful. I'll never forget the feelings I felt when I first saw our flag waving in the breeze. I felt so proud to be an American. To this day, whenever I see our flag, I think of that day in Panmunjom, North Korea.

After we came across the "line," and after we were welcomed back by several General Officers, we were loaded into ambulances and transported to Freedom Village. As we off-loaded the ambulances, we were greeted by several American women. Oh, they looked so pretty, every last one of them. After a brief recovery period, we were led into this huge, temporary building where we were met by a minister, rabbi or a priest. Then came the press, then the paymaster, and then delousing and finally a good hot shower.

Through all these stations (except for the shower, of course) we were offered all the milk and ice cream that we wanted. They

179

were so organized — it was truly amazing. Of course they should have been because they knew who was coming across and when, but even so it was nice to see a little organization for a change. At the paymaster's station they told us exactly how much back-pay we had coming and how much we'd be able to draw. They would only allow partials, for obvious reasons.

After our shower we were issued underwear and a robe. Our next stop was the tailor shop where we were measured for our uniforms. Then it was off to be fitted for our shoes and then it was time for lunch. The lunch menu included everything one could imagine as long as it wasn't fried or spicy. After lunch it was time to pick up our tailor-made uniforms complete with patches, stripes, hash-marks, etc. Then we were issued our campaign ribbons and badges.

After that, we were loaded into choppers and flown to Inchon for processing to ship home. We were disappointed when we learned that we were not going to fly back to the States. They told us that it was necessary to go by ship so that we could received physical examinations and de-briefing, which was a must before we could go home on leave. We had no idea of what we were going to be subjected to once we got out on our own, and the many sessions we had with the psychiatrists on board certainly helped prepare us for life in the real world.

Harold Kaschko

It was exhilarating to be released from captivity after being held for 1,011 days by the Communists in Korea. It was one of the happiest days of my life. Peace talks had dragged on for nearly two years before an agreement was reached. Many of us POWs thought we would end up in Siberia or some other remote place like that and would never return to the USA.

Edward Sheffield

Some few days after the treaty had been signed at the neutral zone, they announced to the other groups that they were going to be repatriated, but never told me anything.

One morning I came out of my hole in the ground to go to work... there was a truck parked on the road with several other men aboard. The guard motioned for me to get on the truck. Through talking with the others aboard the truck I found out they were reactionaries also, and we knew we weren't going to the neutral zone to be released, but instead were hauled away back in the mountains to an old house and double guards were posted around us. None of us was all that bad; we just weren't cooperative with their Communist doctrines.

However, they told us that we would finally be released if we wouldn't cause any more trouble. They also told us that some of the men back at camp who needed medical attention had been released already. That made everyone's hopes rise, and later we heard that others had been released.

The Chinese wanted some volunteers to stay over there since the Americans had 5,000 of their men captured who refused to go back to North Korea and China. So they had no one to turn to, but the ones who had collaborated with them.

At first, none volunteered, then they told them like this, "We don't force you to stay here, but when we turn you over to your authorities we have the right to turn your records over along with you. The Chinese did keep a daily record of every man's actions and activities, but they still only got a few to agree to stay. Two months later our time came.

We loaded on a truck and went to the railroad station. We crawled aboard cattle cars for the journey south to the neutral zone. The cars were a little cleaner and not so crowded as they were three years before. I stood in the door as we traveled south and thought how fortunate I was to be among the thirty percent left.

The bridges, the towns and the railroad stations along the way were shattered to the ground. Bomb holes big enough to bury a tank were everywhere. The ever present sight of women working in the fields, the women on the railroad sections with shovels and spades—they looked so worn and pathetic. I felt these women never had much of what we in America call femininity, certainly war was not their idea.

When we reached the neutral zone, we were transferred to the officers' company and awaited repatriation. Finally, my number came up. About 10 of us were loaded on the back of a truck with one Chinese instructor and one driver who drove us to Freedom Village. The 30th day of August, 1953, was the happiest day of my life. Tears came in my eyes, and I was sort of choked.

The truck wheeled around and a two star general was standing there beside a big tent. He said, "Welcome home, son. You're free now." Everyone was so nice to us. They kept asking if there was anything we wanted. I said, "Yes, I would like to sleep in a bed one night." They assured me that I wouldn't have to sleep on the ground anymore. It took sixteen days to come to San Francisco by ship. They ran us through a medical examination during that time.

I caught a plane from San Francisco and arrived home the 19th day of September, 1953.

After Operation Big Switch

Operation Big Switch started August 3, 1953 at Panmunjom, South Korea. Across Freedom Bridge came truck after truck carrying men who had been prisoners of the Communists. All but twenty-one were returning to freedom. All, that is, who had been reported by the Communists. Another group of Americans who had not been reported but were known to be prisoners of the Chinese were four fighter pilots, an entire B-29 crew, and two civilians. The Korean War did not end for them until August

1955. They finally were returned to freedom through the British crown colony of Hong Kong. Returning prisoners in Hong Kong told stories of seeing many hundreds of American prisoners still being held in labor camps in Siberia.

Three of the fighter pilots were kept together and granted mail privileges by the Chinese, who permitted them to receive three letters per week, one from their parents, and two from friends. The Chinese again were demonstrating to the world their lenient policy by permitting the captured Americans to send and receive mail.

Capt. Harold E. Fischer said after repatriation that all of his letters were dictated and censored. Each letter was handed to a guard with the envelope unsealed. It then would be censored and recopied before the envelope was stamped and mailed.

The Chinese security section handled the prisoners' mail. They refused to let the Americans put stamps of the envelops because it was believed that they would put messages on the backs of the stamps, or stub the perforations into a coded message.

There is a list of 389 names of U.S. Military Personnel that the U.N.C. hands to the North Koreans each year for an accounting. These men were known to have been in Communist hands at the cessation of hostilities. The names are listed in the Appendix, under the section entitled Honor Roll of Forgotten Americans.

This section taken from various sources

CHAPTER NINE

"A PROMISE KEPT," THE STORY OF JOHNNIE JOHNSON

In August of 1953, when the newly released prisoners of war made the long trip home from Panmunjon, Korea, each man brought his memories home with him. Appalling memories of torture, starvation, disease, filth, and death. Memories that would last a lifetime. One of these brave Americans brought home something else. Smuggled out inside of a small empty toothpaste tube was a precious cargo, something he had nearly paid for with his life. Inside the tube was a faded and worn handwritten list of nearly 500 men and women he had seen die from starvation, disease, or at the hands of their North Korean captors.

P.F.C. Wayne A. (Johnnie) Johnson, of Lima, Ohio, had spent over 36 months in the prison camps along the frozen Yalu River which separated North Korea from Manchuria. He was a survivor of the brutal death marches lead by the infamous North Korean guard known as "The Tiger."

Soon after his capture on July 11, 1950, Johnnie began to realize that because of the horrible situation they were in, knowledge of those he saw die might be lost forever. He was haunted by the fact that their families would never know what happened to them, and at that point made a promise not to let that happen. So, starting with stolen scraps of paper and the stub of a pencil, he began to record information about the those around him he watched struggle and die. He secretly wrote the name, rank, unit, date of death, and hometown of each. He eventually chronicled the deaths of close to 500 people. In spite of the constant fear of torture or death if his actions were discovered, he persisted in his quest. He even went as far as to make two complete lists, carefully hiding one in a wall and the other under the floor of

184

his hut. When the list he had hidden in the wall was found by a guard, Johnnie was interrogated, beaten and threatened at gunpoint. Even this could not persuade him to stop. He intended to make good on the promise he had made to himself and to the families, no matter what the cost.

When the joyous news came that they were being released, Johnnie had to quickly devise a way to get his list home safely. What precious little they had was being taken away. There didn't seem to be any place to hide the list from his captors. Then in the last few days, the prisoners received soap, toothbrushes and toothpaste from the International Red Cross, the first of such luxuries they'd seen since their capture. Johnnie immediately emptied and cleaned out his toothpaste tube and carefully pushed his list inside, and in this way was able to bring it home with him.

More than forty years later, on August 3, 1996, Johnnie was finally recognized for his valiant deed and awarded the Silver Star for valor. He has also received the deep personal reward of being able to share information with the some of families of the people on his list, telling them about the last days of their loved ones' life. At last he was able to feel his dream of long ago was fulfilled, that his promise to the families was kept.

[Johnny has graciously sent a copy of his list to be included in this chapter.]

"ROSTER OF THOSE WHO DIED IN CAPTIVITY"

Part I-Soldiers
[Last name, First name, rank, unit, date of death, hometown]

ADAMS Robert I. 1/LT 34/24 11-(15 or 16)-50 MA
ADAMS Charles W. PFC 34/24 12-25-50 Blandon PA
AHERN Gerald 41st British Marines 5-7-51 London England
ALBRECHT John A. PFC 21/24 1-31-51 Pittsburg PA
ALEXANDER Jack D. PFC 21/24 11-19-50 Eildeauer WI
ALFORD Raymond PVT L/21/24 2-27-51 Atlanta GA
AMBEAU Donald F. PVT L/21/24 11-1-50 Escanaba MI
AMPON Joseph CPL L/21/24 1-20-52 Chicago IL
ANDERSON Douglas R. CPT Med/21/24 8-14-51 Rockford IL

ANDERSON Larry J. PVT 19/24 12-25-50 Battle Creek MI
ANDERSON Omar Lee CPL 21/24 2-5-51 Frydek TX
ANDREWS Shirley B. PFC 21/24 7-16-50 MA
ANGELL Eugene L. PFC C/19/24 9-25-50 WI
ANZALDUA Baldomero SGT 21/24 4-17-51 Raymondville TX
ATEN Fred W. PFC 34/24 10-24-50 NJ
AYO Albert J. PFC 19/24 1-10-51 Bronx NY
BAER Donald Le PFC 34/24 12-3-50
BAILY Charles V. CPL L/21/24 1-22-51 Holly MI
BAKER Walter R. PFC 21/24 1-12-51 Rockbridge IL
BAMFORD Charles SGT 15AA/7 1-24-51 Ontario CA
BARNES Herbert R. PVT 19/24 5-3-51 Lonaconing MD
BARNETT Raymond PFC 8-50 Seattle WN
BARON John PFC 21/24 1-25-51 Pawtucket RI
BARRICK George 1LT L/21/24 11-7-50
BARTER Charles T. MAJ S3/63/24 5-3-51 Mt Vernon IN
BAULK Richard E. PVT 19/24 1-11-51 Detroit MI
BEAHM Thomas J. PVT 21/24 1-16-51 Bethlehem PA
BECKHAM Larry E. PVT C/19/24 2-24-51 Lutherville AR
BEECHER Robert PVT 21/24 1-22-51 So Miami FL
BENNER Warren W. PFC 21/24 1-8-51 Chester PA
BERARDI Thomas H. PFC 21/24 7-11-51 Bellingham MA
BERFORD Bobby PFC 11/24 11-4-50 Lynchburg VA
BERGE Ralph O. PVT 21/24 12-26-50 Clearwater TX
BERGERON Joseph E. PVT Med Co/34/24 1-16-51 Waterbury CT
BERGMAN William J. 1/LT 34/24 6-18-51 Little Rock AR
BERRIER Jackie G. PVT L/21/24 1-5-50 Kansas City MO
BEVELS Charles M. CPL 1/21/24 12-24-50 Biloxi MS
BILYEU Michell G. PVT 21/24 9-26-50 OR
BISHOP Arthur L. PVT 21/24 11-22-50 San Angelo TX
BISSELL Janes R. SGT 57FA/7 6-2-51 Barton OH
BLOCK Robert S. PVT 19/24 11-4-50 Lyle MN
BOLLES Lloyd PVT 34/24 4-13-52 MI
BOOKS Arthur H. 2/LT 52/24 11-1-50 Norwood OH
BOONE James L. PVT 63/24 11-3-50 AR
BOR Felix V. PFC 21/24 11-12-50 Detroit MI
BORDEAU Alfred C. PFC 21/24 4-29-51 Bay City MI
BOTSFORD Philip A. PFC 34/24 10-29-50 Manchester NH
BOWSER Lemuel R. PFC 21/24 2-22-51 Elmbank PA
BOYER Charles E. CPL L/21/24 1-28-51 Benton Harbor MI
BOYIDDLE Silas W. PVT L/21/24 10-27-50 OK
BRADLEY Edgar N. PFC 21/24 11-15-50 Hon AR
BRANDENBERG Kenneth CPL 21/24 10-30-50 Norwood OH
BRINGE Donald P. PFC 63/24 3-18-51 Milwaukee WI
BROCKMAN John J. 1LT 1/21/24 12-12-50 Tampa Springs FL
BROWN Arthur L. PFC 21/24 1-19-51 Cincinnati OH
BROWN David Q. PFC H/19/24 11-13-50 Farmington MI
BROWN Joseph CPL 21/24 7-51 Briggsdale OH
BROWN William PFC 34/24 11-25-50 Weissport PA
BUFF Jack Y. MISGT 19/24 10-28-50 McAlester OK
BUNTING Worth L. CPL 21/24 1-8-51 Ahan NC
BURNES Francis CPL 34/24 9-2-50 Santa Monica CA
BUSICO Ernest PVT 19/24 3-3-51 NY
BUSKIRK George E. PVT 21/24 1-28-51 Topeka KS

BYERS Charles E. PVT 21/24 12-27-50 Fort Plain NY
CAKS Joseph PFC 34/24 9-28-50
CALAWAY William E. PFC C/19/24 10-24-50 Quincy IL
CAMMARANO Thomas A. PVT 34/24 11-2-50 Brooklyn NY
CARMAN Lyle H. PFC 21/24 12-7-50 Marietta OK
CARNES Harry Z. PFC 63/24 11-22-50 Detroit MI
CASPER Charles D. PFC 21/24 1-9-51 Eure NC
CHARLES Madison CPL 21/24 11-3-50 North Chatham NH
CHARLES Raymond M. PVT 19/24 27-9-50 OH
CHERRY Richard F. 19/24 9-26-50 TX
CHEFF Louis PVT 34/24 12-28-50 Niagara Falls NY
CHOAT Lloyd L. PVT A/19/24 11-1-50 Lonoke AR
CHRISTENSEN Jerry C. SFC HQS/34/24 12-10-50 Dalton MN
CHRISTIAN Stuart B. PFC 21/24 3-21-51 Richmond VA
CHRISTOPULOS Clayton PVT 34/24 34/24 Salida CO
CLARK Glen M. PVT 21/24 11-16-50 Springfield WV
CLARK O.C. Jr. PVT 21/24 2-28-51 AL
CLARKE Harry B. PFC 19/24 4-27-51 Dunnellen NJ
CLOSSON Archie J PVT 21/24 4-21-51 RI
COLFORD Wilber B. PVT 21/24 10-31-50 Fairfield ME
CONNICK Karl F. PFC 21/24 6-18-51 West Chazy NY
CORONA Jainie PVT HVY MTR/19/24 4-24-51 EL Paso TX
COTLAND Miral PVT 34/24 10-31-50 Bronx NY
COUNCIL William PFC 63/24 11-4-50 Pittsboro NC
COX Jansen C. 2/LT L/21/24 12-28-50 Woodlawn VA
COX Lester A. CPL 21/24 10-31-50 Lincoln NE
COX Robert C. CPL L/21/24 1-8-51 Richmond VA
CUMMINS Zolton PFC C/19/24 10-31-50 NY NY
DAGGETT Calvin A. PFC 63/24 11-9-50 Stamford NY
DAILEY Richard M/SGT 21/24 11-14-50 Auburndale MA
DANIEL Richard A. PVT 21/24 10-31-50 WA
DANOWSKI Alex SFC L/21/24 3-17-51 Ashley PA
DAVIS George P. PFC 21/24 6-15-51 Pawhuska OK
DAVIS Leo C. PFC 21/24 11-14-50 NY
DAY Donald PVT 34/24 10-30-50 Cincinnati OH
DEAN Alvin C. PFC 21/24 5-18-51 New Orleans LA
DECICCO Leo M. PFC 34/24 9-2-50 Hoboken NJ
DELUCA Leslie J. PFC A/19/24 12-3-50
DEMMIN Dale A. PFC 34/24 1-11-51 Peoria IL
DETAMORE, Robert G. PFC 34/24 10-30-50 WV
DIEKMAN Lester H. CPL 52/24 11-29-50 Readlyn IA
DIRKSEN Abraham Jr. CPL 34/24 5-8-51 Blackwell OK
DITHER Elwood L. CPL 63/24 11-2-50 Kansas City MO
DOBBS J.B. PFC 34/24 11-5-50 Mellette OK
DOWLING James R. PVT 21/24 10-15-50 GA
DOXIE Paul SGT 34/24 11-1-50 Ontario CA
DOYLE Lawrence A. PFC D/19/24 10-28-50 Baltimore MD
DRISCOLL Herman 2/LT 34/24 9-7-50
DUBOSE Cayatt R. PFC 21/24 5-27-51 Tampa FL
DUFNER John PFC 34/24 11-21-50 South Gate CA
DUNCAN Lester A. PFC 34/24 4-8-51 Frederick OK
DUNHAM Leland R. MAJOR 1st BN/34/24 8-7-51 Littleton NH
DUNN Francis PFC A/19/24 10-27-50 Troy NY
EASTERDAY Charles We PFC L/21/24 11-16-50 Ann Arbor MI

EASTON Edward D. CPL 63/24 11-25-50 —AR
EATON John D. PFC C/19/24 5-8-51 Sulphur IN
EBENSPERGER Clarence CPL G/19/24 11-2-50 Utica.NY
EDGE Edward C. PFC A/19/24 11-20-50 Seaside Park NJ
EMMOTT Robert P. CPL 63/24 7-17-50 NY
ESTES Edward E. PFC 34/24 2-7-51 Canehill AR
EVANS Joseph K. SGT 21/24 1-2-5- Macon GA
FABBI Earnest PVT 21/24 12-20-50 Carthage NY
FAHRMEYER Kermit PVT 34/24 9-29-50 KS
FALLOW Richard PVT 34/24 2-2-51 Fort Dodge IA
FANCHER Harold S. PFC 21/24 5-7-51 Johnstown NY
FANNIN Clyde CPL 24G? 11-51 Tyler TX
FARONE William M. CPL 21/24 10-31-50 Watertown NY
FINE John PFC 21/24 1-22-51 Pittsburg PA
FINE Richard M. PFC 21/24 2-9-51 Monongahela PA
FITZGERALD Gerald PFC 34/24 12-12-50 Syracuse NY
FLEMING John PVT 63/24 1-12-51 Philadelphia PA
FLETCHER Robert S. CPL 19/24 1-9-51 Manchester NC
FLOOK Grady H. SGT HQ BTRY/52/24 11-14-50 Alhambra CA
FLORCZYK Edward S. PVT 34/24 10-26-50 NY
FRANKLIN John D. JR. PFC A/19/24 6-6-51 Salem NJ
FRANTZ George A. PFC L/21/24 12-5-50 Indianapolis IN
FRECHETTE Charles J. PFC 21/24 10-21-50 MI
FREUND Alyoisis J. SGT HQS 1BN/19124 1-5-51 Fond Du Lac WI
FREYTAG Reuben W. SGT 34/24 1-20-51 Wartburq TN
FULLER Donald PFC 34/24 1-8-51 Stockton CA
FULLERTON Harold D. PFC L/21/24 10-1-50 PA
FUNA John F. PFC 21/24 1-5-51 PA
FURLOW Robert D. PFC 21/24 5-3-51 Mechanicsville NY
GAILEY Robert G. CPL 63/24 2-12-51 Smiths Ferry PA
GARCIA Roger PVT 34/24 3-20-51 Los Angeles CA
GARZA Nickolas C. PVT 21/24 12-20-50 Rockdale TX
GEARHART William PVT M/21/24 1-3-51 Fort Indian Town Gap PA
GEDNEY Robert E. PVT 34/24 12-9-50 Cleveland OH
GENDILO James F. PVT 21/24 11-4-50 Santa Clara NY
GEORGE Edward PVT 34/24 11-22-50 Dallas PA
GEORGE Edwin PVT 21/24 IL
GIBSON Charles V. PVT 21/24 12-50 KS
GILLETTE Robert L. PFC 34/24 1-11-51 Alanson MI
GIRONO Emil SFC 34/24 9-6-50
GLASS, Cecil R. PVT 34/24 3-31-51 Louisburg MO
GOHL Lavern Pe PFC 19/24 10-21-50 Williston ND
GONZALES Joe PVT 3D ENG/24 12-29-50 Montebello CA
GRAFF Herman L. JR. CPL 34/24 11-17-50 Knox City MO
GRAHAM William CPL 21/24 11-27-51 Bordentown NJ
GRAMBERG Bernard 1LT AF-27/25 12-10-50 HI
GRESSENS Norman J. CPL 34/24 9-28-50 Ashland PA
GRIFFITH William G. PFC 34/24 11-1-50 Pittsburg PA
GROGBAN Harold PFC 12-13-50 Batelian OH
GROSS Myron E. PVT 21/24 1-14-51 Sundale PA
GUIDRY Joseph CPL 21-24 7-3-51 Marrero LA
GUSTAFSON Harold W. PVT 34/24 12-21-50 Madinsonville TN
HAGGARD Bille M. PFC L/21/24 6-26-51 Savannah TN
HALBERT George R. JR. PFC 21/24 6-1-51 Hermosa Beach CA

HALEY Richard A. 1/SGT 1/21/24 8-11-50 Auburndale MA
HALLUM Leonard D. PVT 34/24 6-9-51 Cookeville TN
HAMILTON Milton SGT 34/24 2-5-52 Beloit KS
HAMMOND Robert T. PFC 34/24 11-2-50 Ilion NY
HANNON Arthur PFC 21/24 11-23-50 Gardner IL
HANSEN Dan H. PVT 21/24 12-10-50 Correctionville IA
HANSINGER Nicholas J. PVT 21/24 10-28-50 Los Angeles CA
HARBOUR Ronald E. PFC 34/24 12-9-50 Colfax IA
HARDY Edgar W. SGT 21/24 5-11-51 Nowata OK
HARRINGTON James H. PVT C/19/24 10-4-50 Brooklyn NY
HARRIS Howard K. PFC 34/24 11-4-50 Providence RI
HART Michael J. JR. PFC 24/QM/24 9-12-50 IL
HARTMAN David K. PVT 34/24 7-50 MI
HARTMAN Roger w. 2/LT 52/24 3-8-51 Santa Fe NM
HAYMAN James R. PFC 21/24 10-28-50 Tampa FL
HEATH Richard C. SFC 21/24 3-18-51 Richfield Springs NY
HEFFLEY Edgar S. PVT 21/24 11-14-50 Chicago IL
HELMS Eugene CPL E/19/24 10-29-50 Pittman OH
HENNESS Jimmy E. PVT 63/24 12-11-50 Wichita KN
HENSLEY Bird SGT TACPs/ USAF 10-31-50 Cawood KY
HENSLEY Eldred PFC 21/24 11-5-50 Hullinus WV
HESS Kenneth PVT C/19/24 2-7-51 Concordia KN
HICKS Chester S. PFC 63/24 12-23-50 Madisonville TN
HIGGS William D. JR. PVT 34/24 11-2-50 VA
HILL Donald G. PVT 21/24 1-24-51 Riverton WV
HILL James C. PVT 19/24 1-14-51 Detroit MI
HILL Melvin J. PFC 52/24 11-18-50 Negaunee MI
HOLENCIK Joseph P. PFC C/19/24 3-16-51 Egypt PA
HOLLAND William PFC 21/24 6-11-51 Cincinnati OH
HOLMAN Albert C. JR. PFC 34/24 6-6-51 Statesville NC
HOULIMAN Patrick PFC 34/24 12-23-50 Lawrence MA
HOWARD Ralph A. PFC 63/24 11-20-50 Lacona NY
HUDSON William PVT 34/24 12-18-50 Niles MI
HUTTON Donald J. CPL 63/24 11-4-50 St Louis MO
IZU Isamu PFC HQ Co/3rd Bn/21/24 7-12-51 Kaalalila HI
JESTER William F. 2/LT 3Bn/21/24 5-26-51 Indianapolis IN
JESTER William R. PFC L/21/24 6-16-51 Vevay IN
JIMENEZ Victor P. PFC C/19/24 4-16-51 San Antonio TX
JOHNSON Dewitt W. PFC 34/24 12-30-50 Doniphan MO
JOHNSON John E. SGT 21/24 1-9-51 Council Hill OK
JONES Arthur CPL 21/24 10-31-50 Baltimore MD
JONES Dale R. PFC 21/24 7-12-51 Piqua OH
JONES Thomas D. PFC 52/24 1-1-51 Coalton WV
JORTHEN Harry PVT 21/24 11-22-50 Cleveland OH
KACAR Stanley J. PVT 34/24 7-5- Youngstown OH
KAILIANU Robert W. CPL D/19/24 12-23-50 Honolulu HI
KEKCA Joseph K. PVT 21/24 9-26-50
KELLY Ernest SGT 21/24 9-6-50 Washington PA
KELLY Robert T. PVT 21/24 1-16-51 Pittsburg PA
KENDIG John P. PFC 63/24 11-20-50 York PA
KIM George PVT 34/24 12-14-50 Honolulu HI
KINGSLEY Willie L. M/SGT 34/24 11-17-50 Birmingham AL
KING Ralph PFC 21/24 2-6-52 New Albany IN
KISER Henry G. SGT 21/24 6-25-51 Paris KY

KIVLEMAN Allen F. PFC HQS/34/24 11-3-50
KLIMSEY Joseph W. JR. PVT A/21/24 1-2-51 Cleveland OH
KNAPKE Anthony L. PFC A/19/24 11-4-50 Minster OH
KOCH Kermit K. PVT 21/24 5-3-51 Frederickburg TX
KOLBERG William V. PFC 21/24 12-28-50 Keyser WV
KRISTENOFF George W. 1/Lt 24 Recon/24 4-29-51 Pengilly MN
LANTZ Rupert PFC 19/24 12-25-50 Beloit WI
LASSIC Kenneth PVT 21/24 11-22-50 Whitefield MI
LASSITER Donald T. PFC 34/24 11-20-50 Ripley TN
LAYTON Robert 1/LT 28B/USAF 4-51 Tulsa OK
LEBIEDZ Joseph CPL 19/24 11-3-50 Cambridge MA
LEE Charles PFC 34/24 1-6-51 Honolulu HI
LeMATTY Donald G. PFC 63/24 11-1-50 Keokuk IA
LEWIS Warren G. 2/LT M/21/24 12-6-50 Cartersville GA
LIEBEG Robert W. PFC 19/24 3-1-51 Brainerd MN
LIPES Richard PFC 19/24 12-23-50 Lewisburg WV
LINGLE Keith L. CPL 63/24 1-1-51 Coalwood WV
LOGSTON Edward PFC AAF 11-4-50 Richmond CA
LOOMIS Otis W. CPL C/19/24 12-25-50 Caledonia NY
LORENZ Robert E. PFC 63/24 10-28-50 Chicago IL
LOVE Robert J. PVT 21/24 11-14-50 Mansfield OH
LUKITSCH John J. PFC C/19/24 10-27-50 Allentown PA
LYDAN John S. JR. PFC 21/24 12-5-50 Lewistown ID
MACGILL Henry 1/LT C/19/24 7-50 NC
MACNAIR-RAGA Hector PVT 34/24 1-16-51 NY NY
MACOMBER Wayne B.CPT HQS/1ST BN/19/24 7-19-51 Oakland CA
MAGNUS Donald F. PFC 21/24 1-4-51 Evansville IN
MAHONEY Kenneth PVT 21/24 8-3-50 MA
MAJESKE Arthur JR. PVT 21/24 1-1-51 West Allis WI
MALDONADO Victor J. PVT 34/24 11-27-50 NY NY
MALONE Francis P. JR. CPL 19/24 1-29-51
MANN William C. PFC HQS BTRY/52/24 3-3-51 Indian Mount TN
MANROSS Thomas M. PFC 19/24 11-14-50 Titusville PA
MARDEN William PFC 21/24 11-4-50 WN
MARSH Harold SGT 34/24 8-50 Oshkosh WI
MARTIN John A. CPL D/19/24 5-2-51 Ridgeway TX
MARTY Albert C/19-24 17-7-50
MATHEWSON Ward M/SGT 21/24 7-16-50
MATTHEWS Richard F. SGT 34/24 10-31-50 Sacramento CA
MAYNARD Edward W. 1/LT HQ BTRY/63/24 6-20-51 Baltimore MD
McCABE Donald PVT A/19/24 11-4-50 Brooklyn NY
McCLAIN Fredrick F. SGT 34/24 11-2-50 OH
McCORMICK Billy G. PVT 34/24 11-6-50 Santa Paula CA
McDONNELL John J. PFC 34/24 11-14-50 Philadelphia PA
McELROY Joseph A. CPL 34/24 12-13-50 W(?)port PA
McGILL William PVT 21/24 12-18-50 Lock Haven PA
McGRATH Ross R. PVT 63/24 11-2-50 MA
McINTYRE James T. PFC 21/24 12-28-50 New Albany IN
MCKINLEY Ralph H. PVT 21/24 5-5-51 Atlanta GA
McNARY Walter D. PVT 34/24 11-22-50 East Detroit MI
McQUEEN Norman SFC 63/24 1-16-51 OK
McSHANE Edward P. PFC C/19/24 12-14-50 Pittsburg PA
MELCHIORRE Joseph D. PFC 21/24 3-19-51 Utica NY
MELLINGER James PFC 34/24 11-2-50 Billingdale OH

MENTOZ Paul SGT G. 21/24 7-3-51 St Louis MO
MERSHON David F. PVT A/19/24 11-4-50 Portsmouth OH
MEYERS Guy PVT 34/24 10-31-50 Boston MA
MIELKE Robert PVT C/34/24 10-31-50 Kenosha WI
MILLER Paul LT US Navy 11-15-50 Flat Rock AR
MITCHELL Rubus JR. PFC HQ CO/19/24 11-4-50 New Orleans LA
MITCHELL William B. JR. PVT A/19/24 7-29-50 Jackson MS
MITCHELSON Thomas P. PFC 34/24 9-24-50 WY
MIRTH Philip PFC 63/24 7-50
MOMPHER David T. PFC 24REC/24 10-29-50 Springfield VA
MONROE James H. PFC C/19/24 11-2-50 Meridian ID
MONTGOMERY Harold W. SGT 21/24 1-3-51 Madera CA
MORAN Joseph PVT 34/24 11-26-50 Johnstown PA
MORENO Raymond M. PFC 21/24 5-17-51 Los Angeles CA
MORGAN Melvin H. PFC L/21/24 12-6-50 Stanfield NC
MOSS William R. PFC 21/24 1-18-51 MA
MURDOCK Jackie L. PVT 34/24 10-29-50 Crawfordville IN
MURPHY Michael D. CPL MED/34/24 11-14-50 Oklahoma City OK
MURPHY Robert M. PFC 34/24 5-27-51 Fairchance PA
NAZELROD Earl C. PFC 34/24 4-14-51 Oakland MD
NEIMANN Robert 2/LT 1ST BN/21/24 8-50 IA
NELSON Oscar PVT 19/24 10-26-50 Detroit MI
NELSON Woodrow W. PFC L/21/24 10-19-50 New Biochoices OH
NICKELS Robert A. PFC 21/24 1-3-51 Toledo OH
O'HARA William T. PFC 19/24 11-21-50 Milwaukee WI
OLES Peter PVT C/19/24 12-8-50 Batavia NY
Ollero Luciano F. PFC C/19/24 5-23-51 Philippine Islands
OLSON Sigurd C. PVT 21/24 2-5-51 Bethel ME
OLTMAN Charles R.L. PVT 63/24 1-28-51 Springfield MO
OMION Vernon J. PFC 34/24 12-25-50 Foreston MD
OSTROWSKI Chester PFC 21/24 11-20-50 Onamia MN
OXNER Harvey PVT 19/24 7-28-50 Bri—— AR
PALLESEN Robert G. PVT 63/24 10-30-50 Racine WI
PARKS Ralph L. CPL 19/24 3-15-51 Carlyle IL
PASTUZEK Walter PVT 21/24 12-17-50 Philadelphia PA
PEARSON Raymond E. 2/LT SERVICE/BTY/63/24 1-24-51 Crawfordville IN
PEETERS Marcel C. PVT 19/24 1-21-51 Allanson MI
PERRY Fletcher CPL 19/24 9-7-50 Hilton GA
PETERSON Donwin R. PFC C/19/24 8-5-51 Osakis MN
PHILLIPS Elda JR. PFC 34/24 10-30-50 Grandview TX
PIERCE Fredrick E. PFC 34/24 11-4-50 Edgerton WI
PITRE Charles D. JR. 34/24 11-30-50 Alexandria LA
PITTIS Gilbert L. PFC 19/24 10-31-50 SmithvilleFlats NY
PITTMAN Irvin W. CPL Hq Co 3rd Bn/34/24 11-7-50 Burlington NJ
PLOTNER Gerald R. PVT L/21/24 3-6-51 Prospect OH
POLKA Francis SGT C. 19/24 1-11-51 Melvindale MI
POSEY Harold T. PVT 21/24 11-8-50 Cleveland OH
POSIVAK Michael J. JR. CPL 21/24 1-1-51 Philadelphia PA
PRATT Glen L. PFC 34/24 11-4-50 Lowell WN
PROVOST Leonard E. PVT 21/24 2-14-51 Santa Clara NY
RABURN Cleon SGT L/21/24 12-26-50 Baconton GA
RABOYE Ronald PVT 21/24 1-1-51 Alexandra VA
RADANOVICH Harry T. PFC 21/24 11-20-50 Rockford IL
RAILLING Thomas CPL 63/24 1-14-51 NY NY

RAINEY William CPL 11-50 Milton WV
RANDALL Elgin CPL 21/24 5-7-51 Anniston AL
RARICK Ronald SGT 34/24 11-1-50 Hudson MI
REED Lee B. PFC 34/24 11-30-50 Organ Cave WV
REED Ray W. PVT 34/24 11-26-50 Detroit MI
RHOADS Edward PFC G/19/24 1-52 Tucson AZ
RICKENBACH Adam L. PFC 34/24 11-4-50 Reading PA
RIVERA Fernando JR. PVT 34/24 11-2-50 Hilo HI
ROBINSON George PVT 63/24 9-12-50 Pittsburg PA
ROCKWELL Clyde T. PFC 21/24 11-22-50 Butte MT
ROGERS Raymond JR. M/34/24 8-50 or 9-50
ROMO Angel P. PVT 1/21/24 11-4-50 Whittier CA
ROSE Albert E. PFC 21/24 12-15-50 West Frankfort IL
ROTH Bernard F. 2/LT 11/24 10-26-51 Dayton OH
ROY Floyd A. SGT 21/24 7-3-51 Cloquet MN
RUDDELL James C. Jr 1/LT HQS/1STBN/19/24 1-21-51 Ft Hamilton
RUSSELL Gordon C. SGT 63/24 12-30-50 Caniesville IL
RUSSELL John W. SFC 34/24 10-28-50 Lawton OK
SADDER William PFC 34/24 11-10-50 Altoona PA
SALMON Donald W. PVT 21/24 10-22-50 M——lersud NJ
SAMMS Jack C. PFC G/19/24 11-13-50 Ashland KY
SANDERS Gene A. PFC 34/24 11-1-50 Greenville CA
SCHMOLLINGER James E. PFC 21/24 11-2-50 Platte City MO
SCHOULTHIES George L. PVT 21/24 10-30-50 Calif., KY
SCHRECENGOST Paul M. PVT 26AAA 11-4-50 Mayport PA
SCHUMAN John H. CPL 3ENG/24 3-1-51 Ridgefield NJ
SCOTT Amos PFC 19/24 1-52 Rosehill VA
SCOTT Floyd E. PFC A/19/24 11-11-50
SCOTT Neal R. PVT 34/24 1-5-51 Hilisboro OH
SESLER Philip PFC 3ENG/24 11-17-50 Smock PA
SEXTON Talinage J. PFC 21/24 11-3-50 VA
SHACKELFORD Howard J. PFC 63/24 11-2-50 Oklahoma City OK
SHARP Raleigh T. CPL 63/24 12-5-50 Guthrie OK
SHORTER James W. PFC 63/24 10-31-50 Davis NC
SIEGMUND Earl V. CPL 21/24 11-3-50 N———— OH
SIMS Holly S. PVT 21/24 2-2-51 Witchita KN
SIRMAN Donald 1LT 8AF 7-7-51 Hartford CT
SKEENS Irvin J. PFC 34/24 3-20-51 Goldvein VA
SKERO Charles M. PFC B/34/24   6-22-51 Mt. Pleasant PA
SKINNER Kenneth L. PVT 34/24 1-9-51 Abingdon IL
SMITH Billy E. PVT I/21/24 11-4-50 AL
SMITH George R. PFC L/21/24 12-12-50 Whitehall MT
SMITH John J. SGT 34/24 1-11-51 Gastonia GA
SMITH Leonard CPL 7M BN 2-3-51 Tampa FL
SMITH William L. PFC 21/24 2-20-51 York PA
SMITHSON Donald CPL 21/24 11-22-50 Gaywood MD
SPARKS Donald D. JR. CPL 52/24 11-4-50 Hawthorne CA
SPECHT Wilfred G. CPL 21/24 12-4-50 Saginaw MI
SROGONCIK George J. PFC 21/24 1-8-51 Mt. Pleasant PA
STALLINGS Vernon D. PVT 21/24 11-1-50 Mooreston NC
STANSBURY William H. JR. PFC 34/24 11-2-50 Kansas City KN
STEELE Clyde D. CPL 24Rec/24 12-10-50 Charles City VA
STEPHENS Robert D. PFC 21/24 1-14-51 Clayton KN
STEWART Robert E. PFC L/21/24 12-26-50 Detroit MI

STOUT Johnnie O. PFC F/19/24 11-14-50 Old Hickory TN
STRAWSER Paul S. PFC 34/24 11-22-50 Ashley IN
SUMNER William G. CPL 21/24 12-12-50 Greer SC
SUMPTER Bill S. CPL C/19/24 11-7-50 Kanokatto MO
SUNSDAHL Roy L. PVT 19/24 12-4-50 Cambridge MN
SWANSON Richard P. PVT 34/24 2-12-51 Enfield MN
SWEET Richard L. CPL C/19/24 12-19-50 Huntsville TX
SWEITZER William C. PFC 34/24 11-11-50 Altona PA
SZCZEPANSKI Anthony A. PFC L/21/24 11-4-50 McKees Rocks PA
TATE Hershel L. SGT 34/24 1-12-51 Beersheba Springs TN
TAYLOR William PVT 34/24 11-22-50 Greencastle IN
TEIXEIRA James C. SFC 63/24 11-21-50 NJ or CA
THOMSON Keith ENS/US Navy 1-3-51 Macomb IL
THORNTON Cordus H. 1/LT 2nd Plat/L/34/24 11-1-50 Dallas TX
TIERNAN John PVT L/21/24 7-29-50 NY
TITUS Robert E. PFC 19/24 11-23-50 Fairfield IN
TODD Blanton SGT 21/24 2-3-51 Orlando FL
TOMASZEWSKI Waclaw A. 2/LT 34/24 1-2-51 MI
TORMAN George PVT 34/24 5-27-51 Arnbridge PA
TREXLER Rayfield A. PFC 34/24 11-2-50 Breinigville PA
TROSS Eugene E. PFC 21/24 12-23-50 St Louis MO
TYLER Charles R. PFC L/34/24 6-14-51 Reyno AR
UNDERHILL Vigil CPL 578FA/7 8-5-51 Tampa FL
VAN DEWERKER Patrick W. PFC 34/24 11-4-50 Bingham Canyon UT
VANN Harvey T. M/SGT 21/24 1-6-51 Franklin TX
VANNOSDALL Gilbert CPL 1st Marine Div 11-21-50 Bronx NY
VAN WINKLE Calvin A. PVT 21/24 2-16-51 Ft Calhoun NE
VARNER Edmund S. PVT 34/24 2-5-51 Summit NJ
VARNEY Basil JR. PFC 34/24 9-25-50 KY
VERCOLEN Albert L. SGT 34/24 7-20-50 Rochester NY
VIARS James E. PVT 21/24 11-27-50 Baymeadow VA
VINCENT Albert A. PFC 21/24 11-4-50 ——eerhey MO
VINCENT William E. PFC 21/24 12-20-50 St Louis MO
WAGONER James C. PFC 34/24 12-17-50 Kannopolis NC
WALTEN Thomas PFC 34/24 11-4-50 Bambridge NY
WARD Delmer R. PFC 1BN HQS/19/24 Greenvalle TN
WARREN Everett PFC HQ/19/24 10-28-50 Meiqs GA
WILLIAMSON Claud H. PVT L/21/24 11-12-50 Weissport PA
WILNER William H. PVT 21/24 6-1-51 CA
WILSON David H. PFC L/21/24 11-26-50 ——oha IA
WILSON Earl PVT 21/24 12-12-50 Cromwell KY
WINLING Earnest PVT 21/24 11-4-50
WINTER Gerald A. PFC A/19/24 11-3-50 Berwick PA
WISE Arthur F. PVT 3ENG/24 11-22-50 Pomeroy OH
WOODRING Raymond L. PFC 21/24 11-2-50 Sallinville MD
WRIGHT Chester A. PFC L/21/24 1-13-51 Battle Creek MI
YOST Edward F. PFC A/19/24 11-2-50 ——ville PA
YUMASZ Tony F. PFC 19/24 11-2-50 ——ville MI
ZAMORA Anselmo PFC 21/24 2-24-51 North Brownfield
ZUVER Robert L. PFC 21/24 12-10-50 Mena CA

Part 2-Civilians

BASTIN, Therese 11-30-50 Carmelite Nun from Belgium. Had TB. From Carmelite convent in Seoul. Formerly Irene Bastin. Born 1901. During WW II at age 13 she joined a resistance group, "La Dame Blanche". Arrested in 1918 by Germans and released for lack of evidence.

BULTEAU Joseph 1-6-51 French priest. Age 50 when captured. Member Paris Foreign Mission Society. Born 1901. Came to Korea in 1927 - got sick and had to return home. Was drafted into the French Army WW II and captured by the Germans and released because of illness. Returned to Korea after WW II.

BYRNES Patrick 11-25-50 American. Bishop and Apostolic Delegate to Korea. 67 years old when captured. Was with Maryknoll Missionary Society and came to Korea in 1922. In 1932 he went to Kyoto Japan. Was not interned by Japan during WWII and maintained his parish during the war. Returned to Korea in 1948 and was stationed in Seoul.

CADARS, Joseph 12-18-50 French. Member Paris Foreign Missionary Society. 70 years old when captured. Was a Lt in French Army during WW I and went to Indochina. Went to Siberia as chaplain for his unit. Born 1897. Became a college professor. Stationed at a monastery in Taejon South Korea.

CANAVAN Francis 12-6-50 Irish Colomban Priest. 35 at capture.

CLAIRE, Mary 11-6-50 Irish Anglican Nun stationed in Seoul. Was a school teacher before becoming a Nun. Came to Korea during WW I and had to leave during WW II to return when peace came. Was injured in a fall a few weeks before the death march.

DeVRIESE- Mechtilde 11-18-50 Belgian Nun. Carmelite Mother. Was Godelieve DeVriese before becoming a Nun. Born 1888. Went to Smyrna Turkey when she became a Nun about 1917. The Insurrection started and she barely escaped with her life.

EDOUARD, Beatrix 11-3-50 Shot on death march. French Nun age 76 at capture. Was assigned to the St. Paul of Chartres Sisters' Orphanage in Seoul. Before she became a Nun she was Anne Marie Edouard. Born 1875 and came to Korea in 1906. Brought no teeth into captivity and was starving to death.

ELTHINGHAM Walter 11-17-50 American from PA. Was with the ECA, Economic Cooperation Administration in Seoul. Was a mining engineer.

EVANS, William 12-12-50 American Mining Engineer. 50 years old at capture. Born and raised in Japan and interned by the Japanese in Korea during WW II. Stationed in Seoul. Wife Korean living in Tokyo. Son, William Jr. on ROSTER. He was 4 years old when father was taken by North Korean Army.

FUNDERAT 11-3-50 Shot on death march. White Russian age 69.

GOMBERT, Antoine 11-12-50 at 4pm. Brother to Julien. French and member of the Paris Foreign Mission Society. 76 at capture. Stationed in Seoul. Ordained in 1900 with brother and they left for Manchuria but the Boxer Rebellion broke out during the trip and they were diverted to Korea. Was Chaplain to the Carmelite Sisters in Seoul.

GOMBERT, Julien 11-13-50 28 hours after his brother, Antoine died. French. Same Society as brother above. Was 74 years old when captured. Was Chaplain to the convent and orphanage of the Sisters of St Paul of Chartes in Inchon.

HUNT, Charles 11-26-50 English Anglican Missionary stationed in Seoul. Came to Korea during WW II. Member of the Royal Geographic. Society of Asia. Was published and was President of the Korean branch at capture.

HALE, George Died Autumn 1950. American Engineer working for South Korean Government on a power plant on a barge in the Han river by Seoul that produced electricity for American agencies, in Seoul. Was married to a Korean and his brother in law turned him in to the Communists.

JOHNNY 11-3-50 Young Korean who may have worked at the dependent housing area in Seoul before the war. Shot on Death March.

KIJIKOFF Ilian 12-17-52 age 58. Russian Monqol Cossack. Was nicknamed Emily Post by the women because he lectured them on etiquette.

KISH, Ernst 6-29-51 Jewish Medical Doctor from Vienna, Austria. Was a Medical Doctor of note. Was an accomplished pianist. He was arrested by Hitler and went to both Dachau and Buchenwald. Lost everything during WW II including most of his relatives. With all his worldly goods in one suitcase he left for the Methodist Hospital in Shanghai, China where he stayed a few years. The Communists came and forced him to leave. He came to the United States and for a short while had a job at a hospital in New York. This poor man was denied permanent asylum in America and came to the Methodist Hospital at Kaesong in South Korea. He was there a few weeks when the Communist came for him.

LEONOFF 12-9-50 White Russian 70 years old when captured.

MATTI Alfred 11-30-50 Swiss. Manager of the Chosin Hotel in Seoul. 48 at capture. Was in Shanghai China when it fell to the Japanese before WW II. Because he was Swiss he was not arrested and ran the International Red Cross in Shanghai during the war. After the war he departed for home with his wife and two boys but the ship went down in heavy seas off from the Philippines. One son drowned. Matti, his wife, and son were in the sea for many hours before rescue.

SMIRNOFF 1-6-51 White Russian.

VILLEMONT Paul 11-11-50 French Priest with Paris Foreign Mission Society. 82 at capture. The oldest in our group. Born 1868 and came to Korea in 1892. Was stationed at St Pauls of Chartes Sisters' Orphanage in Seoul. Brought no teeth into captivity and starved to death.

Unresolved Names From Johnson's List

BURROUGHS SGT CA
LA——Y John PFC 21/24 11-14-50 Philadelphia PA
RIVRI——, Dick or Richard PFC 21/24 11-5-50
SCHWARTZ 34/24 11-50 Altona PA
THOMPSON 1950
KILBURN Gerald K/21/24 1-52 Charleston WV

CHAPTER TEN

HOMECOMING

Jack Chapman

My homecoming was great. After awhile, I had a hard time coping with all of my freedom. I started drinking, etc. I was in the hospital for a week, nerves.

Yes, my family was different around me, and looking back, I wish they had taken things a little slower and given me time to adjust. There was too much pressure on me to get back into things. Most of the people I knew, school mates, etc., were very nice and then there were those who didn't think that we had any business being in Korea.

Richard Rook

My homecoming wasn't all a happy occasion. Along with my wife and daughter, my sister, Lois, was at the dock to greet me when I disembarked from the ship. I didn't give it a second thought until she said, "Dick, there's something I have to tell you." She told me that my mother had died in March of 1952, and they didn't tell me for obvious reasons. Like most teenagers, I had done many things that I was sorry for and my stay in North Korea made me realize how badly I had mistreated my mother. I had made many promises to God that if I got out of the mess that I was in, I'd make it up to her. Now I would never get the chance to even say, "Mom, I'm sorry." I've told this story to my children and my children's children and I've never been able to tell it without crying. This time is no exception.

I lived in a small town, Ashton, located in northern Illinois, with a population of 950, and that's counting chickens and dogs. The American Legion and the V.F.W. paid all expenses to fly my wife and daughter out to San Francisco to meet me when I got off the troop carrier. I thought that was just great for small veteran posts in my small home town to do. Well, that wasn't all they did. We flew into Chicago and having been raised in Chicago, about 50 or 60 relatives were there at the airport to greet me. They had a huge banner that said, "WELCOME HOME DICK."

Not being around people like these for so long, it was difficult for me to cope. After several hours embarrassing myself by not being able to remember some people who I had known all my life, we finally got started on the 100 mile trip to the little town I lived in. When we were about 10 miles from town, at a popular crossroads, we were met by—I have no idea how many—cars, fire engines and police cars, which then escorted us the last 10 miles with sirens and lights blazing away. All of these vehicles had signs in their windows that said, "WELCOME HOME DICK".

We lived in a small apartment on the main street of town and when we finally got there I thought that we would be alone at last. No such luck. In front of our apartment were at least 2,000 people and everyone of them expected me to remember him or her. My wife came to my rescue when she realized I was in trouble. She would say, "Honey, (that's when I was still her honey) you remember Mrs. so-in-so, don't you?"

After about four hours, we finally made it up to our apartment. The next day the American Legion Post Commander came up to the apartment and told me that the Fall Festival was going to be held in our honor and that a collection had been taken up with the towns people and also the surrounding countryside, and that a check for $1,645.00 would be presented to me at the conclusion of the Festival. I know that $1,645.00 doesn't sound like much today, but it was a lot back then. I purchased a new Pontiac hard-top convertible, with everything on it, for $3,300.00. That's when a dollar would buy a dollar's worth of goods.

Getting back to my homecoming, there were "WELCOME HOME DICK" signs in every store window and every car in town. They even had them painted on the sidewalks and on the streets.

You don't mind fighting for people like that. It's hard to believe that the same people treated the veterans from the Vietnam War so badly. Those guys got a bum deal.

Harold Kaschko

When I returned from Korea, our son was nearly five years old, and I was a stranger to him. He wanted to spend his time with his mother or grandmother, and he didn't know how to act with a father.

Coming home was not the same as it had been at the end of World War II. However, my hometown of Dundee, Oregon, had a welcoming home celebration for me. They presented my wife and me with a silver tea service which we greatly appreciated, and it is still one of our treasured possessions.

About November, 1953, I was asked by the Chamber of Commerce in my hometown to attend a dinner meeting. After dinner, they asked me to tell about my experiences as a prisoner of the Communists. I was reluctant to say anything as I had signed a Certificate that I would not disclose military information to unauthorized persons in connection with "Personnel Escaped, Liberated, or Repatriated From a Hostile Force". [See Appendix for a copy of this certificate pertaining to Circular 131.] I did tell them that the treatment had not been good and that many died in the POW camps from lack of food and medicine. Because I said very little, the people looked at me and probably thought I was some sort of a dumb bird.

Over 40 years later, at our Korean ex-POW Reunion in San Antonio, Texas, in November, 1994, ten people from the Department of Defense came to talk with us. They gave us a copy of a letter from a Senior Attorney with the Department of Defense stating that Circular 131, Headquarters, U.S. Army Forces, was no longer in effect and could not even be located. [See Appendix for a copy of this letter.]

After returning from Korea I was assigned to Ft. Lewis, Washington, with the 209th FA Bn. and later in the 1950's to the 2nd Inf. Div. Arty. and the 4th Inf. Arty. My last assignment was Reserve Component duty in Montana. I retired from the Army in 1962 as a Lieutenant Colonel.

James H. Ransier

Don and I were in the 55th Army Hospital together. My feet healed to the point where I was discharged from the hospital prior to Don. When I left I had orders with me that stated, "I was to report to Camp Drake (near Tokyo) to await transportation home." From the time we were picked up by "L" Company of 32nd RCT, we had been told by just about every doctor we saw that we were headed home.

When I arrived at Camp Drake, I found about 200 men also waiting for transportation to the states. I was eventually ordered to report to the station master's office, where I was told that I was to report to the 55th Army Band, in Osaka, Japan, as a drummer for the band. I was speechless, but I did manage a "Thank you" and took off for the supply room. I was back in time and boarded the train. All the way to Osaka I tried to think of the name of the Sergeant who sat down to drink beer with me and must have ended up helping get this assignment. I was paying so little attention to him that I had no idea as to who he was. Even to this day, I often pray to God thanking him for sending that sergeant to me.

I only spent three or four weeks with the band. At one of the last rehearsals I had my first indication of the problems I would have for the rest of my life. After the rehearsal, we all headed back to our rooms. We were quartered in a tall office building in downtown Osaka. As we headed for the elevators I suddenly felt like I was going to cry. Not wanting to have anyone see me crying, I headed for the stairs and went up the stairs to the roof.

200

Once on the roof I had a good cry and wondered what brought it on. I went on sick call the next day to talk with the doctors about it.

A week later I again had orders to report to Camp Drake to await transportation home. This time I was only there three to five days and left for San Francisco on a troop ship built to carry about three thousand men and on this trip carried about two hundred and fifty. After arriving in San Francisco, I was given a plane ticket and flew to Fort Dix, New Jersey. There I was separated from the service and caught a plane home.

I arrived home in July of 1951. About two months later I began to have bad headaches. The Veterans Service Officer for my county called to welcome me home and suggested that I should go to the VA Hospital for a check up. If I didn't do it within 12 months of leaving the service, it would be very difficult to prove any problems I might have to be service connected.

In addition to my headaches, I guess I brought the war home with me. After seeing the doctors I was awarded a disability rating of 40%, 30% for gunshot wounds and 10% for battle fatigue (bad nerves). (By 1980 the name of this condition was changed to Post Traumatic Stress Disorder.)

It wasn't long before the nightmares started, and the crying spells began to come more often. I didn't realize it at the time, but it was determined that a good deal of my problems were due to my blaming myself for the three men and myself getting captured and for the deaths of Foreboard and McLaughlin. Also for the misery that Don Faudskar and myself went through as POWs.

I went to work at a music store as a bookkeeper in a town about ten miles from my home town. I worked there a little over a year and liked the work. In 1953 I received an offer to go to work at the bank in my home town. I figured that the banking business held more of a future for me, so I took the job.

Andrew (Chief) Aguirre

When I came home from WW II, the war had been over for a year and all of the home coming celebrations had ceased and the people were busy trying to get back to normal. Not many noticed my coming back other than my family, and even they were sort of apathetic. I did not waste much time and got out of the service and went back to pick up the pieces where I had left them, which was going back to work in the truck farms where they were raising vegetables.

When I came home from Korea, I had just gotten out of the Chinese POW camps that were located in the Manchurian/North Korean border at the Yalu River. I came home by boat and during the trip I was de-briefed and interrogated extensively to find out if I had been brainwashed and if I had become a Communist and how much. The government at the time had heard so much of Americans being brainwashed by the Chinese Communists that they were naive enough to believe some of the guys had actually turned Communist. Even the guys who stayed behind had other thoughts soon after they lived under that system a few years. They all requested to return and did return, except for one, who in obtaining Polish citizenship forfeited his American citizenship.

Even after we were released and were civilians, the interrogation did not stop. There were always some government agents investigating somebody and asking questions about so and so. After a few visits from these government agents, I got mad and refused to answer any questions until they could obtain paperwork which gave them the right legally to make me answer their questions. I guess they never really had a legal right to question me, as they never returned.

The topic which one might think was more important to the country's security was military information. They did interrogate us on military matters, but the time spent on this topic was minimal. Before coming home, and during the trip home, we were treated like we had the plague in that we could not intermingle with non-POWs aboard ship and had separate and secluded areas to move around in. I did not let this bother me and in a matter of weeks after coming home, I left the Marine Corps. I got married eleven days after coming home. Then I went to work at my old job, enrolled in night school under the mm Bill where I finished my high school and went to two years of college at a community college.

After WW II, I was treated like any returning mm in that, though I was not treated as royalty, I was genuinely welcomed back by my old friends and most of the neighborhood. The only ones who resented my return were the 4-F'ers. These were the ones who never went into the service and in my absence had taken over what few good jobs there were. They were moved in order to give me back my old job.

After Korea, I was treated a little like a dignitary by those very close to me and treated with kid gloves by those who did not know me, as they were not sure how to treat a person who had been a POW. They had read so much of the deprivation and suffering of POWs that they thought of us as being a little off the track with quick temper and easy to get riled. One could see the unsure and questionable expression on the face of new acquaintances when introduced. Then, after talking a few minutes, I could see the acquaintances relax and become friendlier and hospitable.

After WW II, there were many changes in the community, as many factories which had been built during the war were now in existence. Also the war had drawn many workers from around the nation to come work in the war factories. Many of these stayed and did not return to their native state. Many service men who had been stationed in the San Diego area liked the area so much they settled here. Where there had once been many lemon orchards and celery fields there were now many housing projects. There were now freeways where there had once been two lane roads. The border station was rebuilt from one incoming two lane station to about 15 lanes. The isolation of neighborhoods ended as was opened to the influx of many people.

After I came home from Korea, the first thing I noticed about the community was how flat it was. This was strange as we had previously lived where there were mountains in every direction one looked.

My family was not too noticeably different around me because my family was never too close. There was no such thing as hugging or kissing and compliments for achievements did not exist. It was like every member was too busy with himself to take notice of what the others were doing. Our poverty prevented us from celebrating holidays like Christmas as everybody celebrates, with gifts and large dinners and Christmas trees. Christmas day was no different than any other day. There was never any exchange of presents among the family. We would rise and have the regular breakfast of fried beans and tortillas and coffee. Holidays like Thanksgiving were even less noticed.

This is perhaps why there was no hugging or kissing when I arrived home at two in the morning. My dad was the only one that got up to converse with me, and even then the conversation was not too long. The rest of the family members stayed in bed, and I did not see them until the next morning. My mother treated me like I had not been away and very casually and indirectly asked me if I was going to give her any money. When I had been home I was one of the principal providers and during WW II I had sent an allotment home. After W.W. II, I was the one, together with my dad, instrumental in buying the first home the family ever owned.

When I returned after WW II, I did not see any of the allotment I had sent home, so when I went to Korea I decided that I would not come home broke, and instead of sending an allotment I saved it and had a small chunk upon my return. I did not interface with the family too much after getting back. I got married eleven days after coming home and with the back pay (close to $ 5,000) and my compensation for subsistence as a POW (approximately $2,500), I managed to buy a home, get furniture for it, get a car, and establish my own household. I started night school and went back to work, so I was too busy to interface with my family.

204

After WW II, I felt I returned as a mentally sound person. I was different because of the exposure to war. I had matured a lot and could not tolerate things done in a haphazard way. I carried a grudge for awhile against all those who had not gone to war, but that wore off. I was not one of those that dove under the table every time a car backfired. I was single and frequented lots of bars and got home drunker than a skunk. There were many bar room brawls in which I was a participant. I was very lucky that I never seriously hurt anyone or got myself hurt. I was more a young man letting off steam than a mentally disturbed person.

It was different after Korea. I was seven years older and had been through more than I had been in W.W.II. It was not a big battle that I came home to fight, but it was a battle trying to keep and maintain stability. I was always dreaming of being back in the prison camp. I would treat the most insignificant arguments with my wife as something big and blow it out of proportion. Thank God she had the tolerance to stand by me and overlook them.

I would wake up at night and go outside in the dark and start crying. I would cry mostly for the guys who had had died in the Korean War. And to this day I still feel depressed when certain states of things trigger the recollection of some incident from the past. Many a time out in the forest in winter, in the dark of the evening amidst the snow, I can hear the POWs crunching the snow and coughing and murmuring to each other as we once did while walking in the dark night, not knowing where we were going, nor where we had been, nor where we were. We were just lines and shadows moving in the darkness of the night.

Before WW II, I thought of myself as a teenager, a green horn who thought he knew it all like an adult. While actually, I still satisfied myself with teenage activities like going to the movies, playing games with the neighborhood kids, spending much time at the beach, spending lots of time playing the slot machines and really enjoying the amusement parks with all the rides, including the rollercoaster. I would love the carnivals and above all, the circus. I enjoyed all this in the company of my young friends. This was what I thought of myself before WW II. After WW II, I saw myself more mature, secured, and more selective of my friends. Girls replaced the companionship of young friends whenever possible.

After Korea, I thought of myself as an ordinary veteran who had come home and was now trying to make a living. This was what I thought I was and was trying to be, but in reality, I was a confused, bewildered, lost individual who moved more from instinct and habit.

Richard Makua

My homecoming was happy and confusing. I just wanted to do all the things you dreamed about while being a POW.

Things weren't too good for me then at home, especially when my mom and dad were on the verge of a divorce then. It took me awhile before I got myself together. I did see that progress had gone on in my community and in the world while I was gone.

People didn't treat me any differently. I was not congratulated for my efforts. Why should I be? There were others who were left behind.

Joseph Wilson

I was released on August 12, 1953. I was happy to be home. My brother who was in the Army was also home, here in California, where we have lived for many years. It was nice. I had left in 1945, at the age of 18, to be a merchant seaman for five years, to help rebuild Europe. Then I went on to be in the Army.

My wife, Rose, saw a change in me after being a POW. I am not married to her now. I am now married to my wife, Helen, and we live in Los Angeles.

Wayne A. (Johnnie) Johnson

I was repatriated at Freedom Village, Panmunjom, Korea, on August 28, 1953. I returned home to Lima, Ohio, and later moved to Phoenix, Arizona, where I have lived for the past 20 years.

CHAPTER ELEVEN

"GOOD AND HONORABLE MEN," LIFE AFTER THE WAR

Post Traumatic Stress Disorder, PTSD, is a product of all wars. It is very real. Its long ranging and multi-faceted effects on a human being are devastating. In writing this series of books I have seen how it can affect the lives of veterans, WW II through Desert Storm, and, even as a child, saw it in my own grandfather, a veteran of WW I. I have personally lived with the effects of PTSD since my husband came home to me from the war in Vietnam in 1970. But never had I seen it take such a toll as it has on these brave men who spent so many months in what can truly be called "Hell's Frozen Inferno."

In researching PTSD I found an article that I would like to offer here, in part:

"Costly Moment of Terror"
by Daniel Goleman

"A single instance of overwhelming terror can alter the chemistry of the brain, making people more sensitive to adrenaline surges even decades later, scientists are finding. This sensitivity to adrenaline surges is a major factor in post-traumatic stress disorder, in which people can experience normal events as repetitions of the original trauma....

For the brain changes to occur, scientists now say, people have to experience the stress as catastrophic, an overwhelming threat to life or safety and one over which they have no control....

'Victims of devastating trauma may never be the same biologically,' said Dr. Dennis Charney, a psychiatrist at Yale and director of clinical neuroscience at the National Center for Post-Traumatic Stress Disorder. 'The more intense the trauma, and the longer it lasts, the more likely it is to result in post-traumatic stress ... And although the symptoms can last 40 years or longer, they clear up in some people, either spontaneously or through therapy.'

208

Researchers say the findings [of new scientific research] may hold a promise of relief for those who suffer the symptoms of PTSD.

Jack Chapman

Our cause was simple and just, but our objectives in the Korean War were frequently confused in the public mind.

The Korean War had three aspects. There was the Civil War aspect—North Koreans fighting South Koreans for control of a divided country. There was the collective aspect—the first United Nations' attempt to stop a treaty breaking aggressor. And there was the Cold War aspect—the Western powers blocking the expansion of Communist imperialism.

The causes of the war, United Nations objectives and the need for American intervention were not clearly delineated in the public mind. This lack of understanding prevailed among citizens and American fighting men. The Communists attempted to exploit to the fullest this condition in both international propaganda and in dealing with our prisoners of war.

I personally feel that the President was doing the right thing at the time. We weren't prepared to fight the Communists, but we did manage to stop them from accomplishing their goal. I do believe that there were American POWs still left behind after the Korean War.

As to the question about whether I would I do it all again, my only reply is I would do it again, only to preserve the Americanism born and inbred in me. I consider myself a 100% patriotic American. My advice for anyone entering the military today would be to make the best of it. My personal opinion is that I feel that every young person should serve at least one year after completion of high school.

Besides the battles, the thing I remember the most about the war is all the great people I met in a number of prisoner of war camps. I still maintain contact with many of them. We have our reunion every year, and also keep in touch by mail, phone calls and as a member of the Board of Directors for the past 12-13 years and vice-president of our association, The Association of Ex-POWs from the Korean War Inc. We also exchange over 80 Christmas cards a year with my brothers of the Korean War.

As for my life being affected by my experiences in the war, I know that I never take anything for granted anymore. I like to be clean, have clean clothes, be warm, etc. I felt more guilt after I survived the horrors of being a POW and so many others died such terrible deaths. I have not participated in any counseling. Healthwise, I am rated with a 100% service connected disability, 40% paralysis of sciatic nerve, left, 40% paralysis of sciatic nerve, right, paralysis of all radicular nerve groups, 20%, P.T.S.D. 50%, and I have traumatic arthritis, skin disorder, lung disorder, and headaches.

My nightmares are no longer serious, although they were for a long time. Once in a while I still dream that I am in North Korean captivity. I am aware in those dreams that I have been there before, some of my friends and the guards are there with me. Occasionally I dream of being taken to the various places in North Korea where we once barely existed ...

Richard Rook

I feel that President Truman did the only thing he could have done at that time, because the war began with a surprise attack against a people who were unable to defend themselves. We accomplished, in my opinion, two things of real importance:

Number one, very simply, we stopped the Communists from accomplishing their goal of spreading communism throughout the world. Maybe we didn't stop the overall spread of communism but at least we stopped it in Korea where it was their first attempt to spread out.

Number two, and probably the more important, was that it woke us up for the second time in less than 10 years.

After WW II, we believed our own propaganda that there would be no more wars because we formed the UN, we cut our armed forces back to dangerous levels. There was no attempt to improve the weapons or equipment in general. All ammo was dated as far back as 1942. The "C" rations were packaged during WW II and almost everything was obsolete. I had to wait until my squad leader was hit before I got a chance to get a feather type sleeping bag. All they had when I got there was the "blanket" type, and it got down to 20 and 25 below zero every night. After Korea things changed considerably with the development of new and better weapons such as the M-16.

I believe the war was worth it because it was our first chance to let the Communists know that the West wasn't going to "lie down and roll over." However, I do feel that war is a terrible situation to be in, and I feel that every avenue should be exploited before we start shooting at one another.

I consider myself a patriotic American, and I do feel secure about my life now because I feel that we have built the strongest, most effective and the best equipped fighting force the world has ever seen. If I were asked to, I would fight again because I feel that this country is worth fighting for. I've been in several countries on the other side of both oceans, and I haven't seen anything to compare with what we have here. I had a college professor, Dr. Parker, who said something I have never forgotten. He had escaped Hitler's Germany in 1939 and moved to this country. He told us that he was not only anxious to pay income taxes in this country but was very proud to be able to pay them. This has always stuck with me; it's something I've repeated to my children over the years.

As far as how I feel about the North Koreans now, I don't like their form of government, and I don't think I could ever be converted. We weren't captives for more than two days before they started their "brainwashing" lectures. They tried to convince us that our government was evil and no good for the masses, and yet most of the North Koreans were starving to death. Once, while being marched through a village in the North, we passed in front of this mud hut. There on the ground in front of this hut were six or eight little carcasses, all skinned out and ready to cook. Do you know what they were??? They were RATS!!! And these stupid people are telling us that their way is better than ours.

Another non-selling point came about after we had undergone approximately two years into our stay with our captors. We were fed twice a day, and every day after our 4 o'clock meal, a little old blind woman, led by two small children, was allowed into our compound to gather up the slop that we threw away. Of course there wasn't much left from our meager rations, but it didn't take long before we, each of us, left a little something for her. We tried to give her food outright, but the Chinks wouldn't let us so we did it our way. These were just two of the incidents we witnessed, there were plenty more. Do I hold any animosity toward the people I fought? No, I don't dislike the people I fought, but I don't like their form of government.

I don't know how many POWs were kept against their will after Operation Big Switch, but I do know that 23 or 26 stayed behind of their own free will. I knew two of them personally. They have all returned to the United States, and as far as I know, none of them was punished, except for receiving dishonorable discharges.

I don't feel guilty about anything that happened on line except when I was captured, because I was alive, and so many others weren't. I felt more guilt after I survived the horrors of being a POW. So many men died such terrible deaths that to this day, I can't think about them without crying. In fact, I'm crying as I write this, so I'm going to get off this subject right now.

As to how my experiences have affected my actions today, I can tell you that I never take ANYTHING for granted anymore. It was the little things that were missed the most, matches, toilet tissue, soap, toothpaste, a toothbrush, and a razor are just a few of the things that every one of us take for granted.

My memory recalls one thing in particular. Before I was called back into the service, whenever I went to my sister's house in the winter time, I hated to sit on her toilet because right next to the toilet was a heat register, and when the furnace was on, it was, what I thought at the time, too hot. Well, you can guess what I thought of every time I had to bare my behind in 20 and 25 below zero weather.

My family knows what it's like to eat at the same table with a man who spent time as a POW. To this day I can't stand to see people waste food. My own children weren't so bad because they grew up in a different period and expected me to come down on them for not cleaning up their plate. My grandchildren are a different story. They shouldn't be because their parents, at least one of them, should know how fortunate they are to just have food. My wife usually feeds the grandchildren first so they're away from the table before I get there. This move maintains the peace.

I have several medical problems which are typical for most returning POWs. I'm going to give you, verbatim, my personal problems right off of a report from the Board Of Veterans Appeals in Washington, DC:

"The veteran's service-connected disabilities include post-traumatic stress disorder, rated as 30 percent disabling; the residuals of frostbite of the feet with peripheral neuropathy and episodic neuritis, rated as 30 percent disabling; the residuals of an injury to the lower back with degenerative changes, rated as 20 percent disabling; the residuals of dysentery with irritable bowel syndrome, rated 10 percent disabling; the residuals of malnutrition, avitaminosis with ascariasis, beriberi, dermatophytosis, and onychomycosis, rated as 10 percent disabling; pulmonary fibrosis, noncompensably rated; the residuals of a gunshot wound to the face and right leg, noncompensably rated; the residuals of malaria, noncompensably rated."

We ex-POWs of the Korean War meet once a year in various cities around the country. Friendships formed under the conditions that POWs endured together are forever. At our reunions we have a ball and very seldom are any "war" stories told. All of the funny things that happened in the various camps are the only things that are discussed. This year our reunion is in Sacramento, and I can't wait to see my friends.

Henry Wadsworth Longfellow said it best, "Ah, how good it feels—to touch the hand of a good friend."

I came out of Korea with dozens of life-long friends, but two stand out from the others. Their names are Joe Nickols and Lew Villa. Joe was my sleeping partner. I know that doesn't sound exactly right, but I don't know how else to say it. I had better start explaining what the situation was. We didn't have any heat in the mud huts we lived in and to keep warm at night we had to "cuddle" with someone; well, Joe was my cuddle partner. Lew was the company clown. There's one in every outfit. If it hadn't been for Lew and his antics, I'm sure that fewer guys would have come home.

Joe Nickols and I were in the same squad together and to this day are very close friends. I mentioned earlier that on cold winter nights he was my "cuddle buddy." He was also my "mother hen." Every time the Chinks took me to headquarters, he would start praying for my safe return. We both said a Rosary every night in bed—he still says his every night after all these years. Our first meeting after 30 years was in the St. Louis airport in 1987. Without a word spoken, we just stood there and hugged for at least a full minute. My wife said that people passing by were really staring at us. It was in St. Louis, the same year, that I first saw Lew Villa, after 34 years.

I remember that the night before I was captured, after being surrounded for three days, we were told by Battalion to break out and head south to Hill 894. They were sending in a Ranger company to bring us out. This was good news to our ears because we were getting worried about our well-being, and we were also getting mighty hungry. After suffering several casualties, we got off the hill and headed south to Hill 894 and freedom. To make a long story short, the Ranger company never showed, and we were taken the next morning.

214

It wasn't until several months later and after we were established in North Korea that I found out why that Ranger company
never showed up. They ran into the same problem that we did,
thousands of Chinese soldiers with real guns. Two members of
that Ranger company became very good friends of mine—Rip
Ratigan and Lew Villa. He's the same Lew Villa who I mentioned
earlier as being the company clown. After I found out that he
was the one that was supposed to save me and didn't, I couldn't
resist giving him the needle. One of the few things the Chinese
didn't take away from me when I was captured was a picture of
my wife, Jo and my daughter, Jerie. Whenever I would give Lew
a hard time about not coming in and rescuing us, he would say,
"To make it up to you, Rooker, I'm going to get the kid something." Every time he would say that, I would say, "If you don't,
Lew, I'm going to kill ya." All the time we were together, there
weren't too many times that we'd meet that these words weren't
exchanged. It just became the thing to say. (Strange huh?)

After we were home a few months, a package, addressed to
Jerie, arrived in the mail. It was a beautiful hand-made dress that
fit her perfectly. We had her picture taken in it and sent it to
him. Because he kept his word, I didn't have to kill him.

There is one other person who must be mentioned in these
writings. Most people, when they first find out that I was a POW,
say something like, "It must have been so hard on you, how did
you do it?" Certainly, it wasn't a picnic for me, but at least I
knew that I was alive. My family on the other hand had no idea
of my well-being. I can't imagine what it must have been like
when my wife received that MIA telegram. It must have been
devastating for her. In the telegram they don't use the milder
term "MIA" but rather the much harsher, "Missing In Action."
We have never discussed this, but I'm sure she imagined the
worse. Is he dead, is he wounded and alone somewhere, is he
lost and frightened or is he a POW? I'm sure all of these
thoughts went through her mind. How terrible that must have
been for her. Even after she found out that I was alive, it didn't
get any easier for her. On the other hand, I knew that she was
alive, I knew that she wasn't being mistreated, and I knew that

215

she and my daughter would want for nothing because I knew that the people in my small hometown of Ashton, Illinois, would not permit it. She knew nothing about what I may or may not have been going through.

If any of you have chosen to enter the military, you are about to embark on a very interesting journey. Of course this is my own personal opinion, based on my own personal experience, but I feel every young person, whether male or female, should enlist after completion of high school. In most cases you will come out a lot better person than you were when you went in. The most important thing I can tell you is to be prepared to learn how to take orders. If you can't take orders, then I suggest you take up something else. The discipline in the service will make a real person out of you.

Harold Kaschko

Today I can say, YES, I certainly consider myself a patriotic American. I am old, but I would fight again for our great country, the United States of America. I have visited 68 different countries, and I would not want to change my citizenship to any. Our nation has some problems, it is not perfect, but it is the best I have seen. I believe that the war in Korea was worth it, because it helped to cause the downfall of communism. I learned a great deal about communism as we Korean POWs were forced to attend indoctrination classes about Communism.

After I retired from the military, I worked at Boeing for nearly 22 years and then retired in 1984. I have been married 44 years to a wonderful wife, Marie, and we have two sons, an archaeologist and a medical doctor. We have three grandchildren. I was able to revisit South Korea three times, in 1975, 1983, and 1986.

As far as my health and how my experiences in Korea directly affect my actions today, I was very fortunate that I was never wounded in combat during either World War II or Korea, however, I suffer from Peripheral Neuropathy in both legs and the VA has rated me at 40% disabled because of it. I had beriberi

216

as a POW which was caused by malnutrition and the lack of vitamins. I also am affected by Post Traumatic Stress Disorder or PTSD.

I'd like to quote here some facts about PTSD from a brochure from the Post Traumatic Stress Disorder Outreach & Counseling Program of the Washington State Department of Veterans Affairs:

"PTSD can happen to anyone. It is often described as a 'normal reaction to an abnormal situation.'

"Traumatic events—war, combat, natural disasters and other life threatening experiences—have always been a part of human existence. However, the impact of these events on the survivors was not well understood until recently. Counseling efforts with returning Vietnam-era veterans and their families highlighted the special influence that such out-of-the-ordinary events have upon survivors.

"Vietnam-era veterans have been especially prone to PTSD because the healing properties associated with homecoming were largely denied returning veterans. Many Vietnam veterans tried to forget where they had been and avoided the important work of talking out their experiences. All warfare is filled with many experiences that are horrible and require extraordinary behavior to survive. The attitudes at home either support and justify the suffering and sacrifice, or they act to give another message. They can lead to social withdrawal, suppressed feelings, and anger. This happened to a large percentage of Vietnam veterans."

And, of course, that would apply equally as well for Korean veterans. I have listed the following as my own personal symptoms of PTSD:
1. Guilt feelings for losing (plus or minus) 100 men in my battery at the Kunu-ri roadblock on 30 November 1950. I did the best I knew how; by hindsight, it could have been better.

2. Guilt feelings for being captured. Anger for signing peace appeals in order to stay alive.

3. Anger because many men died needlessly on the 8th U.S. Army race to the Yalu River because higher HQ's drastically under estimated the strength of Chinese forces in North Korea.

4. Anger because of a lack of command decisions from HQ's 2nd Infantry Division and HQ's 2nd Division Artillery for actions to be taken by artillery battalions during the road-block.
   Rear guard, 23rd Infantry Regiment, withdrew and deployed via Sinanju Road about 3:00 p.m., 30 November. About 10:30 p.m., 30 Nov., after battalion C.O. was critically wounded, executive officer ordered all artillery pieces to be destroyed and trucks to be set on fire, then fight out on foot. Kaschko was to lead the column.

5. Korean POWs were not treated very well upon return to USA. The official government policy was that the POWs didn't do very well in the Korean War. Many interrogations, court martials, boards, etc. continued on for four years.
   In 1990, I found out that General Eisenhower was responsible for the deaths of some 750,000 German POWs who were held in U.S. Army POW camps during World War II.

6. Some flashbacks (dreams, and nightmares.)
   World War II - all death related.
   Korea - death related to both U.S. and enemy deaths.

7. Can't stand loud noises, such as firecrackers.

8. Nervous, quick tempered.

I have attended counseling at the Seattle VA Medical Center from November 1989 to the present date of May 1995.

I retired from the U.S. Army as a Lieutenant Colonel on 1 August 1962, and as a retired officer and veteran of both World

War II and Korea, I would offer these suggestions to anyone entering the military today:

Keep your eyes open, listen with your ears and keep your mouth shut (unless you are an authority and know something about what you are talking about.) Try to improve yourself and excel in everything that you do.

Edward Sheffield

Since returning home and since discharge from service, I have continued to serve my community and our people in various ways. I was a member of three civic clubs, one for 17 years and a charter member of another of which I am now on inactive status. I went through the officer ranks to Lt. Governor of a district. I served ten years as a volunteer fireman and a volunteer deputy sheriff.

I am now retired with my wife of 42 years, Jamie. Since my military days I've worked as office manager of a local dairy for 5 years, worked in a local bank 5 years and climbed the ladder to Vice President of the largest financial institution in North Florida and retired with 15 years of service. I am now on total disability as the horrible experiences of the Korean War and imprisonment has left its toll.

One thing I would like to add here is a letter I wrote to talk show host, Geraldo Rivera, after viewing one of his shows on television:

02/22/90

Geraldo
P.O. Box 684
NY, NY 10108

Dear Geraldo:

I was watching your show on Feb. 5 when you were focusing on death row in Alabama and was inspired to write this letter.

First; I want to say that I agree with you that America needs to see more of this type showing, which could perhaps be a deterrent for crime. On your show there were varying opinions about the death penalty being a deterrent for crime. I'm not offering my opinion in that regard. However, I do feel that a very effective deterrent would be to somehow instill in people and especially the younger men, women, and students the glory of giving in some worthy way instead of taking.

I am a former prisoner of war who spent 37 1/2 months on death row in Korea, along with many others. It was not for taking, but for giving for our country and our people. I am one of few who survived but we also died a little every day and our guards or executioners were not all compassionate. In fact, they delighted in torturing us. There were hardly a day went by without a rifle being pointed at my head and expecting to feel the bullet any second, many did.

I noticed the nice looking plate of food being passed through the little window. We didn't have that, or good water, or a warm room, or even a bed. No doctors, no medicine, or a funeral for those who died or were executed. Well, so much for that.

We must all realize that unless we give back more than we take, our future will continue to be uncertain. I am near 60 years old and proud to still be giving. I'm a member of two civic clubs, a volunteer fireman, and a volunteer deputy sheriff. We can find the time when we want to, to pay something back for so much received.

Respectfully,

Ed Sheffield

James H. Ransier

When the war was over for me, yes, I did come home to fight another war. It was a war within myself. When I returned from Korea in 1951, I was awarded a monthly compensation based on a disability of 40%. The disability was based on gunshot wounds of the feet and on a nervous condition. The nervous condition shows itself as depression with a frequent tendency to cry and have bad dreams.

As a younger man I was better able to hide and cover up these problems but over the years it has become very difficult

220

to do so. The bad dreams the past few years have been few and far between, but have been replaced by many sleepless nights during which I cry quietly and lie awake thinking of Korea.

After the war, I worked in banking, and I enjoyed banking very much, but signs of depression were beginning to show at times and the urge to cry continued to surface now and then. I became manager of the loan department near the end of 1955. In 1966, I was promoted to a branch manager and with my wife and two children moved to a suburb of Buffalo where the branch was located. It was about this time that I began to realize my memory was not as good as it used to be. It was not yet a real problem, but I was a little bit concerned.

In 1968 I was at my desk, when I suddenly had a very weird feeling come over me. I had the feeling I could no longer stay at this job or at the bank. I got up, told my secretary I was going out to make some customer calls and did not know when I would be back. I walked to my car and sat there feeling that I had to get away from everything.

I drove around probably thirty minutes more until I thought of the VA Hospital in Buffalo. I went there and said I needed to see a psychiatrist. The end result was, I did see a doctor and I stayed a week in the mental health ward realizing it was the best thing I could have done.

As a result of my stay, I began to see the psychiatrist on a regular basis until 1970 when we moved to Florida where I took a job with a much smaller bank, feeling that this was just what I needed. For a time it did help very much. But the symptoms of what would later be referred to as P.T.S.D. (Post Traumatic Stress Disorder) were to continue to increase. I still had the bad headaches that started in 1951, anxiety and depression were increasing. By 1980, I could take no more of banking. I had enjoyed the business, the people I had worked with, and the customers. But my own condition was beginning to interfere with the quality of my work and I wanted to leave before others would notice.

My wife and I purchased a liquor store in Greenville, South Carolina. After moving to Greenville in January 1981, I started seeing doctors at the VA Clinic in Greenville and the VA Hospital in Columbia. The end result to date has been an increase in my disability to 60% due to the worsening of my nervous condition. The diagnosis was of severe headaches and depression, caused by an inability to forget and put to rest the Korean experience because I blamed myself for the events that took place. During one of my last visits with the doctor in Greenville, he said that I should not hesitate to tell and retell my experience as a means of removing the pressure and the burden of guilt that I have kept within myself for so long.

By 1982 I could no longer take the daily routine at the store and decided to try and find other work. I tried a number of jobs after that.

From 1982 until 1987, I received treatment from the VA Clinic and a private doctor. In 1987, this doctor suggested that I go to the VA Mental Health Hospital in Augusta, Georgia. The doctors there recommended me for a permanent disability rating of 100%. As a result of this disability rating, I quit my job at the Post Office and have not been employed since. This was a real blessing for me. To those good folks who have asked me how I like retirement, I have told them, "It hasn't solved my problems, but it sure beats working."

The blame for all that happened the morning we were captured, I have for some reason placed upon myself. It has affected my life in many ways. It has drained me of much physical and mental energy and has prevented my enjoying life to the fullest.

I hope I will someday rid myself of all this guilt. I am trying but I know I must try harder. At any rate I'll do my best.

As for my health problems, I would not hesitate to place headaches at the top of the list. They are with me most of the time, night and day, since they started in 1951. Taking medication for them day and/or night is the only way to make them go away for awhile, but that doesn't always help.

Number two on the list would be depression. I've been taking medication for it since 1981.

Number three is guilt. I told a therapist at one session that my own logic convinces me that it was not my fault that the four of us were captured, lined up and then shot with an automatic weapon. Then one man was shot through the head because he could not stand when we were ordered to. A second man was shot through the head because he couldn't keep up as we started our march to North Korea. But something inside keeps telling me all the time, "But you should have done something." She said it was my subconscious mind, and it was not yet convinced. We then went through several sessions of hypnosis. But as luck would have it she took a job at a hospital and was no longer available.

The fourth problem, crying, is very difficult to deal with particularly when I'm not alone. Sometimes I cry for no apparent reason. Other times it's because I'm reminded of Korea. But the one that was the most difficult for me to understand is the feeling to cry when people are nice to or want to go out of their way to help me. This the doctors tell me is due to the low opinion I have of myself, and I am not deserving of kindness being shown to me. All this because I blame myself for us being captured and shot.

Occasionally, now, in a parking lot a person will notice the POW plate on my car and ask me if I was in the service and a POW. I will answer, "Yes." The person may then put his hand out to shake my hand and say something like, "I want to thank you for fighting to keep our country free." I feel very proud to have served my country, but to have them walk over to thank me, leaves me with tears in my eyes and hardly able to thank them and to tell them how much I appreciate their telling me. As they leave, I hope they understand the situation.

There are two things I learned by going to the VA Hospital in Augusta as many times as I have. The first, there is no cure for PTSD. The best they can do is teach you how to cope with it. The second, is the older you get the more difficult it is to cope with. For me, since 1951, it has indeed been a lifetime problem affecting just about everything I've done and decisions I've made. I complain about my headaches now and then but overall God has been very good to me. He brought me safely out of Korea, let me spend twenty-eight years in the banking business which I enjoyed very much and has blessed me with a wonderful wife who I dearly love and who loves me enough to put up with all my problems, and He has given us two children we love very much. Who could want or ask for anything more?

There is one more story I'd like to add here. After arriving home in July 1951, I could not help but wonder how Don Faudskar was doing. So I wrote a letter to his home address he had given me while in the hospital in Japan. The letter was returned and stamped, "Not known at this address, no forwarding address."

For the next 33 years, I felt even worse about myself because I was convinced that Don would not have any of the problems I was having. He wouldn't let the war effect his life like I had.

Sometime in the summer of 1984, in my effort to find Don, I called several departments of the government in Washington. I had no luck with any of them except when it was suggested that I place an ad in the VFW magazine. I felt it was a good suggestion and although I was a member of the American Legion, I placed the ad in the VFW magazine without even thinking of placing it in my own Legion magazine.

In the meantime, and, of course unknown to me, Don was living in Hoquiam, Washington. A friend of his had been trying for years to get Don to join the VFW Post in Hoquiam. Don would always say, "No, I just don't want to join or get involved in any military-type organization." Finally, his friend decided to solve the problem by going to the VFW Post and enrolling Don in the VFW. He paid Don's dues and then took the membership card to Don's house and handed him the card and said, "Now you are a member of the VFW."

Don accepted the card but was not very happy about it. His view of the situation changed considerably when on August 10,

1984, the first issue of the VFW magazine was delivered to his house. He sat down right away and began to thumb through it and stopped at a page full of personal ads. He then did something he had never done before. He read each ad and did not stop reading until he came to the ad I had placed. He tried to call me, but got no answer. He then sat down and wrote to me. Upon receipt of his letter, I called him, and we had a long talk. I was very sorry to hear he also was having problems, but it made me feel somewhat normal. We both felt that if we could have lived within walking distance or a reasonable drive of each other, we could have talked often and probably both been better off.

We also determined that both his records and mine were destroyed in a warehouse fire in St. Louis, Missouri. When I first found out from the VA that they could not verify my claim of having been in Korea and was a former POW, I brought in all my documentation to prove it. They accepted it, and I have had no problem since. But Don did not have anything to prove he had also been in Korea and a POW, so I sent him copies of all I had in 1984, and he was finally able to apply for and receive a service connected disability rating.

Carolyn and I have been out to visit Don and his family twice since we made contact. We still wish we were living closer, but at least we can talk on the phone and write back and forth. I believe it has helped us both now that we can keep in touch.

What I have written in this book I hereby dedicate to my loyal and loving wife, Carolyn, and to my good friend and POW buddy, Don Faudskar, and his loyal and loving wife, Robbie. Our wives have stood by us through good days and bad. I realize it has often been difficult.

I feel that any woman who can stand by a husband with PTSD must truly be an angel who will find herself most welcome when it comes her time to enter heaven.

Andrew (Chief) Aguirre

There are many who would say that the Korean War, sometimes called the Forgotten War, was not worth it—depending on what your role was during the war. I think Korea was worth it because it was the first time the United States faced the Communist threat head on and stopped them from overtaking South Korea. It also helped for the first time to unify the United Nations to a common cause. Korea and the death of Stalin were the beginning of the end for the cold war and the U.S.S.R.. Viet Nam was to be the last war supported by the U.S.S.R.. Shortly after that, the U.S.S.R. started to fall apart, and the end of communism began and the cold war came to an end.

There was a four star general in charge of the United Nations command in Korea who, after blundering the war and underestimating the Chinese and nearly loosing all of the Tenth Corps on the east side of Korea, thought that we should use nuclear weapons. Just as he underestimated the Chinese, he was underestimating the Russians and their nuclear capability. He was a frustrated individual who had once been hailed as a military genius for the Inchon Landing and was blinded to reality by so much praise that had been bestowed upon him. After the Chinese came into the war and practically annihilated all the UN troops, he became disorientated and blamed everybody but himself for the fiasco and debacle which befell the UN troops. He tried to regain his broken stature and military bearing by wanting to use Chinese Nationalist troops in Koreas in addition to bombing the Chinese mainland and to lay a wall of radiation across the Korean Peninsula. The use of nuclear weapons, to me, was not acceptable as it would have escalated the war into a nuclear holocaust.

It is possible the war could have been avoided by including Korea within the perimeter of defense established by the Department of Defense in the years prior to the Korean War. Korea was excluded, and this was perceived by the Communist block, especially North Korea, as a message that the United States would

226

not go to war over South Korea. This is clearly written in many history books of the Korean War.

The aspect of the American effort I am most proud of was the effort made by the President, Dwight David Eisenhower, then recently elected President in 1952. In 1953, he took a stand putting all the previous roadblocks to peace aside and told the Chinese Communists that unless peace came to Korea he was going to unleash new weapons that were of the atomic kind and that all the stalling had come to an end, and there were would be no more haggling and stalling. The Chinese wasted no time in dropping a lot of their longtime demands and quickly reached an accord with the United Nations.

One lesson we should learn is that we should not go to war again unless the country as a whole including the American People and Congress is in full agreement and behind it. As an example of this, look at the Gulf War. It did not last long because every American supported it, and the mighty power of the United States and its allies was unleashed against Iraq. On the contrary, in Viet Nam and Korea the wars were not all-out wars, they were limited wars which restricted the military and committed them to an unwinnable war which prevented total victory.

When the U.S.S.R. crumbled and Yeltsin took power, he helped form a Russian/American unit to look into the possibility that many American Prisoners of war in Korea had been shipped into Russian soil for exploitation of technology and equipment. These were mostly F86 Sabre Jet Pilots and Sabre Jets themselves. During this period of time, the Sabre Jet was the most advanced American Jet fighter and had many features which were superior to the Russian MIG. During the Korean War, the Russians created agencies just for this purpose—to obtain F86 pilots and if possible Sabre Jets themselves. All Korean and Chinese were under orders to pass on to the Russian agencies any F86 pilot they captured. The Russians would determine if the pilot was worth taking into Russia. The Joint American/Russian unit never recovered any pilots but interrogated many Russians who were involved in transporting American pilots into Russia for the information they possessed. The joint Unit also ran across many people who reported many live sightings. Yes, I believe many POWs stayed behind involuntarily.

I cannot say that I hate the war and that wars must be automatically hated by everybody. There are a lot of people who think wars help cull the nation's undesirable youth. By undesirable they mean those long-haired drug addicts who never seem to bathe and are parasites on society always sticking their hands out for something to be given. These individuals are a burden on society as they swell the Welfare offices, any state or federal health program, offices, and contribute nothing back in the form of taxes. They become a stigma in any neighborhood, and people do not trust nor want them around because where one comes, more will follow. I have learned long time ago to not dwell too much on the past and accept those things that happened in the past as part of one's life. Since one cannot change the past, then we have no choice but to live with it. I can not say I hate the war because it was the war that indirectly or directly made me what I am today, and I think I am well off financially with lots of friends and a wonderful family.

On the positive side, many of the experiences I had as a POW do affect my actions today. Today when I feel bad for whatever reason or I tend to fall in moods of depression for whatever the reason or think that I have a big problem, I think back to the problems we had at the prison camp. Problems with food, clothing, medical attention, disease, diarrhea, body lice infestation, intestinal worm infestation and all those hardships associated with extreme cold temperatures such as frost bite, and I come to the conclusion that I do not have any problems at all, and my imaginative problems are minimized to a very tolerable level. On the negative side, I have been accused of being too blunt and straight forwarded and crude and not very diplomatic in my association with certain people. I think it is because I value and prize my friendship with POWs due to the similarities we endured and went through in the past, that for me these are my true friends, and I will even go as far as calling them brothers. The elation and happiness I feel when I talk with them, especially those from the Korean war, is true and genuine while when I interface and talk with non-military related persons, it is sort of put on and one that is done more for necessity than enjoyment.

I have kept in touch with many of my old buddies. Some of them were in the South Pacific and Okinawa in WW II, some were in my tank battalion in Korea, one was in Tienstin, China. The ones I keep in touch more are the buddies who were in the prisoner of war camp with me. Even though I was in the Marine Corps, most of these buddies were in the Army, and we meet every year some place in the country for a four day reunion. In between the reunions we call each other, send letters or keep in contact with the Internet on America Online. The non POW buddies that I keep in contact most are the people from California. All these buddies are the only really good friends I have, and I try to preserve and maintain the friendship so that I will always have company and many good friends to share my present life with. Some of these buddies that I have close contact with were people I met in the Marine Corps 50 years ago. Most of them I met in Korea 44 years ago. I am 70 years old and most of them are in that age bracket, and we will keep in contact until we die. This is the type of camaraderie and friendship that war can produce.

My outlook after being in the war is that of a man who has experienced the many facets of war, negative and positive. I experienced the excitement, adventure and yes, even the thrill of combat. The years and age have changed this 70 year old man and diminished the drive of an active 'do-er' to a retired onlooker and a side line spectator. Without knowing it I have slowly succumbed and given in to the position of an elderly grandfather with grandchildren, a son and a daughter of whom I am ever so proud and, above all, a wife that has stood the test of time and our marriage. All in all, I am surrounded by family members that I am most proud of, and I wish every person in my position had. I look forward to the future with expectations of many happy and contented years.

I have health problems that developed due to the war and seem to accentuate with age. To name a few, I have severe frost bite and a micro valve in the heart that does not function well. I have Pernicious Anemia, facial spasms on the right side, knees that have deteriorated to the inducement of crippling and legs and feet that will swell up after some stress due to walking. I had peptic ulcers, and I had night blindness at one time. I had beriberi of the lower extremities and goiter inflammation under the mouth. I developed boils in camp and much dry skin. These are just a few that I remember and currently have. There were many more which time has erased from my mind.

I do not feel guilty about any of my war experience as it was not my choosing to participate in the wars. I was just an instrument that was called upon to participate by people in government and by the President of the United States. I was urged and encouraged to fight and annihilate the enemy by the Marine Corps, while still an immature person, under the threat of repercussions should I refuse. The guilt is not mine, and if blame for conduct in the war is to be pointed out, then let it be pointed to the system, government policies, and attitude of the people at the time that selected all those immature, young, teen age boys to do the dirty work of war.

I started to attend counseling in California after I retired and had lots of time on my hands. I went mostly to be with those who had undergone POW experience and the camaraderie that existed among the counseling group. Most of the time the sessions were controlled by the same individuals, who without knowing it, always kept repeating the same thing, while those who never said anything kept saying nothing. In one group the therapist was a woman who knew nothing about war and, without knowing it, used pity to console the attendees. Pity is the worse thing to bestow on anybody, in war time or any other time. This will make the recipient weak and susceptible to self pity. Pity, and especially self pity, can destroy a man's character and ability to withstand and endure strenuous stresses which he is called upon to endure. In the prison camp if you felt sorry for anybody, you never let him know it. You kept it to yourself because the moment that person knew you felt sorry for him he would stop the struggle to survive and indulge in self pity with much crying, which prevented him from taking care of himself and would depend on others to take care of him. When help was offered, it was offered conditionally. Like, look, I am going to help you this time but you better get off your ass and do it yourself the next time as I have enough on my hands taking care of myself, just as the rest of the guys here have enough taking care of themselves.' Some times the cynic in me thought these persons in the sessions exaggerated their emotions to justify and help them win their compensation claims. I could never let myself open up when called upon to relate some traumatic experience of the past.

There is one thing I wish I could have done differently, not during the war but after the war ended and I came home and that was that I wish I would have attended and gone to school under the G.I. Bill instead of wasting all that time in bars and gallivanting around. If I would have attended college and used the G.I. Bill in WW II and then later on in Korea, I would have been able to get a masters degree and would have been in a position to get a better position in the employment department. The schooling I did get after Korea under the GI Bill opened many doors for me and helped me get positions that would have never been gotten if I had not gone to school.

I do feel secure about my life now. I think I am one of the luckiest persons in the world because currently I am enjoying freedom from want in areas of money, friends, home, automobiles and family. Through years of working and decisions of my own making, I have achieved security and accumulated those necessities required to live the rest of my life in a very comfortable position. I feel secure that in an extreme need, I would find some way to achieve it.

I feel very patriotic and proud to have served my country, especially during celebrations like the Fourth of July, Veteran's Day, and Memorial Day when in the company of my fellow veterans we participate in parades and carry the colors. I feel even prouder when spectators cheer and applaud us as we march by.

At my age (70) I do not think anybody is going to ask me to fight again and even if they did, I do not think I could physically be able to, even if I wanted to. But I am sure that just as they asked me to fight again in Korea after fighting in WW II, and should the nation call me and I was physically fit, I would not hesitate to go again.

It is very gratifying to have Korean children and grown ups come up to us, shake my hand and thank me for saving their country when they find out I am a Korean War veteran. Yes, I would have to say that it was worth it.

My advice to anyone going into the military is to keep your ears and eyes opened and your mouth shut. You will develop pride in what you are doing and slowly start to accept the facets of training as a personal challenge. You will start to enjoy the competition as you compete against time and your buddies. You will start taking pride in the many things you do such as marching in the parade field, your excellent performance with the weapons at the firing range and your accomplishments in physical and scholastic areas.

In Korea, I kept going because it was expected of me. I had an obligation to myself as a Marine and to the Marine Corps and to all those wonderful guys I was with at the time. I could not just think of myself in this war because I was not by myself. I was part of a fighting unit that had a reputation to maintain. I do not think too many American fighting men think of themselves as being independent of the branch of service they are in or their units. They think of themselves as part of a team, and the team spirit is always there to maintain team adhesion and cohesion. To quit and not keep going is to let the team down, and if everybody in the team felt the same way, then there would be no team. There are certain standards which a fighting man must maintain and to quit and not to keep going is not one of them.

Looking back, the best thing I remember about the war was the many wonderful guys I met and interfaced with and the wonderful experiences which helped mold me into a man from a teenager. If it had not been for the war I would have never gotten out of the barrio and most likely would have gotten involved with gangs and sooner or later would have crossed the law. Another thing I remember (that the military did for me) was all the many places I visited which otherwise I would have not seen, places like Hawaii, Guadalcanal, the Russell Islands, Tulagi, Ulithi, Okinawa, Tientsin, China, Kobe, Japan, and North and South Korea.

Richard Makua

I feel they should have let the war in Korea continue through China and kicked ass. Maybe we wouldn't have the trouble we have today. I do not think we should have used nuclear weapons, though.

We could have avoided the war by letting the other countries fight their own problems. No, I do not think the war was worth it. If there was one lesson that I would like us to learn from the war it would be this: Stay out of it!

Of what aspect of the American effort was I most proud? That I was an American. And do I feel guilty today about any of my war experiences? No, I don't!

My experiences in the war do affect my actions now. Being in the hole for three months, by yourself, it either broke you or made a man of you!

I have flashbacks of what I have seen and what I had done to me. I cannot forget. I go to the VA all the time for my health. I see the psychologist every other week about my flashbacks. Sometimes it gets worse, and sometimes it gets better, but I still have them. I do not feel secure about my life. Yes, there is something I look back at and remember that I wish I could have done differently. When it comes to how I feel about the people I fought against, I mind my own business. What did I hate the most about the war? Getting shot at.

We have a reunion every once in awhile of the people I was with in Korea. I do feel that there were American POWs still left behind when we came home. Those who stayed back or those who they kept, I wouldn't know. Those who stayed back should be shot.

If I have to do it all again, I would, if I was younger. I'm proud to be an American. My outlook on life now, after being in the war, is that I wish I was overseas kicking ass. My suggestion to anyone entering the military today would be to learn all you can from it and take it like a man.

Joseph Wilson

We could have avoided the war by talking, making peace, not going to war. Not having to go to war to help other people to be free. But the government took so long to talk to the people and so many vets were killed. If the peace talks hadn't have taken so long, we could have made peace easy.

I am a happy person, before and after the war. I happened to have learned to be a proud American Black, to be a good worker, to work hard, and I've learned that you can make it because you learn to let what happened stay in the past. But also to do good in school, do not let race keep you down. If you are poor, white, black, Latin, we made it [possible] for you to be free, by going to war. I have learned to say that we are blessed to be born in America. I try each day, as a vet, to help my vet friends who are not doing too good, by being in a vets' group, and working for those who did so much to free others and to keep America free.

Never let race make you not a good American. We are all one people in the U.S.A.

As far as my "outlook on life," I have learned to say that we did our job to free the other people. So maybe we did do a good job. We need to make sure we have good people in the government, not for them, but to take care of all Americans, to help our people to live a good life, even if we will always have poor here.

234

If I could do one thing differently, I would like to try to keep up on some of my fellow POWs and try to learn how they are doing. Also, I would work more to try to help the POWs who did not come back to the USA. I know so many are still there, and I feel we should do more to help them.

There were 21 POWs who stayed in Korea (after the war). Some of them came home after about 15 years, but some are still there; they have stayed on there. They also have said that the last one was sent to Russia. But the government did not seem to care about the POWs.

Life was good to me. I have worked and done really well. My health is OK, only my feet are not too good. I have done OK. I learned to work for the vets, to try to help them get what they need. So I feel I am doing OK—by helping them. I am retired from the Los Angeles Unified School District. I have worked for many years with the American Legion, as a Service Officer, and Commander of the Will Rogers Post #539. I have worked hard to make sure that we have a National POW/MIA Recognition Day each year on the third Friday in September. Here is a letter that I wrote and sent to many people in our government:

"One Day For Our POW MIA"

"America, give us one day, National POW MIA Recognition Day, the 3rd Friday in September to fly the Day POW MIA flag on this day. We did what we were told. Some made it home, but others are still there. Look and hope the day will come when they'll be home too. Let us not forget them but if you give us this day we will be happy for that day, but it will be nice if you let it stay some more days. Let the POW MIA flag fly all over the land for all to see. We did not forget you, we must do all we can and to work each day to do what we can to bring our POW MIAs home. They are our brother, father & sister. They are our American vets, who were sent there to help to free others. But now's the time to help free them. Do what you can to free our POW MIAs now. The war is over if we don't help them to be free. You will say I had no time to help free you.

Ex POW wish

Joseph Wilson"

[A friend of Joseph's wrote the following touching tribute to him....]

"JOSEPH WILSON"

Commander - Will Rogers Post 539 Inc.   1988-89, 1989-90

Chef de Gare Pacific Sunset V-1336   1992-93, 1993-94

"In Joseph Wilson we have a Veteran for all seasons, a Legionnaire with compassion and determination, and a Forty and Eighter with will to help, wrapped as a caring man. For years since joining the American Legion, Joe has had a mission in mind, to alleviate the suffering and pain of his former comrades-in-arms. As service officer he has seen that no veteran feels the injustice of work undone.

Performance of duty is not new for Joe Wilson. As a merchant seaman from 1945 to 1950 he was part of a formidable armada with the task of rebuilding Europe and a devastated world. His most memorable trip as a seaman was a shipload of European "War Brides."

Destiny would eventually catch up with Joe, entering the Army he thought it would be an uneventful tour of duty, meantime the relations between North and South Korea grew worse by the day. When hell broke loose, Joe Wilson was shipped to Korea. At that time the all black 25th Infantry division, with a long history of service to Country was part of the army of occupation doing police duty in Japan, turned some of its components to the United Nations in Korea and Joe was attached to the 24th Regiment, K Company, which was one of the first to resist the attack of the crack Chinese trained North Korean Army.

Joe served with distinction and along the way was awarded the Good Conduct Medal, the Combat Infantryman Badge, two Bronze Stars, one Silver Star, and the Purple Heart for wounds received at the 38th Parallel.

The winds of war changed and a wounded MIA soon emerged as a POW of a brutal and sadistic captor; which explains the fuel that drives his quest for a national recognition that a problem does exist. His efforts, coupled with other activists, have been recognized to the extent that the President signed a proclamation to adopt the 3rd Friday of September when the Flag of the National League of MIA/POW Families shall be flown at the White House, the U.S. Departments of State, National Defense, Veterans Affairs, Selective Service Headquarters and the Viet Nam Memorial; this not being enough, Joe is currently engaged communicating with each State Governor and legislature urging them join the Federal government and endorse the proclamation honoring the Flag of the Nation League of MIA/POW Families.

You would think that this is all there is to give, not to a man on the go as Joe is. The Viet Nam Memorial Wall replica is visiting the Southland? Joe Wilson is at the vanguard of citizens and legionnaires that visit it and work for a successful stay. Veterans need moral support? Need rehabilitation? Joe, as a member of La Societe des Quarante Hommes et Huit Chevaux (40 & 8 to you) has been appointed by Correspondant Nationale Robert Law VAVS Deputy Representative to the VA Medical Clinic, Temple and Alameda. Joe not only visits and cheers the sick, he is conductive in many a way to their rehabilitation with his classes in floral creativity or, "Flowers by Vets".

Joseph Wilson is indeed a 'Veteran For All Seasons.'

Theo Baudoin, Jr.

In July, 1953, a Cease Fire Agreement was signed, and in August I was exchanged in Operation Big Switch. On September 14, 1953, I was welcomed home with a parade in downtown Texas City, Texas. I am a self-employed floor contractor and live with my family in Dickinson, Texas.

I have talked to many high school classes here about my POW experiences and have written a book of my own about my experiences, and plan to self-publish it soon. Also, I have created

237

a detailed model of one of the prison camps I was in, "The Mining Camp". This display, along with other memorabilia I have collected, has been shown at various events, including conventions of the American Ex-Prisoners of War and the Korean War Ex-POW Association.

The following is an excerpt from an article that I wrote for the May, 1993 Ex-POW Bulletin (Volume 50, No. 5, of the American Ex-Prisoners of War Bulletin):

"American POWs in Korea"

"Lately much is being written that Americans did not do as well as other United Nations personnel held as prisoners of war in Korea. They state facts and quote figures that are deceiving unless they are put into their proper order. Some have said Americans were soft, ill trained, lacking leadership from their officers, and in the end were unable to face life in captivity. I would agree that some of these statements were true, but the same facts and figures that are available show Americans did just as well as other UN personnel while in captivity. As we examine the facts and figures we must remember that Americans supplied over ten times the troops of all United Nations combined, with the exception of the South Korean forces.

It is said that 2,625 Americans died in captivity the first year, but only nine died in the last year and a half. It is also assumed that a major factor contributing to these deaths was the inability to adjust to the harsh reality of captivity. These assumptions are wrong. The main reason is that we were starved. Our food ration at the time of our high death rate was one cup of boiled field corn per man per day, which is not enough food to maintain body weight, and hardly enough 10 sustain life. Sometimes it was not cooked long enough for our systems to digest it. The bitter cold sub-zero weather, having to sleep in crowded unheated buildings on dirt floors, made our survival nearly impossible. At this time we were all infested with blood sucking lice. Most of us had bloody dysentery, and some came down with pneumonia. The figure of 2,625 American deaths comes from eye-witness reports we gave our government when we were released; we lost that many more. We did not know their names. Many died on the long marches to the prison camps.

In order to better understand the American POWs struggle to survive, let's look at these figures. It is said that 2,836 of the 2nd Division were captured, and of that group 47% died in captivity. Most of these were captured in the last three months of 1950 when the Chinese entered the war. 1 was in that group, and many more were captured. We estimate that 60% died while in enemy hands. The figures for the 24th Division are even greater. Most of these men had been captured in July and August 1950 by the North Koreans. They had captured 1, 177 known, with 48% dying while prisoners of war. In contrast, the 40th Division (National Guard Unit) sent to Korea in 1953 had 16 reported captured, with 6% deaths. The 45th Division had 33 known captured and no reported deaths.

It is easy to see that when Americans were given the bare minimum food, clothing and shelter they survived. It is also evident that in the first six months of the Korean War the enemy did not seem to care. Prisoners of war just did not have the necessary food, shelter or medical attention. Very few of the badly wounded survived.

By late March 1951 the Communist Chinese started their propaganda education (so-called brainwashing) program. At this time food rations were improved and increased. At Pyuck-tong Camp 5, over 1800 men had died in the past three months. In January I had been on my group's first burial detail. We carried 28 men to the top of a hill in our camp. Here, in a trench dug out for a gun emplacement, we dropped our dead. The ground was frozen and no graves could be dug. The Yalu River was frozen with four foot thick ice. Later, in April, I saw the dogtags of over 1600 men. Many more had died that did not have dogtags. My dogtags had been taken from me at the time of capture.

Many times the 229 Turkish prisoners that were held captive by the Chinese Communists are compared with Americans in the ability to survive. It is said that they had no deaths reported while prisoners, and it was "due to discipline esprit de corps that they were able to overcome their ordeal as prisoners of war." The facts are, the Turks were a 5,000 man battalion and had just arrived in Korea. Their first battle was fought near the Kunu-ri roadblock. About 28 Turks were captured near Kunu-ri along with us, and they were on the marches to the Mining Camp and later to Pyucktong Camp 5.

I remember at Pyucktong in January 1951. Each morning a Chinese guard would take them out on a wood detail. They were a small unit and were able to forage for extra food from the Koreans. They were very resourceful, and masters at "scrounging," as GIs called it. The Turks were located to the south of my company area at Camp 5. At times I would walk down to the road separating their area from ours, and I would trade with a young Turk. He was able to get tobacco from the Koreans. They were better able to heat their buildings and divide their rations, since they had a small group. It is said none died, but I remember that one wounded Turk was said to have died. Most Turkish POWs were captured after April 1951, after rations had been increased and deaths had ceased. By war's end they had reported 717 dead and 2,413 missing in action or unaccounted for.

At Camp 5, Americans were not able to go on wood details, and in many cases, some of us did not get our daily rations. The facts are the strong took away from the weak many times. On the other hand, the Turks, being more familiar with this type of food, cooked their rations. The Chinese were cooking ours at this time. Americans adapted well, and soon we were cooking our own rations and making sure each GI received his ration. In the end, Americans, given the same conditions to survive, did cope as well as any other United Nations personnel.

Wayne A. (Johnnie) Johnson

After returning home, I was a night club owner, personnel and labor relations manager in steel, hotel and motel manager, and general manager and lounge owner, among a few other things. I am divorced, retired, and live in Scottsdale, Arizona. I'm on total disability primarily due to my imprisonment. I enjoy pro football, fishing, pool, and the casinos. I am pretty much a loner, with no relatives living in this part of the country.

I am a member of VFW #1275, Lima, Ohio, DAV #20, American Legion #29 of Glendale, Arizona, and The POW-WOW Chapter of POWs and KWVA of Phoenix, Arizona. Also, the American EX-POW Association, Korean Ex-POW Association and the 24th Infantry Division Association.

APPENDIX

U.S. Army Certificate pertaining to "Circular 131" (Inchon, Korea - 1953)

C E R T I F I C A T E

I certify that I have read and fully understand all the provisions of Circular 131, Headquarters, United States Army Forces, Far East, 1953, subject: Disclosure of Information in Connection With Personnel Escaped, Liberated, or Repatriated From a Hostile Force, to Include Evaders of Capture in Enemy or Enemy Occupied Territory and Internees in Neutral Countries, and will at all times hereafter comply fully therewith.

I understand that disclosure of military information to unauthorized persons will make me liable to disciplinary action.

I realize that it is my duty during my military service, and later as a civilian, to take all possible precautions to prevent disclosure, by word of mouth or otherwise, of military information of this nature.

Name (Print) __Harold L. Kaschko.__ Signed _Harold L. Kaschko_

Grade_ Capt ___SN_ 01167491____ Dated_ 7 Sep 1953_ Place_ Inchon Rep] Depot

Unit___ 8057th Army Unit P.O. 971_ Witness___ M/Sgt. C. Adams

Department of Defense letter pertaining to "Circular 131"(Washington, DC - 1993)

DEPARTMENT OF DEFENSE
OFFICE OF GENERAL COUNSEL
WASHINGTON, D.C. 20301-1600

July 29, 1993

MEMORANDUM FOR LTC MARTIN WISDA

SUBJECT: Debriefing of Korean War POWs

By your memorandum you requested this office determine the validity of a Certificate, purportedly signed by Korean POWs, prohibiting the disclosure of miliary information to unauthorized persons. It would appear from its language that the Certificate was issued pursuant to a 1953 Headquarters, U.S. Army Forces, Far East, Circular 131. We understand that you have been unable to locate a copy of the Circular.

Based upon the Certificate's language, this office is doubtful that DoD could enforce the prohibition as a matter of law or would desire to enforce the prohibition as a matter of policy. Additionally, since we presume that any future discussions between POWs and DoD representatives would be authorized, the prohibition on unauthorized disclosure of military information, in this context, would not appear to apply anyway.

We believe that DoD can also formally relieve the POWs from their obligations under the Certificate or cancel the Circular. Since it does not appear that the document can be located within OSD, we suggest the an inquiry be made to the Department of the Army. In addition to possibly locating a copy of Circular 131, the Army may also be able to shed some light on the document's status and the procedure for cancellation if that course of action is deemed necessary.

Albert H. Dyson, III
Senior Attorney
Office of Deputy General Counsel
(International Affairs & Intelligence)

242

THE STUDENTS' QUESTIONS

How did you react when you found out you were going to war?

What was your reason for going to the war?

What type of unit were you in?

How long were you in the war?

How much training did you have before going?

What was your service occupation during the war?

What were some of your objectives on your missions?

What kinds of weapons did you specialize in?

Did you leave a girlfriend, boyfriend, or a spouse behind?

What branch of service were you in and what was your rank?

Were you drafted or did you enlist?

What was it like to be in a war?

When you were there did you fully understand why you were fighting and what you were fighting for?

What was your opinion on the war at the time you were there?

What did you rely on the most to keep sane during the war?

How long did it take before you ran out of coping skills?

What was your Christmas like there?

What was your birthday like there and how old were you?

How long did it take you to adjust a little to being there?

What was your worst or most frightening experience?

Describe some people that you best remember.

Did normal happenings like sleeping or eating come hard to you?

What was the food like?

What was the local people's reaction to seeing you and the other troops?

Where were you stationed at?

What was the hardest thing to deal with personally?

Was it hard being away from home a long time?

What was the hardest thing for you to do?

What was the closest you got to being killed and how did it happen?

How much did disease or illness affect the operations?

Were there any discipline problems during combat?

What kept you going when you were fighting so far away from home?

Did you see a lot of prejudice among the Americans you were with?

Describe the type of battles you fought in.

Did you ever think of deserting?

Were you ever wounded?

What do you remember the most about the war?

In spite of the fighting did you have very many good times or very much fun?

What were living conditions like for you?

Were alcohol or drugs used where you were at?

What is the best thing you remember during the war?

Did you make friends with any of the local people? Tell about it if you did.

Did you ever actually kill anyone? If so, how did it feel?

Did any amount of training ever prepare you for actual combat?

Were communications home open and free or did censorship occur often?

Did you ever go against your commanding officer's instructions when you felt they were not right?

Did you ever have a face to face battle with the enemy?

What was it like to have someone die in front of you?

Did you witness any of the atrocities of war that we hear about today?

What was it like fighting?

How did you feel when you saw your friends die?

Did you agree with what you were fighting about?

What did you do while waiting?

Were you scared?

Did you ever have to give medical aid to another soldier? If yes, please explain.

Was there much close friendship in your platoon? Did most members like and respect your leader?

What kept you going when you were fighting so far away from home?

At that time did you think that the President was doing the right thing and that the war was fought right?

What was it like coming home?

How did people treat you when you got back?

When you came back from fighting had your community, the world, changed in any way? How?

How was your home life after the war? Was your family any different around you?

What was your life like when you came home? Were you congratulated for your war effort?

How were you mentally after the war was over? Did you come home to fight another war?

Do any of your experiences in the war directly affect your actions today?

What did you think of yourself before and after the war?

Have you kept in touch with any of the people you were stationed with?

Of what aspect of the American effort were you most proud?

Have you had any health problems because of going to war?

What kind of outlook do you have on life after being in the war?

Do you feel guilty today about any of your war experiences?

Have you been involved in any kind of counseling as a result of your war experiences?

Do you look back at the war and remember one incident that you wish you could have done differently?

What do you hate most about the war?

Do you yet feel secure about your life now?

If you were asked to fight again, how would you feel about it? Would you fight or not?

What feelings do you have toward the people you fought against now?

Do you consider yourself a patriotic American?

Do you think the war was worth it?

Should we have used nuclear weapons?

How do you think we could have avoided the war?

What is one lesson that you would like us to learn from the war?

Were there any American POWs still left behind?

How do you think American's feel about today's armed services?

I am leaving for basic training in 13 days. Do you have any suggestions for me?

OPERATION LITTLE SWITCH

Pows Released April 20, 1953 - April 26, 1953

Abraham, K. Uylsses Pfc
Akers, W. Charles Pfc
Anderson, G. Edward Sgt
Armstrong, J. Samuel Pfc
Ball, L. James Pfc
Barnes, R. Thomas Pfc
Beck, L. Earl Pfc
Beck, L. Earl Pfc
Blanton, O. Paul Pfc
Bowling, E. Vernon Pvt
Boyer-Garcia, H. Angel Pvt
Britt, P. Joseph Pfc
Brook, R. William Pvt
Broomhead, S. Martin Ens
Brown, L. Marvin Pvt
Bullock, W. James Cpl
Camden, A. Willam Pfc
Christie, Gilbert M/Sgt
Clements, E. Paul Pvt
Conley, L. William Cpl
Contreras, E. Ernest Cpl
Coogan, J. James Pvt
Cordero-Ramos, E. P. Pvt
Cortez, Hermenzildo Pfc
Cottel, T. Wayne Pvt
Cottle, T. Wayne Pvt
Cox, Tally Pfc
Cuttin, A . Harry Sgt
Cuttin, A. Harry Sgt
Dandreo, Vincent Cpl
Daniels, F. James Sgt
Daniels, L. White Pfc
Daniels, L. Willie Pfc
Dean, W. Zach Capt
Del La Garra, Albert 2nd Lt
Dix, F. Charles Pfc
Dunn, L. Robert Pvt
Dunn, R. James Pfc
Edwards, B. Sam Pfc
Elmer, Ray Pfc
Fetty, C. Thomas Pfc
Fleming, W. Robert Pvt
Franklin, M. James Pfc
Garcia, M. Jose Pvt
Gray, W. George Pvt
Green, W. Martin Capt

Gregory, G. Arthur Pfc
Hart, F. George Pfc
Hartman, R. John Pvt
Heath, T. Joe Pfc
Heinke, R. Williams Pfc
Herndon, Roger Pvt
Herrera, A. Pedro Pvt
Hichcox, H. Robert Pfc
Hilcord, R. William A/3C
Himpel, E. Carl
Howard, L. Albert M/Sgt
Huebener, E. Wayne Pfc
Humphrey, A. Louis Pvt
Jackson, Theadore Pfc
Jankouits, M. John Jr. Pfc
Jewell, L. Joe Cpl
Jones, M. Roy 1st Lt
Juern, A. Theodore Pfc
Kaver, A. Virgil Pfc
Kelly, M. Neal Sgt
Kerkstra, Louis Pvt
King, John Cpl
Kirchenhausen, W. Carl Pvt
Klozik, A. Paul Pfc
LaClaire, S. Peter Pvt
Lacy, E. Jimmy Cpl
Lang, P. David Pfc
Lawley, Odie Sgt
Lee, Robert Pfc
LeGay, K. Donald Pfc
Ludlum, W. David Pfc
Luther. C. Alexander Pvt
Martin. B. John Pvt
Mateo-Rodriguez, A. Pvt
Matta, John George
McCahon, D. Phillip Sgt
McCollum, Walter M/Sgt
McCurley, D. Herman Sgt
McGhee, F. Benjamin Pvt
Medina, H. Raymond Pfc
Melendez-Osorio, Juan Pfc
Millens, R. Orville Cpl
Mincey, F. Harry Pvt
Mitchell, J\Fon Pfc
Mitchell,. H. Walter Sfc
Moreland, G. Wiliam Pvt

Morrison, O. Richard Cpl
Muldrow, N. Fredrick Pfc
Neighbors, Gerald Sgt
Noland, L. Almond Pfc
Ortiz-Rivera, Juan Pvt
Osorio-Jimenez, N. Pfc
Oven, L. Richard Pfc
Patrick, J. Willie Cpl
Paul, F. Frank Pfc
Penn, R. William HM
Petersson, E. Lionel Pfc
Philpot, F. Robert Pvt
Picerno, Joseph Pvt
Pinkerton, Lee James Cpl
Pizarro-Baez, Alberto
Poloch, S. John Pfc
Polston, D. John Pvt
Powell, M. Levi Cpl
Powers, J. Robert Pvt
Preston, Cech Cpl
Purvis, E. Harry Cpl
Ritenour, W. Everett Pfc
Robertson, Jesse Pvt
Robinson, L. John Pfc
Rodriguez, Seerino Pvt
Rogers, W. George Pfc
Roherbaugh, L. Vernon Pfc
Rose, A. Donald Sgt
Rubin, Tibor Pfc
Rutherford, A. Virgil Pfc
Sacco, Charles Pvt
Schaur, F. Paul Pfc
Schedell, A. Thomas
Shaw, W. Robert M/Sgt
Shinagawa, Shinayo Pfc
Smith, F. Clifford Pfc
Smith, M. Charles` Pfc
Smith, W. William Pfc
Steinke, C. Fred Pfc
Stell, C. Robert Pfc
Sulivan, Reggie Alan Pfc
Todd, R. Lester Pvt
Trabbucki, J. Wiliam Pfc
Treffery, H. Wendell Cpl
Vampran, Ambrow Pvt
Villega, B. Elias Cpl

Villegas, B. Elias Cpl	Watters, L. John Cpl	Wiseman, M. Earl Pfc
Wadill, H. Thomas	Weinbrandt, L. Robert A/2C	Witt, L. Harold Pfc
Wagner, L. Kenyon Cpl	White, E. Robert Pfc	Woodhouse, J. Melvin Pvt
Warren, L. Vernon Cpl	White, E. Robert Pfc	Zidal, P. Eddie Pfc
Warring, M. Wilber Pfc	White, H. William Sgt	

[Listing compiled by Sgt. Andrew (Chief) Aguirre, U. S. M. C. R., former Korean War POW, from news reports in 1953]

OPERATION BIG SWITCH

Pows Released August 3, 1953 - September 5, 1953

Aarnspiger, H. Meil Sgt
Aaronson, Phillip S/Sgt
Abbot, H. William Cpl
Abbot, N. Robert Lt Col
Abbott, D. Richard S/Sgt
Abrahamson, S. M. Cpl
Acevedo, L. B. Pfc
Achee, R. Edward Pvt
Acosta, Roy Cpl
Adair, Sammie Cpl
Adams, S. Ralph Sgt
Adams, W. John Pfc
Adams, L. John Sgt
Adams, R. Joel Cpl
Addington, J. H. Cpl
Adelmann, G. W. Cpl
Adesso, J. Jerry Pvt
Aguinaga, Luis Sgt
Aguirre, Andrew Cpl
Ait, A. James
Akers, F. William M/Sgt
Aldeis, A. Manuel M/Sgt
Alexander, L. Sfc
Alford, A. Junior Pfc
Alfred, Boyd
Allemond, D. R. Sfc
Allen, Millare Capt
Allen, B. John Cpl
Allen, Clifford Cpl
Allen, E. Joe Pfc
Allen, M. William Sgt
Alley, E. Ronald Capt
Allison, A. William Pfc
Almendarez, R. Cpl
Alston, C. Ira Pfc
Althiser, M. Rae
Amador, Luis Sgt
Anderdon, G. L. Sgt
Andersen, J. Alvin 1st Lt
Anderson, R. P. Cpl
Andrews, Malcom Pfc
Andrews, O. N. Sfc
Andrews, E. Harold Cpl
Anguino, J. Benito Cpl
Antonis, J. Nick Pfc
Applegate, O. Bert M/Sgt

Aquilera, Vincent Cpl
Arakaki, Kazumi Cpl
Arakaki, T. Henry Sgt
Aramino, J. N. Pfc
Arceneaux, J. L. Pvt
Archambauit, J. L. Cpl
Arekano, Daniel Cpl
Aria, Armando 1st Lt
Aria, Raymond Cpl
Arians, I. Robert Sfc
Arias, R. Robert Cpl
Armour, D. Harlan Pfc
Arnold, D. Clifton Cpl
Arroyo, Fernando Cpl
Ascue, J. Jose Cpl
Ashpole, D. Robert M/Sgt
Atkins, R. George Cpl
Atkinson, R. E. Cpl
Atwell, F. Daniel Sgt
Aubrey, L. Carl Lt. Col
Auman, C. Neil Pvt
Austin, Julian Jr. Pfc
Austin, L. Maxir Sgt
Avery, E. Willis M/Sgt
Avilan, R. James Cpl
Aviles, Pedro Pfc
Ayalin, Hillarion M/Sgt
Aycoth, L. Hermen Pfc
Ayotte, A. Clifford Cpl
Bacher, F. Alfred Cpl
Bacote, D. James M/Sgt
Badgett, Sylvester Pfc
Badke, K. Kenneth M/Sgt
Bafs, Carl Sgt
Bagwell, M. Ralph Lt. Cmdr
Bagwell, R. James M/Sgt
Bailey, Lawrence Cpl
Bailey, M. N. Harvey M/Sgt
Bailey, A. William Cpl
Bailey, D. Robert Sgt
Bajo, Emiliano M/Sgt
Bakely, A. F. Sgt
Baker, D. Jerry Pfc
Baker, I. Rodney Sgt
Baker, R. Jerome M/Sgt
Balamenti, Sam Cpl

Bales, C. James Pfc
Balkcom, M. W. Pfc
Balkenship, L. R. Sfc
Ballenger, L. G. Cpl
Ballie, W. Fred Sgt
Balwin, G. Kenneth M/Sgt
Banash, P. Alfred Cpl
Banks, C. Clarence Pfc
Banks, H. Johnnie Sgt
Banks, L. Robert Cpl
Bannister, A. K. Cpl
Baranski, A. A. Cpl
Barber, H. James Pfc
Barber, J. Julius Pfc
Barbhart, M. H. Sfc
Barcczykowski, W. Pfc
Barcus, A. Floyd Sgt
Barkdull, H. D. Sgt
Barker, O. Elldo Cpl
Barkovie, Robert M/gt
Barnard, C. Earl Pfc
Barnes, E. A. Pfc
Barnes, Richard Cpl
Barnes, L. Dallas Cpl
Barney, L. Richard Cpl
Barrett, E. Franklin Pvt
Barricks, L. William M/Sgt
Bartholomew, E. C. Pfc
Bartholomew, F. S. M/Sgt
Bartom, E. Clyde Cpl
Barton, E. Donald Cpl
Basset, M. Richard Cpl
Bassett, J. Kenneth Pfc
Batdorff, L. Robert Pfc
Battle, A. Jr. Pvt
Baudoin, Theodore Cpl
Baugh, G. Uylsses Cpl
Baxter, David Pfc
Bayes, J. Charles Cpl
Bayes, Thomas Jr. Sgt
Baylis, B. R. Sgt
Bayman, F. Harry Sgt
Bdeck, F. Edward Cpl
Beadleson, J. H. Cpl
Beale, W. George 1st Lt
Bean, J. Thomas Cpl

Beanba, Edwardo Pfc
Beasley, Leonard Pfc
Beattle, E. Rodney Cpl
Beaudry, A. John Cpl
Beaupre, W. J. Sgt
Beaver, H. James Spt
Becker, J. A. Sgt
Bedroslan, N. R. Pfc
Bedwell, L. C. Cpl
Beerbower, W. H. Cpl
Belcher, O. Roy Cpl
Belden, E. H. Pfc
Bell Richard 1st Lt
Bell, B. Hartley Pfc
Bell, Leonard Pfc
Bell, Lester Sfc
Bell, E. Enoch Cpl
Bellamy, Jesse Pvt
Bemerer, Albert Sgt
Bender, G. Paul Pfc
Bennet, W. James Sfc
Bennett, Conley Pfc
Benoit, E. Clifford Sgt
Bentley, K. John Pfc
Berchem, Wick Cpl
Berman, I. Bernard Cpl
Berry, Elmer
Berry, A. Thomas Cpl
Berube, E. George Sgt
Best, W. Donald 2nd Lt
Best, Oscar Sgt
Bettinger, L. S. Major
Bickam, Lemiah Pfc
Biere, J. Randall Sgt
Billeck, A. Edwin Cpl
Billman, Y. James M/Sgt
Bingham, M. G. Sgt
Bingham, H. Jesse Sgt
Birchard, J. S. M/Sgt
Bishop, D. Robert Cpl
Bishop, E. Carl Cpl
Bishop, E. Ralph Sgt
Bittner, R. Donald Cpl
Black, A. Richard Cpl
Black, J. Richard Sfc
Blackburn, G. Otis Cpl
Blackburn, L. W. Pfc
Blair, D. Jackie Pfc
Blazavic, L. R. Lt
Blevin, R. John Cpl
Blewitt, R. Robert Pfc
Block, M. Richard Pfc
Blodgett, D. Irving Cpl
Boax, Aaron Jr. Sfc

Boden, C. Chester Sfc
Bohimann, L. E. Sfc
Bolden, Daniel Cpl
Boles, J. Oliver Sgt
Bolinsky, J. Walter Cpl
Bolton, Curtis Pfc
Bolton, Harry M/Sgt
Bond, Leroy 1st Lt .
Bonestky, W. R. Pfc
Boody, A. Claude M/Sgt
Booker, V. Jesse Cpt
Booth, D. Clyde Cpl
Booth, Nathaniel Pvt
Boren, W. Claude Capt
Borer. F. William Sfc
Borie, E. Harry Sgt
Borrelli, Frank Cpl
Boston, R. D. Jr. Cpl
Boswell, G. William 1st Lt
Bouldie, A. C. Pfc
Bounds, B. L. 1st Lt
Bourbeau, Phillip Sfc
Bourgeois, E. J. Cpl
Bourgoin, A. J. Sfc
Boutwell, L. N. Cpl
Bowditch. J. A. Cpl
Bowens, W. J. Pfc
Bower, Lahman Cpl
Bowles, W. John Pfc
Bowling, Mathew Pfc
Bowling, C. R. 2nd Lt
Boyd C. Charles Sgt
Boyd, H. Robert Pfc
Boyd, O. William Sfc
Boyd. R. Charles Cpl
Bozarth, R. H. Sgt
Bracamonte, R. A. Pfc
Bradley, H. N. Cpl
Brand, H. Ralph Sgt
Brandon, V. Lloyd Sfc
Brandt, H. Howard Sgt
Branett, E. George Pfc
Brannon, D. T. Cpl
Brannum, L. Carl Sgt
Brantley, P. C. Sgt
Brasswell, D. T. Sfc
Braun, E. Paul Pfc
Brave, G. Robert 1st Lt.
Brazee, D. Fredrick Pfc
Brecklin, L. Henry Cpl
Breton, E. Joseph 1st Lt
Breweer, A. Dewey Pfc
Bridgewater, E. L. Pfc
Briggs, M. Frank Pfc

Brightman, A. R. Pfc
Brinegar, Lucian Pfc
Brittain, E. Dewey Sgt
Britton, D. J. Pfc
Brock, B. Charles Sfc
Brockes, T. John Sfc
Brockhaus, C. F. Sgt
Broner, R. Riley 1st Lt
Brooks, E. Robert Sgt
Brooks, L. Roberts Pfc
Brooks, O. Charles Cpl
Brooks, W. Al Cpl
Broughton, Gilbert Cpl
Broussard, L. Roy Pfc
Browa, J. Ira Sgt
Brown, A. Robert Pfc
Brown, Fred Pvt
Brown, T. Harold Cpl
Brown, A. Robert Sfc
Brown, B. Wiliam Pfc
Brown, C. Archie Cpl
Brown, C. Johnnie M/Sgt
Brown, D. John Sfc
Brown, G. Alfred Cpl
Brown, L George Cpl
Brown, L Herbert Sgt
Brown, O. Clyde Cpl
Brown, S. William Sfc
Brown, T. Harold Cpl
Brown, R. William Pfc
Brown, W. Glenn Sgt
Browning, Jack Cpl
Brunelo, Antony Cpl
Bryant, B. C. Jr. Pfc
Bryant, D. Loren Pfc
Bryant, G. Lonnie Sgt
Bryant, D. John 1st Lt
Bryant, T. James Cpl
Buchanan, H. H. Cpl
Buchanan, J. Billy Cpl
Buell, R. Lester Cpl
Bulinson, H. B. Cpl
Bull, Bernard Cpl
Bullock, T. W. Pvt
Bunce, L. Earl Sgt
Bundy, D. Lyonel Cpl
Burcham, T. Arthur Sgt
Burdelas, J. James Cpl
Burgess, E. C Pvt
Burgess, R. Carl Sfc
Burke, E. Robert Capt
Burke, Stanley Pfc
Burke, W. G. Jr. Sgt
Burke, R. William Pfc

Burkheimer, I. B. Sgt
Burmbelow, L. C. Cpl
Burnett, D. Harold Pfc
Burns, L. Emerson Sgt
Burns, J. Robert MAS
Burress, R. R. Sfc
Burton, A. Charles Cpl
Burton, E. John M/Sgt
Busbee, A. L. Sgt
Bushey, N. Joseph Cpl
Butler, Aubrey Cpl
Butler, Frederick Pfc
Butler, J. David Cpl
Butler, E. Ralph Cpl
Butler, H. Charles Cpl
Butler, J. Millard 1st Lt
Butters, J. Byron Sfc
Byers, W. Lester Sfc
Bynum, T. Simon Pfc
Byrd, T. Roy 1st Lt
Byrd, Wyatt Sfc
Caagel, J. Leamon M/Sgt
CaHill, C. Oscar Pvt
Cain, Allen Sgt
Calderon, J. Arthur Cpl
Caldwell, E. John 1st Lt
Cale, J. Val Sfc
Calirmont, C. Pvt
Callaher, C. Joe Sgt
Cameron, Hayward 1st Lt
Cameron, H. W. M/Sgt
Campbell, Edward
Campbell, E. W. Sfc
Campbell, E. Orbet Pfc
Campbell, J. Harry Pfc
Campbell. B. Paul Cpl
Canaan, C. Gerald Ensign
Canda, Cornelius Pfc
Cannady, J. James Cpl
Cantillo, J. D. Sgt
Cantley, R. Robert Sgt
Cantrell, H. S. 2nd Lt
Caprin, J. William Cpl
Caraveau, N. J. Sfc
Cardwell, D. A. C. M/Sgt
Cargue, E. Coaries Pfc
Carico, N. Glen Pfc
Carlin, E. Joseph Cpl
Carrick, A. Thomas Pfc
Carter, Meifee Cpl
Carter, L. Jerry Cpl
Carter. W. Gale Cpl
Cartex, C. Ira S/Sgt
Carvalho, P. Paul Cpl

Carver, J. Donald Cpl
Carver, L. Roy M/Sgt
Carwell, Henry Cpl
Cash, E. Homer Pfc
Casrswell, B. Ray Sfc
Castlewitz, Manuel Pfc
Cater, A. Robert Cpl
Catle, Hermen HM 3rd
Caulder, L. R. Sgt
Cautl, Arillio Cpl
Cavagnero, Gerald Cpl
Cave, Carl M/Sgt
Celusniack, J. F. M/Sgt
Chagnon, R. Jack Sgt
Champagne, J. H. Pfc
Chandler, C. Harry Pfc
Chandler, Doss Pfc
Chapman, J. F. Cpl
Chapman, R. Paul Cpl
Charging, Kenneth Pvt
Charles, J. Ernest Sgt
Charvat, C. E. Sgt
Chasserau, F. W. Sfc
Chastain, E. B. Pfc
Chavez, Agapito Sfc
Chester, J. Robert Pfc
Chestnut, C. Albert Cpl
Chiarelli, Leonard Pfc
Chickine, L. Albert Pfc
Chiesa, Rafael Cpl
Chikami, B. Akira M/Sgt
Chillis, F. James Cpl
Chisholm, A. J. Cpl
Choma, John Jr. Pfc
Christensen, M. Sgt
Chyers, H. Robert Pfc
Cisak John Pfc
Clark, Clance Pfc
Clark, A. Clarence Cpl
Clark, E. Billy Sgt
Clark, P. Ellis Sfc
Clark, V. Vernon Cpl
Clark, W. Willmer Cpl
Clasyton, A. John Sgt
Clay, W. Jesssie Cpl
Claybaugh, T. Dale Cpl
Cleaves, Van M. T. Pfc
Cleghorn, L. Earl Cpl
Cline, E. Roy Cpl
Cline, W. Penn Sfc
Clinton, P. Willie Sfc
Cloud, G. Donald M/Sgt
Clutter, L. William 2nd Lt
Cobalis, J. Vincet WO(jg)

Coccia, R. Albert Cpl
Cochran, J. Robert Sfc
Cockfield, M. G. M/Sgt
Coddington, D. M/Sgt
Code, C. Charlie Pvt
Cofer, D. James M/Sgt
Coffee, J. Robert Sgt
Cogburn, A. James Sfc
Colbert, P. James Cpl
Cole, Gene 1st Lt .
Cole, W. Thomas Pfc
Coleman, A. D. Sgt
Coleman, Steve Cpl
Coleman, Everett Pfc
Coleman, H. B. Pfc
Coleman, H. C. Pfc
Coleman, Harold Pfc
Colgate, S. T. Cpl
Collet, D. Robert Cpl
Colliet, L. Richard Sfc
Collins, H. James Cpl
Collins, R. Edward A 1/C
Collins, E. Gene Cpl
Combs, H. Charles Sfc
Comeau, L. B. Jr. Sgt
Concepcion, J. T. Sfc
Cones, L. Richard Sgt
Conley, G. Allen Cpl
Conn. P. Thomas Cpl
Connacher, H. K. Pfc
Conte, R. Salvatore Cpl
Contreras, C. H. Sgt
Conway, L. Henry 2nd Lt
Conway, R. M. Pfc
Cook I. Alden M/Sgt
Cook, Lewis Sgt
Cook, Raymond M/Sgt
Cook, Howard M/Sgt
Cooke, L. Charles Pfc
Cookson, J. Arhie Sgt
Cooper, P. Ray Cpl
Cooper, A. George Cpl
Cooper, L. Estly Pfc
Cope, E. Kenneth Sfc
Copeland, B. R. Capt
Copeland, C. Harry Cpl
Copeland, W. W. Sfc
Copenhaver, L. E. Pfc
Copolan, Harold 1st Lt
Corbine, W. D. Sgt
Cordero, Hector 1st Lt.
Corey, E. Charles M/Sgt
Corey, W. Thomas Sgt
Cormier, P. Ernest Cpl

Cornell, C. Mitchell Sfc
Corner, C. Henry Pfc
Cornwell, R. Lloyd Sfc
Cortez, Oscar Cpl
Cortez, Ricardo Sgt
Cosby, E. Samuel Sgt
Cosseti, E. Joseph Cpl
Costegan, J. S. Pfc
Costlow, T. W. Cpl
Coston, Herbert Sgt
Coston, S. Charlie Pfc
Couk, D. Harold WO (jg)
Courey, A. Robert Capt
Covington, R. C. M/Sgt
Cowart, Wallace Sfc
Cowen, V. George Pfc
Coxe, E. Dwight W. O.
Coyle, A. Robert Pfc
Coyle, L. George 1st Lt
Crabtree, T. Albert Pfc
Cram, H Bruce Capt
Crawford, E. R. Pfc
Crawford, W. G. Sfc
Creech, A. Milton Cpl
Creech, Virgil 2nd Lt
Creel, G. Shelby Pfc
Creeson, C. Calvin M/Sgt
Crespo, O. Candido Cpl
Crespo, T. John Cpl
Cress, Patrick Jr. Cpl
Crews, A. William Sgt
Crisp, W. Porter Cpl
Cromble, R. James Sgt
Cross, Alfred
Cross, Sherman Cpl
Croumbly, R. Cpl
Crum, R. Ernest Cpl
Cruz, D. Baldomero Cpl
Cruz, Eddie. Cpl
Cruz, D. Ruben Pfc
Culp, O. William Sgt
Culpepper, E. F. Sgt
Culpepper, J. W. Pfc
Cummings, K. G. M/Sgt
Cunningham, C. W. Sgt
Cunningham, B. D. Sfc
Cunningham, E. L. Sgt
Cunningham, P. T. Pfc
Cunnings, E. R. Pfc
Cuno, T. Francis Capt
Curry, R. James 1st Lt
Curtin, R. Francis Cpl
Curtin, J. John Sgt
Curtis, E. W. Pvt

Curtis, S. John M. Sgt
Curtiss, A. Homer 1st Lt.
Cuthbertson, R. B. Pfc
Cutshaw, Worley Cpl
D'Onofrio, T. P. Cpl
Datry, E. Raymond Capt
Dague, M. Jopseph Sgt
Dahlin, Homer Sgt
Dahms, P. L. Pfc
Dalmazzi, J. Robert Pfc
Daly, J Joseph Sgt
Damiano, Vittorio Pfc
Damron, Allan Cpl
Dangro, H. William Cpl
Darfler, W. Geroge Cpl
Darling, W. Richard M/Sgt
Darnell, W. Melvin Pvt
Darter. C. James Cpl
Dartez, J. Linton Pfc
Daujat, John Major
David, Joseph Sfc
David, P.
David, Leroy Sgt
Davidson, W. C. Sfc
Davies, H. William Pfc
Davis, A. Floyd Sgt
Davis, James Sgt
Davis, M. Richard Cpl
Davis, R. William Pfc
Davis, A. John Cpl
Davis, E. Charles 2nd Lt
Davis, H. Charles Cpl
Davis, H. John Jr. Pvt
Davis, James
Dawson, L. Miles Cpl
Dawson, A. David
Day, W. John Pfc
Day, H. Joseph Sgt
De Armond, E. M. 1st Lt
De Lashmet, B. G. 1st Lt
De Masters, A. J. Lt (jg)
De Smet, A. Albert Pfc
Dean, D. Burl S/Sgt
Deardorf, B. R. Pfc
Deatherage, F. N. Cpl
DeBenedict, J. J. Sgt
Deck, F. Kenneth Sfc
Deck, O. Dean Pfc
DeDengel, J. W. Pfc
Dein, G. Peter Pvt
Del Bosque, A. Sgt
Delany, L. Richard Cpl
Delcastello, A. M. Sfc
Delgado, Tarasico Sgt

Delong, C. James Sfc
DeLuca, J. John Pfc
Demente, L. D. Sfc
Demeo, Joseph Cpl
DeMichele, A. W. Pfc
Deming, A. William Sgt
Demopoulos, Dino Sgt
Dempsey, J. P. Cpl
Denmark, D. H. 2nd Lt
Denny, L. Donald Cpl
Depa, J. Joseph Sgt
DeRoda, E. Genaro Sfc
DeSilva, H. R. Capt
Deumas, J. Donald Pfc
Diaz, Rafael
Diaz, G. Enrique Cpl
DiCato, Joseph Cpl
Dick, F. John Capt
Dick, H. James Cpl
Diggs, N. James Cpl
Dillon, Edward 2nd Lt
Dishon, C. Donald 1st Lt
Disney, B. Donald Cpl
Dittmer, L. T. Sgt
Dixon, Albert Cpl
Dixon, L. John Cpl
Dixon, P. Ralph 1st Lt
Dixon, W. James Sgt
Dixon, R. John Pfc
Dobbins, Frankie Pvt
Dobbs, A. Byron Capt
Dobson, G. J. Pvt
Docs, R. William Sfc
Dodd, E. Lyle 1st Lt
Dodge, Rex Cpl
Doerty, L. Walter 1st Lt
Doherty, L. John Cpl
Doll, Martin Jr. Cpl
Domenosky, F. E. Sfc
Donahue, F. Jack Pfc
Donatelli, P. R. Cpl
Donovan, E. L. Sgt
Doran, L. Carl Pfc
Dorril, J. Willie Sgt
Dorsey, E. Marvin Cpl
Douglass, F. R. Cpl
Douthitt, J. Charles Cpl
Dovel, E. Lloyd Pfc
Dowd, Jack
Dowdy, L. Colquitt Cpl
Downey, D. Earl Cpl
Dowso, L. Thomas M/Sgt
Doyle, E. Arthur Cpl
Doyle, F. Vincent Sgt

252

Drake, H. Brady Sfc
Drake, L. Harlan Cpl
Draper, G. Robert Pfc
Drennan, D. R. Pfc
Driggins, C. W. Pfc
Drummond, E. S. Cpl
Dubreull, J. E. Sfc
Dudukovtch, R. Pfc
Dugger, L. Charles M/Sgt
Duke, Newton Cpl
Dukes, R. Ollum Cpl
Duncan, A. James Pvt
Duncan, W. Solon Pfc
Duncan, E. T. Sgt
Dunlap, E. Junior Sgt
Dunn, D. Jimmie Cpl
Dunning, L. R. Pfc
Duquette, F. N. 1st Lt
Durant, C. Frank Cpl
Durden, E. Carlton Cpl
Durham, L. F. M/Sgt
Durrah, E. C. Pvt
Dutra, F. Joseph M/Sgt
Dwyer, E. Leo Pfc
Dyer, M. Robert Sgt
Early, Earl M/Sgt
Easley, J. Billy Sgt
Eaton, L. Kenneth Sgt
Eaton, Q. Ivan Cpl
Eckenbarger, J. Pfc
Economy, John Sgt
Edward, L. Archie Cpl
Edwards, Irnin Cpl
Edwards, D. F. Pfc
Edwards, E. A. Sfc
Edwards, R. A. Pfc
Effinger, F. Frank Cpl
Egresitz, M. C. Cpl
Eichhorn, J. T. Sgt
Einertson. W. J. Sgt
Eldridge, Johnnie CpL
Eletheratos, T. S. Pfc
Elias, Rafael Cpl
Elliot, M. Donald Pfc
Elliott, E. Charles Pfc
Elliot, E. Willam Sfc
Ellis, O. Alfred Major
Ellison, R. James Sgt
Ellison, M. Paul M/Sgt
Elsbury, B. Irving Pfc
Emert, E. Otha M/Sgt
Emmons, L. Ward Pfc
Englehart, M. W. Cpl
Enos, K. Andrew Cpl

Erickson, L. Edwin Sgt
Erickson, R. W. Pfc
Espinoza, E. Floyd Cpl
Esposito, L. J. Pfc
Essenstein, Sidney Capt
Estabrook, R. W. Sgt
Estell, D. Howard Pfc
Estep, R. Harold Cpl
Estrada, Alphonso Sgt
Ettinger, E. Harry Lt (jg)
Evans, F. John Sgt
Evans, Billy Cpl
Evans, F. William Sgt
Evans, G. Howard Pfc
Evans, H. Ben Cpl
Evans, O. Rodney Cpl
Evans, R. Edward Pfc
Eveland, G. Robert Sgt
Ewbank, O. Robert Pfc
Eyres, L. Thomas Capt
Faconeire, L. D. Cpl
Fahnestock, I. C. Pfc
Fair, E. Claude Pfc
Faler, Dale Ens
Farazier, I. R. Sfc
Farell, S. Thomas Cpl
Farley, E. Roy Cpl
Farmer, R. Clyde Sgt
Feather, B. R. Jr. Cpl
Fedenets, Andrew Major
Fenton, E. Daniel Sgt
Ferguson, D. J. Cpl
Ferguson, J. Billly Sgt
Ferguson, P. B. Pfc
Ferguson, E. C. Pfc
Ferreira, William Pfc
Ferriell, E. Cpl
Festa, K. Robert A/1
Fetterer, L. Vernet Sfc
Fichtner, J. Harry Cpl
Field, E. Horace Pfc
Fields, W. John Sgt
Figgens, R. John Pfc
Figueroa, Victor Cpl
Finley, Erlie Pvt
Fischer, D. R. Sgt
Fisher, Edward Sgt
Fisher, E. Myles Cpl
Fisk, H. Ralph Cpl
Fitzpatrick, F. B. Cpl
Flack, D. Austin Sgt
Flamingo, D. R. Pvt
Flannery, J. A. Sgt
Flattley, G. R. Cpl

Fleeger, R, Harry Sgt
Fleming, C. Lewis Pvt
Fleming, C. William Cpl
Fleming, E. Jr. Cpl
Flore, M. Placido Cpl
Flores, A. Nick Pfc
Flowers, D. James Sgt
Flowers, M. Gerald Sgt
Floyd, B. Rothwell Pvt
Floyd, F. Delmas Sgt
Floyd. E. Herbert Sgt
Flynn, T. John Cpl
Fogle, E. Robert Cpl
Foil, E. Thomas Cpl
Foley, M. James Sfc
Folks, F. Ira Sgt
Folliweller, E. C. Pvt
Fomby, N. Roy Sfc
Foniana, S. A. 1st Lt
Foote, H. Z. Pfc
Foote, L. George Pfc
Ford, E. Joseph Cpl
Ford, H. George Cpl
Foreacre, K. Louis
Forehand, P. Billy Cpl
Forsythe, Fredrick 1st Lt
Forthmen, A. Jewel Cpl
Fortune, E. David Cpl
Foshee, Billy 1st Lt
Foss, H. Sheldon 1st Lt
Foster, C. Richard Pvt
Foulsham, E. G. Pvt
Fountain, Clarence Pvt
Fountaine, A. J. Sgt
Fouts, R. Gerald Pfc
Fowler, E. Harold Cpl
Francione, V. T. Pfc
Francois, A. G. Cpl
Franklin, R. Henry Sfc
Frazee, E. Donald Cpl
Frederickson, A. R. Capt
Freelon, Leo Pfc
Freeman, D. W. Pfc
Freeman, W. John Cpl
Froehlick, E. W. Sfc
Fronapel, L. C. Pfc
Frost, Charles Jr. Pfc
Frost, Elmar Cpl
Fuentes, P. Moises Pfc
Fulk, W. James Cpl
Fulks, E. Harry Cpl
Fulton, F. Edward Sgt
Funderburk, S. Jon Cpl
Furnish, E. Stanley Pfc

253

Gaines, B. Edgar A/1
Gaiser, L. Henry Sfc
Gaither, M. Edward Cpl
Galarneau, L. C. Cpl
Galazia, L. Charles Pfc
Gale, F. Frederick Pvt
Gallagher, C. J. Sgt
Gallardo, D. R. Cpl
Gallegos, G. Max Cpl
Galusha, L. Vernon Cpl
Galvan, Gilberto Cpl
Galvan, Miguel Pfc
Gamboa, S. C. M. Cpl
Gambocurta, H. Cpl
Garcia, P. Abel Cpl
Garcia, R. Andrew M/Sgt
Gardiner, T. J. Sfc
Gardner, C. Fred Cpl
Gardner, G. D. Pfc
Garielle, J. Fred Jr. Pfc
Garmeaux, F. M. Pfc
Garrett, B. Louis Pfc
Gartin, P. John Sgt
Garza, Fred Jr. Cpl
Gaskins, V. June Cpl
Gather, A. Joseph Cpl
Gatlin, E. James Pvt
Gauldine, E. Jack M/Sgt
Gavula, Stephen Cpl
Gay, C. Andrew Cpl
Gaylets, B. Thomas Sgt
Gaynor, J. Melvin Pvt
Gennero, C. Harry Cpl
Geppert, L. Walter Pfc
Germroth, Richard Pfc
Geyer, H. William Sfc
Giannani, A. M. Cpl
Gibbens, M. E. Capt
Gibson, R. Wilbert Pvt
Gibson, T. Paul Pfc
Giesendorfer, P. L. Cpl
Gifford, J. Jack Cpl
Gifforf. F. Milton Cpl
Gilbert, A John Col
Gilbert, J. William Pfc
Gilbert, G. Cecil Cpl
Gilley, E. Floyd Cpl
Gilliland, H. Julian AT/2
Gillman, Thomas Sfc
Gillmer, K Robert Sgt
Ginn, A. Robert Cpl
Giraudo, C. John Lt Col
Girdano, Anthony Pfc
Gladney, Gilbert M/Sgt

Glasgow, W. G. Sfc
Glen, L. Otis Pfc
Glowacki, Steve Pvt
Godburn, M. D. Cpl
Godfrey, M. Larry Sgt
Goelzer, C. James M/Sgt
Goforth, D. J. . Pvt
Goforth, A. Alfred Sgt
Goldlewski, W. R. Pfc
Gomes, A. Joe Sgt
Gonzakes, F. Cpl
Gonzales, G. Cpl
Gonzoles, J. R. Cpl
Goodreau, T. Cpl
Goodspeed, E. M. Pfc
Goodwin, L. A. 1st Lt
Goodwin, P. Jack Cpl
Goolssby, M. Paul Cpl
Gordon, Emmit Jr. Sgt
Gorka, D. Earl Pfc
Goron, Lyle Pfc
Gorr, R. Robert Cpl
Gorski, A. R. Pfc
Graces, Albino Pfc
Graham, P.
Graham, Alfred Jr. Pfc
Grainger, M. Ralph Cpl
Granger, S. John Cpl
Grant, L. Harold Pvt
Grant, Thomas Cpl
Grant, W. Eugene M/Sgt
Grape, W. Richard Sgt
Grauer, E. Furrell Sgt
Gravil, F. James Cpl
Gravitt, L. A. M/Sgt
Gray D. Robert Cpl
Gray, L. Raymond Cpl
Gray, C. Roy Capt
Gray, E. Rex S/Sgt
Gray, G. George Cpl
Gray, L. Vernie Pfc
Gray, S. Paul Cpl
Grebowich, Harry Pfc
Green, C. Willie Pvt
Green, L Pharis Pfc
Greenwell, J. W. Pfc
Greenwood, E. A.
Gregory, F. Homer Cpl
Grenier, Richard Pfc
Grice, Frank
Griffen, M. Donald Sgt
Griffiths, B. Jphn Pfc
Grimmett, Shirley Pvt
Gruarin, J. Albert Cpl

Grueb, E. George Pfc
Grundy, R. Harold M/Sgt
Grussing, Daniel Pfc
Guerra, Edward Pfc
Guerrero, C. M. Pvt
Guerrero, Patricio Pfc
Guitetti, G. Charles CPl
Gunderson, J. Carl Pfc
Guthrie, S. William Sgt
Guzman, R. S. Sgt
Habben, B. Alvin Pfc
Hackney, W. R. Pfc
Hada. Ted Sgt
Hadder, T. Jesse Pfc
Hagerup, T. Erion Sfc
Hale, I. Eugene Cpl
Hale, L. James Pfc
Haley, H. Richard Cpl
Haleyf, Dennie 1st Lt
Hall, H. Cornelius Cpl
Hall, H. Wilofam Pvt
Hall, W. Egbert Pvt
Hall, E. Robert Sgt
Hall, T. Vaughn Cpl
Hamilton, E. W. Cpl
Hamilton, A. R. Pfc
Hamilton, F. James Sgt
Hammett, W. Doyle Cpl
Hammond, M. H. Cpl
Hampton, Tommie Cpl
Hanback, W. John Sfc
Hanbaum, D. Oren Pfc
Hanby, B. John 2nd Lt
Hancock, F. James Pfc
Hancock, W. John Cpl
Haney, W. Oliver Sfc
Hanje, E. Harry Pfc
Hankey, C. Charles Sgt
Hannemann, R. W. M/Sgt
Hanning, M. V. Cpl
Hansen, C. Calvin Sgt
Hanson, H. K. Cpl
Hanson, C. Wlliam Pfc
Haram, M. Robert Cpl
Harbin, B. Joseph Cpl
Harbour, T. John Sgt
Harbrout, B. W. O. Cpl
Hardage, H. Roy Sgt
Hardin, E. Franklin Cpl
Hargiss, D. James Cpl
Hariman, W. Ralph Sfc
Harlan, C. John Major
Harman, M. Findlet Cpl
Harmon, D. Earl Cpl

Harr, E. Vernon Cpl
Harrell, W. James Cpl
Harrington, F. F. Sgt
Harris, J. Huey Cpl
Harris, A. Louis Pfc
Harris, C. L. Sfc
Harris, J. Billy
Harris, T. Audrey Cpl
Harris, W. Herbert Sgt
Harris, W. Ronald Cr.
Harrison, Jake Sgt
Harrison, West Pfc
Harrison, L. Emmet Pfc
Harrison, R. Taylor Cpl
Harrrison, D. T. Lt Col
Hart, F. Charles Pfc
Hart, L. Fred M/Sgt
Hart, W. James M/Sgt
Hartman, L. Ralph Cpl
Hartwell, P. L. Sgt
Haslam, A. Reed Cpl
Hatano, K. Billy Pvt
Hatch V. Verle Cpl
Hatcher, B. Willie Pvt
Hatter, Jesse Pfc
Hauer, N. Victor Sgt
Hauswirth, M. D. Pvt
Havelock, W. G. Cpl
Havener, L. Staly Cpl
Havillin, L Donald Pfc
Hawkins, L. Harold Cpl
Hawley, J. Leroy Cpl
Hay, S. Ralph M/Sgt
Haya, G. Edward Sgt
Hayden, R. James M/Sgt
Haywood, T. H. Pfc
Hazlett, E. Harry Cpl
Head, R. Carl Sgt
Heagy, L. Otis Sfc
Hear, A. Lawrence Cpl
Hearn, F. Charles Cpl
Hearn, S. Joseph Capt
Heath, O. Eldon Pfc
Heath, R. Melvin Cpl
Heddinger, L. C. Col
Hedgeman, E. E. Cpl
Hedlund, F. Harry Capt
Heggett, Laverne Cpl
Hellican, William Pfc
Helmich, P. Robert Pfc
Helms, J. Carl Sgt
Helt, Claud
Heminger, J. L. Cpl
Hemphill, Lorn Pfc

Hemrick, M. K. Pfc
Henderson, E. J. 1st Lt
Henderson, W. W. Pvt
Hendricks, Ray Pfc
Henry, C. Robert Capt
Hensley, O. M. Pfc
Henson, E. Walter M/Sgt
Herbert, Leonard Sfc
Hernandez, Jose Pfc
Hernandez, P. G. Cpl
Hernandez, R. A. Cpl
Herren, L. Milton Pfc
Hess, D. R. Sgt
Hess, H. Ernest Cpl
Hettinger, H. R. Sgt
Hewitt, E. Roy Cpl
Hewlett, Edward Sgt
Hibberd, B. W. Cpl
Hibdon, E. Robert Cpl
Hickley, G. Billy Pfc
Hidalgo, B. Larry Sfc
Higa, K. Henry Pfc
Hikida, R. Y. Cpl
Hill, A. James Cpl
Hill, E. Ronald M/Sgt
Hill, H. George Cpl
Hill, M. Charles 1st Lt
Hill, S. Lemon Cpl
Hill, W. Darin Sfc
Hills, R. Lewis Cpl
Hindman, T John Capt
Hinojosa, A. Joel M/Sgt
Hinojosa, V. R. Sgt
Hinojosa, A. Jose Cpl
Hinton, J. Edgar Pfc
Hitt, W. Jimmy Pfc
Hobbs. Lawrence Sgt
Hodges, James Sgt
Hodges, L. W. M/Sgt
Hodges, T. Carrol M/Sgt
Holden, L. Fred Cpl
Holder, James Pfc
Hollinger, R. B. Pfc
Holloway, D. B. A/1
Holmes, Roxie Jr. Sgt
Homonai, E. Joe Cpl
Honeycutt, C. Pfc
Hood, H. Harold M/Sgt
Hook, George Cpl
Hope, R. James Pfc
Horman, D. Daniel Pfc
Hormanvie, D. A. Pfc
Hotson, O. Wayne Sgt
House, W. Carl Pfc

Householder, L. G. Cpl
Howard, G. R. Cpl
Howard, H. Harvey Pfc
Howay, L. Charles Sgt
Howell, J. Bobbie Sgt
Howell, J. Thomas Sgt
Hoyos, H. H. Rafael Pfc
Hroback, J. C. Sfc
Hubbard, H. W. Pvt
Huber, R. Vernon 1st Lt
Hudson, James Pfc
Huff, G. Henry Cpl
Huff, B. Jame Jr. Pfc
Huffman, F. C. Pfc
Hughes, J. Clyde Pfc
Hughes, Hobert Pfc
Hughes, J. Bobby Pfc
Hughes, L. E. Cpl
Hulon, D. S. Pfc
Humada, Z. Alfredo Cpl
Humphrey, L. E. M/Sgt
Humphreys, E. H. Cpl
Humphries, R. Cpl
Hunges, C. J. Pfc
Hunt, R. James Pfc
Hussey, J. Joseph Pvt
Hussey, P. Donald Sfc
Hussman, R. J. Cpl
Hutchinson, M. H. Cpl
Hynson, H. James Pfc
Iannantuono, D. F. Pfc
Ingalshee, H. C. Cpl
Ingram, E. Lloyd Sfc
Inman, L. Eugene Sgt
Ionadi, Anthony Pfc
Irish, Bradley 1st Lt
Itagaki, J. Geroge Cpl
Ivanushka, Michael 1st Lt
Izbicky, G. Edward 2nd Lt
Izzo, C. Michael M/Sgt
Jackkson, L. W. 1st Lt
Jackson, Amos Jr. Cpl
Jackson, G. C. Sgt
Jackson, Elmer Sgt
Jackson, L. Shelby Sgt
Jackson, T. W. Sgt
Jackson, C. Ellis Cpl
Jackson, W. Noble Sfc
Jackson, W. John Pvt
Jackson, William Cpl
Jacobs, Murray Cpl
Jacobs, A John Pfc
James, Frank Pvt
James, W. J. Jr. Cpl

James, P. Russel Cpl
Jameson, A. F. Cpl
Jarvis, W. Robert Sgt
Jayroe, R. Johnnie Cpl
Jeffers, Howard Cpl
Jeffords, M. J. A/2C
Jenkins, L. Roy Sgt
Jenkins, W. G. Cpl
Jennings, Vernard Sgt
Jennings, F. C. Cpl
Jensen, Raymond Cpl
Jernigan, F. Alfred Pvt
Jeter, E. Frank Sgt
Jett, Richard Pfc
Jetter, J. Carison Pvt
Jewell, W. Charles
Jimenez, R. L. Pfc
Jirek, F. Anthony Sgt
Johnson, C. J. Cpl
Johnson, D. R. Pfc
Johnson, L. Daniel Cpl
Johnson, Robert Cpl
Johnson, Wayne A. Pfc
Johnson, J. John Cpl
Johnson, J. R. Sgt
Johnson, Jesse Sfc
Johnson, L. Duane Pfc
Johnson, O. C. Sfc
Johnson, O. R. Pvt
Johnson, Turner Pvt
Johnson, G. John Sgt
Johnson, C. F. Pfc
Johnson, Rege M/Sgt
Johnston, L. W. Cpl
Jojola, L. Joseph Sgt
Jolliff, E. William Pfc
Jones, A. William Sgt
Jones, L. Kenneth M/Sgt
Jones, L. Robert Pfc
Jones, R. T. Cpl
Jones, Seth Jr. Cpl
Jones, William Sfc
Jones, B. Edwin Cpl
Jones, C. Luther Capt
Jones, E. Dale Pfc
Jones, G. Orville Pvt
Jones, Godfrey Jr. Pvt
Jones, J. Frank Cpl
Jones, J. William Cpl
Jones, L. Robert Sfc
Jones, P. Lloyd Pfc
Jones, T. Nyle Cpl
Jordan, D. Harvey Pvt
Jordan, L. Byron Pfc

Juneau, Joseph Pfc
Kaessner, A. M. Sgt
Kahniack, John Capt
Kammerud, Otis Pfc
Kaschko, Harold Capt
Kaswana, Masao Sgt
Katchmark, D. C. Pfc
Katsaros, Steve Sfc
Kawamoto, L. S. Cpl
Kazcorek, A. C. Pfc
Keen, A. John Pfc
Keene, J. Walter Cpl
Keene, J. Billy Pfc
Keeny, R. Carl Sgt
Kelker, Samuel Pfc
Kelleer, O. Carl Cpl
Kelly, G. Lonnie Sfc
Kelly, L. Donald Pvt
Kelman, Walter Sgt
Kenible, T. John M/Sgt
Kennedy, P. J. Cpl
Kennedy, L. F. Cpl
Kern, H. Henry Cpl
Kestel, E. Reginald Pfc
Kewalewski, R. Cpl
Kiawinsky, W. J. Sfc
Killion, J. William 1st Lt
Kimbrell, W. J. Sgt
King, A. Marvin A/2
King, C. John Sgt
King, J. Billie Pfc
King, M. Edward Cpl
King, O. Guy Capt
King, F. Edwin Pfc
Kinnee, H. Orville Sfc
Kirby, C. Edward Cpl
Kirby, R. John Cpl
Kirk, A. John Sgt
Kirk, W. James Sgt
Kisar, R. James 1st Lt
Klevemano, W. C. Sfc
Klimas, S. Edward Cpl
Kline, F. George Cpl
Klinger, R. Thomas Sgt
Knego, Geroge 1st Lt
Knicley, L. Alfred Cpl
Knipple, R. William Cpl
Knupp, L. Everett Cpl
Koboski, F. E. Sfc
Kohl, T. Robert Pfc
Kohus, E. F. Jr. Pfc
Kolb, B. Leslie Pfc
Konkle, Howard Cpl
Koontz, J. William Pfc

Kostich, Robert Pfc
Kovatch, S. Ernest 2nd Lt
Kral, Robert 2nd Lt
Krammes, J. R. Pfc
Krantz, O. Alton Cpl
Krasko, John 1st Lt
Kreger, S. Walter Cpl
Krentz, J. Darell Cpl
Krueger, H. R. M/Sgt
Kruss, D. Ernest 2nd Lt
Kusmitch, A. John Cpl
Kutys, J. Joseph Cpt.
La Herteux, P. J. H. 2nd Lt
La Blanc, P. R. Sgt
La Pointe, L. Cpl
Lacap, Servere M/Sgt
Lam, N. Gene Capt
Lamb, B. Charles Cpl
Lamphiear, L. S. Pfc
Lane, M. Fred Pfc
Lang, K. Eugene Cpl
Lang, J. Henry 1st Lt
Langell, Irvine Cpl
Langford, L. H. Pfc
Langlois, E. R. Sfc
Langstrom, C. O. Cpl
Lanier, C. Dennis M/Sgt
Lantron, W. N. Major
LaPlante, L. Austin M/Sgt
Larose, M. L. Arthur Sfc
Lashia, J. Roy Pfc
Latham, D. Owen Sgt
Latora, N. Phillip Pfc
Lauri, J. Robert Sgt
Lawing, B. Sammy Cpl
Lawrence, A. R. Pfc
Lawrence, S. M. M/Sgt
Lawson, C. J. Cpl
Lawson, L James Pfc
Lawson, M. John Sgt
Lawson, R. C. Cpl
Layer, E. Eugene Capt
Le Fervre, T. E. J. Sgt
Leamon, J. N. 1st Lt
Ledkins, B. Lonzo Cpl
Lee, John Pfc
Lee, E. Charles Sgt
Leerkamp, G. H. M/Sgt
Legried, G. Darrel Pfc
Lelito, R. Edward Pfc
Lemke, C. Robert 1st Lt
Leon, Daniel Pfc
Leonard, S. H. Cpl
Leslie, J. L. Sfc

Leveillie, R. J. Sgt
Lever, J. Donald Cpl
Leveret, Charis Pvt
Lewis, R. R. Cpl
Lewis, F. James Pfc
Lewis, J. William 1st Lt
Lewis, J. Willie Sgt
Lewis, L. Guy Sgt
Lex, B. Carles Pfc
Lidell, M. Fredricks Sfc
Lieb, E. Theodore Cpl
Liles, S. V. Paul Lt Col
Linfante, Raymond Pfc
Lipper, W. Edward Pvt
Lisetza. H. Frank Pfc
Little, D. Wesley Sgt
Little, L. David Maj
Livaudais, P. Clyde Sgt
Lively, Thompson Sgt
Livesay, E. Carl Sgt
Lloyd, Alan 1st Lt
Llundquist, R. C. 2nd Lt
Loban, John Cpl
Lobatto, E. Joe Sgt
Logan, A. John Sfc
London, W. F. Pfc
Long, Willie Sfc
Long, L. Jessie Pfc
Long, L. Norman Cpl
Long, H. James Pfc
Longtin, P. Ludger Sfc
Lorenzo, J. Michael Capt
Loutitt, N. Charles Cpl
Love, H. Crawford Pfc
Lovejoy, D. Ronald Pvt
Lovern, E. Paul Pfc
Lovin, R. Charles Pfc
Loya, C. Joe Cpl
Loyola, J. Vincent M/Sgt
Lozano, R. Arthur Capt
Lubinski, John Sgt
Ludwig, R. A. Pfc
Lugo, E. Luis Pfc
Lukacinsky, J. R. Cpl
Lukasik, J. A. Sfc
Luksan, E. Edward Sgt
Luna, Eugenio Sfc
Lundquist, C. E. Sgt
Lunn, A. Rosevelt Pvt
Lunsford, L. F. Pvt
Luttrell, John M/Sgt
Lyke, A. Thomas Cpl
Lyles, H. Edward 1st Lt
Lynch, W. Donald Pfc

Lynch, P. Linard Sfc
Lynn, H. James M/Sgt
Lytle, Kenneth Sgt
Maack, F. A. O. Jr. Sgt
MacGhee, F. David Major
Macijeski, C. J. Pfc
Mack, J. Calvin Pfc
MacLean, A. R. Sgt
Madden, E. Lloyd Pfc
Maddox, L. Robert Sfc
Madson, L. Gordon Sgt
Maglera, E. Steven Cpl
Magoria, Joseph Pfc
Mahrenholz, W. R. Pfc
Makua, K. Richard Cpl
Mallonee, Melving Cpl
Manaway, G. Hugh Pfc
Mandarano, A. D. Cpl
Mann, H. William Cpl
Mansfield, F. Willie Cpl
Manuel, W. Donald Cpl
Maravola, A. J. Cpl
Maritn, L. Wayne Pfc
Markham, Arnold Cpl
Marks, E. Richard Lt Col
Marques, A. Jose Pfc
Marry, E. Burton Cpl
Marsh. E. Richard Pfc
Martin, J. D.|
Martin, W. Henry Cpl
Martin, C. R. Pfc
Martin, D. William Cpl
Martin, F. Charles Capt
Martin, G. Paul Sfc
Martin, J. T.
Martin, L. Jack Cp
Martin, S. James Cpl
Martinez, Daniel Sfc
Martinez, Marcos Cpl
Martinez, D. M. Jr. Pfc
Martinez, E. Jose Cpl
Martinez, F. Ramon Cpl
Mascarenas, C. Cpl
Mason, R. Jack Pfc
Massey, R. M. Pfc
Massingberg, S. 1st Lt
Massle, R. Darrel Cpl
Mata, C. Goyo Cpl
Mathermly, M. V. Cpl
Mathews, Elbert Cps
Mathews, H. C. Pfc
Mathis, S. Chester T/Sgt
Mathis, W. Johnnie Cpl
Matlock, J. Benny Cpl

Matzke, E. Delbert Pfc
Maxcey, H. Robert Pfc
Mayer, J. Willibald M/ Sgt
Maynard, D. Eddie Cpl
Mayo, L. Walter 1st Lt
McAbee, W. F. Capt
McAndrews, G. C. Pfc
McCabe, Roger Cpl
McCardle, L. L. Cpl
McCarthur, O. G. Pfc
McCarthy, Francis Sgt
McCauley, Leroy Pvt
McCauliffe, J. R. Sgt
McCelroy, R. J AVO3
McCitire, J. Edgar M/Sgt
McClain, M. E. Sfc
McClean, F. S. Cpl
McClellan, J. D. Lt. Col
McCloud, N. Cpl
Mcclure, Amos Pfc
McCollum, L. H. Pfc
McConaha, Mery Cpl
McCoy, M. John Cpl
McCoy, K. Donald Pfc
McCraw, W. C. Sgt
McDonald, A. Pvt
McDonough, F. M. Cpl
McDuffle, R. A. Pfc
McEntire, G. Carol Sgt
McGee, L. Tommie Pfc
McGee, Marcus Cpl
McGovern, L. E. Cpl
McGovern, W. J. M/Sgt
McGrath, E. R. Sfc
McGreevy, L. R. Cpl
McGregor, J. B. Pfc
Mcguire, M. Robert Sgt
McInerney, P. J. Cpl
Mcintosh, W. Larry Cpl
McKalip, A. K. Sgt
McKelvie, D. John Pfc
McKenney, D. R. Cpl
McKibben, L. H. M/Sgt
McKinney, L. Dan Sgt
McLain, H. Roy Pfc
McLain, W. Jessie Cpl
McLaughlin, N. J. Major
McLean, E. Ernest Sgt
McManus, C. M. Sgt
McManus, E. H. Pfc
McMillian, P. J. Sgt
McMillin, C. Joe Pfc
McMillin, L. G. Jr. Cpl
McMurtrie, H. T. Pfc

McNabb, Everett Pfc
McNamara, J. B. Sgt
McNeil, J. John Pfc
McNell, W. William Pfc
McNell, P. R. Major
McPherson, V. L. M/Sgt
McQuade, H. A. Cpl
McRay, C. Jesse Cpl
McShan, H. L. Pvt
McTaggart, C. W. Capt
Meadows, B. J. Cpl
Meckler, Richard Cpl
Medin, W. John Pfc
Meece, W. David Cpl
Mefford, M. R. Cpl
Megyesi, J. John Pfc
Meir, W. Ralph Cpl
Melendez, S. G. Sfc
Melesio, M. J. Pfc
Mellin, B. R. Cpl
Mello, Ernest
Memering, E. R. Cpl
Mendell, L R. Sgt
Menzia, C. Conrad Cpl
Merilos, V. Ricardo M/Sgt
Merrill, B. Delvin Cpl
Merritts, P. Melvin Sgt
Messer, C. William Cpl
Messman, C. R. 1st Lt
Metcalf, Walter Jr. Pfc
Metz, K. Henry S/S
Meyer, A. Merlin Pfc
Middleton, J. Billy Pfc
Middleton, Frank M/Sgt
Midolo, P. John Sgt
Mikelburg, Albert Cpl
Milantoni, Patsy 2nd Lt
Milgsrt, M. John Pfc
Milholland, J. C. Pfc
Miller, E. G. Earie Cpl
Miller, E. Reinhart Sgt
Miller, B. Paul Sfc
Miller, G. Delmar Cpl
Miller, H. George Cpl
Miller, K. George Cpl
Miller, R. Loris 1st Lt
Miller, P. Arthur Cpl
Millins, Curtis Sfc
Mills, E. Raymond Cpl
Millward, E. G. A/1
Minchew, E. John Sgt
Mindick, S. Richard Sgt
Mitchell, Lawrence Cpl
Mitchell, F. Charles Sgt

Mitchell, O. Harvey Pfc
Mitchell, R. Calude Sfc
Mitchell, J. C. Cpl
Miyamura, H. H. Sgt
Mizer, B. Edward Pfc
Moffett, Rufus Sgt
Moncriffe, Bennie Pfc
Monroe, Franklin M/Sgt
Montanero, R. Pfc
Montano, O. C. Cpl
Montejano, E. Cpl
Montgomery, W. D. Cpl
Montgomery, B. C. 1st Lt
Montgomery, J. H. Pfc
Montoya, Victor Pfc
Montreull, J. T. Cpl
Montz, C. William Cpl
Moody, L. Troy Cpl
Moore, O. Walter Pfc
Moore, S. Martin Cpl
Moore, Clyde
Moore, W. Johnnie Cpl
Moore, W. William Capt
Mora, R. Rafael Pfc
Morales, E. Raul Pvt
Morales, Rodolfo Pfc
Morales, A. Jesus Cpl
Morar, George M/Sgt
Moreno, Raymond Pfc
Morgan, E. Robert Cpl
Morgan, J. Marion Sgt
Morgan, Jerry Sgt
Morgan, C. Jr. Pvt
Morgan, N. C. Cpl
Morita, Hisashi Cpl
Morree, L. Leonard A/1
Morris, H. R. Jr. Cpl
Morris, E Ford Sfc
Morris, O. Lester M/Sgt
Morrison, Joe Pfc
Morse, Thompson Sgt
Morton, H. Lynn Pfc
Mosnicka, J. F. Pfc
Moss, L. X. Cpl
Mossman, W. D. Cpl
Mounts, T. T. 1st Lt
Movinski, J. R. Cpl
Moyer, D. Ralph M/Sgt
Mros, A. Martin Cpl
Mroszka, J. J. Cpl
Muise, J. E. Eric Cpl
Mukai, Takeshi Cpl
Mullins, B. James S/Sgt
Mullins. L. Charles M/Sgt

Munsell, Donald Pfc
Murata, S. Harry Cpl
Murlaschitz, John Cpl
Murphy, E. C. Pvt
Murphy, J. M. Sfc
Murphy, T. Paul Cpl
Murray, Wesley Cpl
Murray, R. John 1st Lt
Murray, R. Thomas Pfc
Murrow, S. Samuel Sgt
Musgrove, Wylie Cpl
MxDonnell, F. R. Sgt
Myatt, Paul Cpl
Myers, E. John Cpl
Myers, E. Max Cpl
Myers, G. William M/Sgt
Myers, P. Paul M/Sgt
Nagyn, J. John Sgt
Naito, Tadao
Nanartowkiez, S. Cpl
Napier, C. Charles Cpl
Nardolillo, J. F. Pfc
Naukarl, E. Robert Sfc
Nava, John Sgt
Nava, Gilberto Sgt
Navarro, G. Jose Cpl
Naville, F. H. Jr. Cpl
Neal, M. George Adan
Negron, A. Jorge M/Sgt
Nehrbass, F. R. Sfc
Nelson, I. Noble Jr. Pfc
Nevill, F. Kenneth Pfc
Neville, Edward Sfc
Newberry, Y. Carol Sgt
Newbury, A. J. Sfc
Newton, W. C. Cpl
Nickens, M. G. Sfc
Niebrand, J. Billy Cpl
Nielsen, J. Henry 1st Lt
Nielson, A. James Sgt
Nieves, M. Alberto Cpl
Nikko, C. Kenneth Pvt
Noble, D. Jack Cpl
Noel, Frank Civilian
Noell, L. Howard Sfc
Noeth, E. George Cpl
Norman, M. Gray Pfc
Norris, D. Alvin Cpl
North, W, Donald Cpl
Norwood, K. W. Cpl
Nothstein, E. E. Pfc
Nugent, R. A. Capt
Nunnery, D. E. Cpl
O'Brien, P. James Sgt

O'Donnell, Bert H. Sgt
O'Keefe, M. Arthur Sgt
O'Keefe, J. John Sfc
O'Neil, L. Robert Sgt
Obenauer, J. Ira Cpl
Oberle, F. Edward M/Sgt
Odom, Tyrols Pvt
Oliver, M. Edgar Cpl
Oliver, P. William Cpl
Oliveras, Pastor Cpl
Ono, Thomas Sgt
Oorino, G. Manuel Sgt
Ordonio, Phillip Sfc
Oresto, V. James Pfc
Ornelas, V. Isaac Cpl
Orr, E Johnnie Pfc
Orr, E. Louis Sfc
Ortega, N. Ruben Pvt
Ortiz, O. David Pfc
Ortiz, Orlando 1st Lt
Ortiz, A. Aurelio Pfc
Osborn, E. Lloyd Pfc
Osborne, H. Henry Lt.
Osbourne, Ed Pfc
Owens, Boss M/Sgt
Pace, L. Robert Cpl
Pacheco, Felipe Pvt
Pacifico, J. Alfred Pfc
Padilla, Solomon Pfc
Page, J. Frank Sgt
Paillete, E. Ted HN
Palacio, F. Marcus Sgt
Palacios, Ricardo Sgt
Palacol, Sefronio Sfc
Panagopoulos, C.
Pantazis, N. E. Cpl
Paquette, G. J. Pvt
Park, Young Cpl
Park, H. C. Joseph Pvt
Parker, F. Edward Cpl
Parker, V. Emmet Sgt
Parmanhox, B. J. Pfc
Parris, Theophila Pvt
Parrish, William Pfc
Paskovich, M. M. Sfc
Patchoski, J. E. Sfc
Patterson, J. Lewis Pfc
Patterson, W. T. Pfc
Patton, F. Charles Cpl
Patton, H. Gene Pfc
Patton, M. John
Paul, E. Donald Pfc
Pavlik, A. Rudolph Sgt
Pavlik, P. Bernard HN3

Pawalina, P. John Cpl
Pawlowski, J. D. Cpl
Peasner, R. T. Jr. Pfc
Peckham, L. C. Capt
Pelse, P. Frederick 1st Lt
Pena-Garcia, Flor Pfc
Pence, D. Claude Pfc
Pendarvis, M. F. Pfc
Penleton, R. R. Sfc
Penton, R. C. Cpl
Pentz, H. E. Howard
Perez, Richard Sfc
Perez, E. Julio Cpl
Periera, Pedro Cpl
Perkins, E. Marion Sgt
Perkins, Evelyn Cpl
Perry, Bobby Cpl
Perry, L. Jakie Pfc
Perry, F. Jack Capt
Perry, G. Glacel
Peters, D. Dale Cpl
Peters, H. Milton Cpl
Peters, L. Robert Cpl
Petersen, A. R. Cpl
Petersen, D. Carl Cpl
Petersen, H. P. 1st Lt
Petersen, W. D. Cpl
Petro, L. Gordon M/Sgt
Petty, F. James Sfc
Phillips, M. Everett Sfc
Phillips, Nathaniel Cpl
Phillips, A. K. Pfc
Phillips, E. J. Pfc
Phillips, L. John Sfc
Phillips, S. Walter Cpl
Philpot, Lee E. Pfc
Pichelli, J. Louis Sgt
Pickard, G. Glen Jr.
Pickett, A Wayne Cpl
Pierce, J. William Sgt
Pierce, R. Billy Cpl
Pierson, W. John Cpl
Pitt, W. Merle Pfc
Pittman, T. K. Pfc
Plath, H. Hermen M/Sgt
Platt, R. Jack Sgt
Poldervaart, A. L. S/Sgt
Pontious, E. W. Cpl
Porter, Arelious Cpl
Porter, W. Fred Pfc
Porter, O. Pearson Sgt
Potter, H. Edwin M/Sgt
Potvin, F. Joseph Sgt
Pough, Albert Jr. M/Sgt

Powazi, John
Powell, R. Jr. Cpl
Powell, S. William M/Sgt
Powell, W. John Cpl
Powers, D. Jack Sfc
Pratt, D. M. Jr. Pfc
Preece, J. Elias Cpl
Preite, F. Agustine Cpl
Presbrey, C. R. Pfc
Preston, N. W. Capt
Price, H. Eugene Cpl
Price, E. Bob Sfc
Price, N. Morris Cpl
Prickett, L. Florice Pfc
Prokop, Olois Pfc
Prosperi, J. Fred Cpl
Provenzano, J. R. Sgt
Publicover, F. U. Sgt
Pucciarelli, J. F. Pfc
Puckett, Gerald Sfc
Puller, L. Bert Cpl
Putt, J. William Pfc
Quails, Ted Sgt
Quinn, V. Patrick Cpl
Raby, S. Richard Sgt
Racer, H. Fred Pfc
Rachel, Leonard Pfc
Rada, A. Stephen Cpl
Ragland, W. D. 1st Lt
Ragsdale. R. Paul Sfc
Rahtigan, C. W. Cpl
Rains, E. Bobby Pfc
Rainwater, W. G. M/Sgt
Ramatowski, T. A. Sgt
Ramirez, Ralph Cpl
Ramirez, E. Joe Cpl
Ramirez. , C. A. Pfc
Ramos, David Cpl
Ramos, F. A. Pfc
Ramos, R. Eugene Cpl
Ramsey, M. J. Cpl
Randolph, George Pfc
Rapier, R. Hugh Cpl
Ratliff, V. Roy Cpl
Rawls, J. Harold Cpl
Ray, R. Donald Cpl
Ray, Vernon Pfc
Ray, L. William Cpl
Rea, S. Vernon Cpl
Reals, D. Donald Sgt
Reed, F. Raymond Cpl
Reedy, L. Doyle Sgt
Reedy, D. John Jr. Cpl
Reese, E. Richard Sfc

Reese, L. Kenneth Cpl
Reeves, E. Henry Cpl
Reeves, W. Gene M/Sgt
Reichi, J. Frank Pfc
Reid, W. Eugene Pfc
Reid, L. Troy M/Sgt
Reilly, R. Eugene Cpl
Remus, W. W. Pfc
Renouf, N. B. Cpl
Reza, Timothy Pfc
Rhoton, H. John Sgt
Richamond, P. Jr. Cpl
Richards, E. H. Pfc
Richardson, L. H. Cpl
Richardson, J. J. Major
Richardson, L. R. Cpl
Richardson, L. R. Pfc
Richardson, W. J. Cpl
Richesson, D. F. Cpl
Rick, E. Curtis Cpl
Rickard, E. C. Sgt
Ricker, G. Lance Pfc
Riddel, Charles Sgt
Riley, J. Donald Pfc
Rinf, Jack Pfc
Ring, C. Jesse S/Sgt
Ring, J. William Pfc
Rippeto, G. D. Cpl
Ripple, L. Howard Pfc
Rising, V. Anton Cpl
Risley, F. Paul Pfc
Ritchie, E. Preston M/Sgt
Rittenberry, R. B. Pfc
Ritter, L. Elridge Sgt
Ritter, R. John Cpl
Rix, A. Lawrence Pfc
Roarbaugh, K. D. Sgt
Roark, Roscoe Pfc
Roatn, E. Frank Pfc
Robbick, L. Arlow Sfc
Robbins, P. E. Pfc
Roberson, O. Jolin Pfc
Roberson, R. Jearl Cpl
Roberts, Lloyd Pfc
Roberts, C. Gaines Sgt
Roberts, Willie Cpl
Robertson, B. A. Sfc
Robertson, D. T. Capt
Robinette, J. C. M/Sgt
Robinson, M. J. Sgt
Robinson, G. D. Pfc
Robinson, M. Alvin Pfc
Robinson, P. A. Pfc
Robinson, R. L. Cpl

Robles, Porfirio Pfc
Rodriguez, Jose Pfc
Rodriguez, C. G. Jr. Cpl
Rodriguez, G. Lupe Cpl
Rodriguez, R. E. Pfc
Rodriquez, F. E. Sgt
Roessler, R. D. W. Cpl
Rogers, L. Harvey Cpl
Rogers, P. George Pfc
Rogers, S. John Cpl
Roldan, Quiterio Sfc
Rollins, E. Charles Sgt
Rollins, L. John M/Sgt
Rollison, W. Harry Sfc
Romberger, M. H. Cpl
Romero, G. T. Sgt
Romero, Louis Jr. Pfc
Rondinoue, M. R. Sgt
Rook, Richard Sfc
Roosas, F. William Pfc
Rosa, E. Fransisco Sgt
Rosado, T. Juan Sgt
Rose, B. Junior Cpl
Ross, Lonzo
Ross, R. Charles M/Sgt
Rotenquillo, R. J. Pfc
Roush, P. Eugene Sgt
Rovezzi, Joseph Cpl
Rowe, L. Powe
Rowe, Venson Pvt
Rowland, Eugene Pfc
Rowley, S. Arden Sgt
Royal, Calvin Cpl
Roysen, M. A. Capt
Royster, H. W. Sfc
Rub, A. Edward Cpl
Rudd, J. Willie Pvt
Rudistil, L. Robert Cpl
Ruff, J. Wilfred Sgt
Ruiz, G. Framk Pfc
Rund, L. Lewis Cpl
Rundgren, E. C. Lt
Runyon, R. W. Cpl
Rush, A. Fred Sgt
Rushinski, Frank M/ Sgt
Rushton, J. A. Jr. Pvt
Ruth, G. Gerald M/Sgt
Ryder, F. Donald Sgt
Rye, Jaye Sfc
Sakasegawa, G. Pfc
Sakerno, Frank Pfc
Saksa, E. Robert 1st Lt
Sakseiski, F. R. Cpl
Salay, C. Gene Pfc

Salazar, R. Jose Cpl
Salcido, P. Frank Pvt
Salerno, Stefano Cpl
Salina, A. A. Cpl
Sampel, M. C. Sfc
San Nicolas, H. J. Cpl
Sanchez, Jose Pfc
Sanchez, J. A. Cpl
Sanders R. Paul Sfc
Sanders, C. W. Pvt
Sanders, D, John Sgt
Sanders, H. Glen Pfc
Sanders, H. H. Cpl
Sanders, H. W. Sfc
Sanders, L. John Pfc
Sankey, Roosevelt Pfc
Santen, V. Henry Cpl
Santoro, Pasquale Sgt
Sawyer, A. Joe Pvt
Saxon, E. Joe Cpl
Saylor, E. Half Pvt
Saylor, T. Harold Sgt
Sayre, M. George Pvt
Schad, G. J. Alvin Pfc
Schade, B. James M/Sgt
Schadler, R. L. Pfc
Schaefer, T. R. Pfc
Schaffer, C. C. Pfc
Schapp, E. Lowell Pvt
Schemer, M. John Cpl
Scherer, James Sgt
Schlichter, B. C. Sfc
Schlinghoff, M. L. Pvt
Schmidt, C. C. Pfc
Schmidt, W. A. 1st Lt
Schminshke, R. D. Cpl
Schmitt, W. Robert Pvt
Schmitz, J. Herbert Cpl
Schnieder, D. R. Cpl
Schommer, P. C. Pfc
Schultz, E. William Cpl
Schumacher, C. A. Pfc
Schuppan, W. F. Cpl
Schusser, J. H. Sgt
Schwark, D. David Cpl
Schwartz, Fredrick Cpl
Schwitzer, C. F. Cpl
Sclae, E. Leslie Pfc
Sconberg, W. L. Sfc
Scott, Jacob Jr. Pfc
Scott, F. James Cpl
Scott, H. Walter Pfc
Scott, J. James Sgt
Scott, K. Mickey Pfc

Scott, L. Eugene Pfc
Scott, L. Rodney Cpl
Seahill, P. James Cpl
Sealey, J. Thomas Cpl
Searles, C. Fred Cpl
Sedgwick, F. Pfc
Sedotal, J. Junius Pfc
Seibert, E. Gerald Pfc
Serafin, Chester Pfc
Serish, M. Gregory Sgt
Serna, Joe Cpl
Serra, G. John Cpl
Serrano, Eligio Pfc
Servatius, L. Reay Sfc
Settles, W. Robert Cpl
Seymor, A. Ruics 2nd Lt
Shaffer, D. Oren Pfc
Shamwell, L. R. Cpl
Shanklin, Milas Pfc
Shapiro, Aaron Capt
Sharp, S. Maurice Pvt
Shartzer, H. J. Jr. Sgt
Shasffer, F. Lloyd Cpl
Shaw, E. John Cpl
Shay, E. David 2nd Lt
Shedd, P. George 1st Lt
Sheffield, C. E. Cpl
Shelby, White Cpl
Shelton, Roderick Sgt
Shepard, D. R. Sgt
Shephard, R. Cpl
Sheppard, F. R. Cpl
Sherrell, R. W. Pfc
Sherrick, V. D. Cpl
Sherron, W. C. M/Sgt
Shiner, R. Johnnie Pfc
Shipes, P. D. Jr. Pfc
Shirlaw, D. Ronald Major
Shockley, N. W. Pfc
Shoemaker, E. M. M/Sgt
Short, G. Donald Cpl
Siebert, L. Arnold Cpl
Sieueman, E. Dale Sgt
Sifford, J. Daniel Cpl
Signorile, Louis Cpl
Silbey, C. Roscoe Cpl
Sim, L. Norman Cpl
Simmons, A. C. Cpl
Simmons, Tyson Pfc
Simmons, H. Jack Cpl
Simpkins, J. T. Pfc
Simpson, C. R. Pfc
Simpson, E. W. Sgt
Simpson, L. Alfred Pfc

Singleton, G. J. Pvt
Sirk, L. Kenneth Cpl
Sirratt, R. Dewey Sgt
Sisson, K. Marlyn Pfc
Sitler, E. Harold Cpl
Sixemore, L. J. Cpl
Sixen, B. Walter Pfc
Skiles, L. Edward Pfc
Skinner, William Pfc
Skipper, J. William Pfc
Skipper, L. Robert Cpl
Slaten, L. Lindsey Cpl
Slater, K. Harold Maj
Slavens, K. Leland Cpl
Slider, E. Carlton M/Sgt
Smalley, D. Dode Cpl
Smallwood, Stevie Cpl
Smith, D. Ira
Smith, A. R. Sgt
Smith, H. Elijah Cpl
Smith, L. Robert Pfc
Smith, Oliver
Smith, S. Dale Pfc
Smith, S. S. Jr. HM 3
Smith, W. George Cpl
Smith, C. Herbert Pfc
Smith, D. Bennie Cpl
Smith, E. Gerald Cpl
Smith, G. Gerald Pfc
Smith, H. Daniel Sgt
Smith, J. B. Capt
Smith, Jerome Sfc
Smith, L. Edward Sgt
Smith, L. John Cpl
Smith, M. James Pfc
Smith, R. Abner Sgt
Smith, S Edwin WO(1g)
Smith, S. Roy
Smith, T. Bob Sfc
Smith, V. John Cpl
Smith, W. James Cpl
SmitH, R. Earl Sgt
Sneed, O. D. Pvt
Solomon, Oscar Cpl
Soria, Edward Pfc
Sorlano, D. Fred 1st Lt
Sorrells, T. David Cpl
Sorrenson, E. E. Sgt
Sorteberg, D. W. Sfc
Soto, H. Ricardo Cpl
Souder, L. Arthur Cpl
Sourbeer, L. A. Jr. Cpl
South, Jimmy Cpl
Souza, Harold Cpl

Spackman, P. T. Cpl
Spano, Joseph Cpl
Sparks, R. J. Cpl
Spearman, L. M. Cpl
Speer, L. Fred Capt
Spencer, C. Erdis Pfc
Spencer, J. W. Pvt
Sperbecl, G. C. Cpl
Spingola, E. K. Cpl
Spivey, John Sgt
Spivey, P. Walter M/Sgt
Sprouse, R. T. Sfc
Spurlock, Kenneth Cpl
Stackley, F. W. Cpl
Stahlman, E. H. 1st Lt
Stallings, E. J. Cpl
Stanfill, F. Herman 1st Lt
Stanford, C. Levis Sgt
Stanley, A. G. Cpl
Stanley, A. G. Pfc
Stanley, L. James 1st Lt
Stanley, W. Milford Capt
Stapp, J. Floyd Cpl
Starcher, J. A. Sfc
Starnes, H. M. Cpl
Stasko, T. James
Staten, R. Donald Cpl
Stauber, C. Calvin
Staudenmayer, E. Pfc
Stauffacher, V. P. Pfc
Stavrakes, C. W. 1st Lt
Stearns, L. M. Cpl
Steege, E. L. Pfc
Steele, L. Adam Pfc
Steiner, A Harold 1st Lt
Stenson, E. Keith Pfc
Stephens, Henry Pfc
Stevens, C. Gary Pfc
Stevenson, A. R. Cpl
Stewart, W. James Cpl
Stewart, C. Willie Pfc
Stewert, C. D. Pfc
Stice, E. Ivan Cpl
Stick, Louis Jr. Cpl
Still, L. Richard 2nd Lt
Stine, L. James Pfc
Stinnette, Henry Sfc
Stinson, R. Jackie Sgt
Stofa, George Sgt
Stogadill, V. W. Cpl
Stokes, J. Henry M/Sgt
Stone, L. Floyd Pfc
Stone, Willie Jr. Pfc
Stone, A. William Sgt

Stone, L. James 1st Lt
Stone, L. Roy Sgt
Stone, R. Clovis M/Sgt
Storud, W. Ernest Sfc
Story, Roy Sgt
Stotts, E. Glen Cpl
Stough, F. August Pfc
Stout, L. Carl Cpl
Stout, V. Arthur Sfc
Stovall, G. Andrew Cpl
Strachan, A. R. Jr. Cpl
Strahan, A. M. Jr. M/Sgt
Strange, C. W. M/Sgt
Strengh, L. D. Sgt
Stricklan, L. T. Pvt
Stringer, A. F. Pfc
Stroup, L. Lester S/Sgt
Struble, T. Maes M/Sgt
Sub, Andrew Jr. Pfc
Suli, T. Thomas Sgt
Sullivan, E. James Sgt
Sullivan, M. L. John Cpl
Surgrue, Daniel Cpl
Sutterfield, L. M. M/Sgt
Suttles, G. James Sgt
Sutton, D. Carl Sgt
Sutton, J. Claxton M/Sgt
Swain, V. L. Cpl
Swanton, G. Lyle Sgt
Sweeney, J. R. Sgt
Sweeny, H. James
Swenson, L. R. Pfc
Swindell, J. Roger Pvt
Sydnor, S. R. Pfc
T. Donald 1st Lt
Tabor, W. Wesley Sgt
Tackes, F. E. Pfc
Tadashi, Sfc
Talbert, A, James Cpl
Talbert, E. Marvin Sgt
Talbert, H. Joe Pfc
Tallon, P. Eugene Cpl
Tamaki, Yoshio Pfc
Tamaye, Goichi Pfc
Tanigawa, Katsuki M/Sgt
Tanner, A. D. M/Sgt
Tarbuch, Joseph Cpl
Taylor, Clayton Pfc
Taylor, C. Calvin Sgt
Taylor, D. William M/Sgt
Taylor, E. Charles Cpl
Taylor, E. Walace Pvt
Taylor, M. Race Pfc
Taylor, O. James Cpl

Taylor, O. Willious Cpl
Teague, E. P. 1st Lt
Teal, F. H. John Pfc
Tenario, F. Sam Cpl
Teriwilliger, R. D. Pfc
Tesso, D. James Sfc
Teston, C. Ottis Sfc
Thielen, M. Robert Pfc
Thomas, A. Benny Sgt
Thomas, G. W. Sgt
Thomas, K. Otis Sfc
Thomas, O. R. Cpl
Thomas, Solomon Cpl
Thomas, H. T. Pfc
Thomasson, C. C. M/Sgt
Thompkins, P. D. Sgt
Thompson, E. H. Cpl
Thompson, J. M/Sgt
Thompson, L. T. Pvt
Thompson, A. C. Cpl
Thompson, B. W. Pfc
Thompson, L. E. Cpl
Thompson, L. Roy Pfc
Thompson, O. J. Pfc
Thompson, P. S. Sfc
Thompson, R. J. Cpl
Thoms, S. N. Pfc
Thornson. F. E. Sgt
Threat, R. Albert Pfc
Tiarks, M William Cpl
Tickell, R. A. M/Sgt
Tinsley, L. Donald Pfc
Todd, E. William Sgt
Tolan, W. Joseph Cpl
Topping, F. E. Cpl
Torkomian, N. 2nd Lt
Torre, G. Julio Cpl
Torres, E Vicente Sgt
Tosquez, V. N. Cpl
Touey, A . John Sfc
Towner, A. M. Cpl
Tracy, R. James Cpl
Traw F. Cecil Cpl
Traynham, L. R. Cpl
Trejo, Gilberto Sgt
Trent, S. Eldridge Sgt
Trevino, Leonel Sgt
Trevino, B. John Cpl
Tripp, S. Stanley M/Sgt
Tritt, Gilbert Jr, Pfc
Trotter, V. John Cpl
Trudo, R. Donald M/Sgt
True, W. Charles Cpl
Tucker, W. F. Sfc

Tucker, E. James Sfc
Tuckerham, D. W. Pfc
Tuom, J. Mervin Pfc
Tupa, S. Joseph M/Sgt
Tupper, J. Carlyn Sgt
Turner, W. Wilford Cpl
Turner, A. Lewis Cpl
Turner, B. Herbert 1st Lt
Tuscano, E. J. Pfc
Tutono, James Pfc
Tuttle, J. Albert Pfc
Twylog, R. George Cpl
Tyler, L. John Cpl
Underly, D. Ronald Pfc
Upshur, Lawrence Pvt
Vadala, T. Guy Sgt
Valdez, Glicerio Sgt
Valencia, Henry Sgt
Van Pelt, H. G. Sgt
Van De Mark, J. B. Cpl
VanDerLinden, P. Pvt
Vann, H. George Pfc
Vannoy, Hale Sgt
Vanryan, Arie Pfc
Varner, J. Russell Sgt
Vasquez, Manuel Sgt
Velasquez, G. Luis Cpl
Verano, Q. Alberto Sgt
Verghies, Stephen Pfc
Veriakis, Michael Cpl
Vernon, H. A. Cpl
Vernon, L. George M/Sgt
Vieu, J. Herman Pfc
Vigil, C. Leo
Vigil, J. Juan Sgt
Viles, L. Kenneth Pfc
Villafana, David Pfc
Villanueva, T. Cpl
Villareal, R. Robert Pfc
Vincent, E. Robert Cpl
Vincent, J. Leonan Pfc
Vincent, P. William Cpl
Vincere, C. John Pfc
Vinson, N. Richard Cpl
Violet, E. A. Jr. Cpl
Viscuso, J. A. Pfc
Vitale, A. George Cpl
Vitruls, J. Billy Pfc
Vivier, J. Ralph Pfc
Vogel, W. Frank Cpl
Volinski, P. Adam Sgt
Vollers, W. Edwin Sgt
Vosberg, V. James Cpl
Vrabel, Paul Sgt

Wakehouse, L. D. Cpl
Walden, T. George Cpl
Walker, M. Perry Pfc
Walker, E. Albert Pvt
Walker, E. G. Jr. Cpl
Walker, H. John Major
Walker, J. Joseph Cpl
Walker, M. Royce M/Sgt
Wallace, J. Billy M/Sgt
Wallace, M. J. Pfc
Walls, W. Tolbert M/Sgt
Walton, T. Robert Pfc
Warble, L. Dallas Sgt
Ward, A. Thomas Sfc
Ward, G. John Cpl
Warner, L. Robert 1st Lt
Warren, L. Don Cpl
Wary, T. Charles Sgt
Wash, Benjamin Pvt
Wasters, Albert Pvt
Waters, Howard Cpl
Watkins, Ficher M/Sg
Watsin, W. John 1st Lt
Watson, H. William Pfc
Watson, Joseph Pfc
Watson, C. William 1st Lt
Watts, Rolan Sfc
Weaver, T. John Sfc
Webb, E. Milton Pfc
Webb, B. Cyril Sgt
Webber, P. Irvin Cpl
Wegrzyn, M. S. Sfc
Wells, A. John Cpl
Wells, G. Tyre
Wells, J. Richard Cpl
Wem, Robert Sgt
Wendling, R. J. Pfc
Wensaul, N. Floyd Pfc
Wertman, P. Albert Cpl
Wessels, P. Harry Pvt
West, A George Pfc
West, V. Richard Cpl
Western, D. Robert Cpl
Westerson, R. J. Cpl
Wetzler, J. Emil Cpl

Whalen, J. Herman Sgt
Wheeler, L. B. Sgt
Wheeless, L. D. Pfc
Wheller, L. H. Jr. Cpl
Whitacker, A M. Sfc
White, C. Thaddess Cpl
White, Durwood Cpl
White, B. Buster Cpl
White, C. Roger Capt
White, P. Charles M/Sgt
Whiteside, K. W. 1st Lt
Whitlinger, B. J. Pfc
Wickersham, R. O. Sgt
Wicks, T. Fred 1st Lt
Wiggle, R. Robert Pfc
Wilburn, E. William Sgt
Wiley, D. Robert Cpl
Wilkens, G. E. Pfc
Wilkerson, J. A. Pvt
Wilkerson, L. A. Pvt
Wilkins, M. R. S/Sgt
Willenborg, E. M. Cpl
William, L. Troy Cpl
Williams, D. H. Jr. Cpl
Williams, Joseph Sfc
Williams, C. James Capt
Williams, E. Lester Cpl
Williams, Edward Sgt
Williams, F. Charles Sfc
Williams, F. Henry Cpl
Williams, L. M. Pfc
Williams, Rosevelt Sgt
Williams, H. E. M/Sgt
Williamson, E. K. Pfc
Willis, N. John Jr. Cpl
Willmeth, B. L. Cpl
Wilson A. Howard Pvt
Wilson, Clifford Cpl
Wilson, Clyde Jr. Cpl
Wilson, Joseph Pvt
Wilson, Robert Pfc
Wilson, D. Robert Sgt
Wilson, E. Donald Sgt
Wilson, E. James Cpl
Wilson, J. Charles Cpl

Wilson, L. Joyce Pfc
Wilson, R. L. Sfc
Wilson. N. Robert Pfc
Wise, H. Robert Capt
Witt, Johnnie M/Sgt
Woodworth, F. Pfc
Wolf, J. William Pfc
Wolfe, Howard Cpl
Wolfe, D. Marvin Pfc
Wolfe, J. Charles Pfc
Wolfe, L. William Sgt
Wollack, P. R. Sfc
Womack, W. W. Pfc
Wombie, H. Emery Sfc
Wood, E. William Cpl
Woodly, F. Perry Sgt
Woods, H. Gordon Sgt
Woodward, C. T. Pfc
Woolman, E. C. Gt
Worill, W. Frederic M/Sgt
Worley, B. Paul M/Sgt
Wright, G. Gerald M/Sgt
Wright, L. Vernon 1st Lt
Wright, M. James Sgt
Wright, R. Porches M/Sgt
Wurden, G. Bill Cpl
Wysoczynski, C. 1st Lt
Yacko, Peter Pfc
Yaw, L. Leo Sgt
Ybarra, C. Joel Sgt
Yesko, D. Daniel Pfc
Yewchn, Michael Sfc
Yoh, L. Herman Cpl
York, E. Edmond Cpl
Yoss, L. Raymond. Pfc
Young, Oliver Jr. Pfc
Young, R. James Cpl
Young, J. Donald Pfc
Young, Y. K. C. M/Sgt
Young. B. Denny Cpl
Zaiser, F. LLoyd Sgt
Zierer, G. Robet Pfc
Zimomra, Mike Cpl
Zodiacal, Q. G. Sfc
Zwiacher, W. John 1st Lt

[Listing compiled by Sgt. Andrew (Chief) Aguirre, U. S. M. C. R., former Korean War POW, from news reports in 1953]

HONOR ROLL OF FORGOTTEN AMERICANS

The following is a list of U. S. servicemen known to have been held as Prisoners of War by the Red Chinese and North Koreans, but never released nor accounted for by the communists after the war:

United States Army
Cpl. Clarence H. Aki
Pvt. Phillip F. Alcorn
Pfc. Isidoro Arrendondo
Pvt. William R. Bastie Jr.
Pvt. Norman C. Bedell
Pvt. James E. Beller
Cpl. Elton J. Bernard
Cpl. Robert J. Besemer
Cpl. Milson Billigmeir
Cpl. Harold R. Boyd.
Pfc. James B. Brock
Pfc. Otis L. Broome
Pfc. Bill E. Brown
Pfc. James C. Brown.
Pfc. Clifford C. Bull
Pfc. Johnnie J. Buster
Pfc. William V. Buttrey
1st Lt. Roger F. Buxman
Pfc. Henry O. Callis.
Cpl. Andrew Carter
Pvt. James G. Chaney
Cpl. Daniel Chavez
Sgt. Roland W. Clatterbuck
Cpl. William L. Clifton
Pvt. Merle L. Cole Jr.
Pvt. Roy G. Cornell
Cpl. Kenneth L. Cozad
Pfc. Paul E. Craig
Sgt. Irvine T. Crews
Pfc. Jeses Cruz-ramos
Pfc. Donald E. Dahms
Pvt. Ezekiel A. Davis.
Pvt. Dave H. Day
Sgt. Casimire T. Demoll
Pvt. Lawrence K. Desau
Cpl. Richard G. Desautels
Pvt. William L. Dick Jr.
Pvt. Donald R. Dickinson
1st Lt. Paul N. Dill
Pfc. Leroy J. Dove
Pvt. Harold B. Dulyea

Pfc. Roger A. Dumas
Pvt. Daniel A. Elias
Pfc. Emil Lee
Pvt. Junior C. Evans
Pfc. Leo E. Fetzer
Cpl. Ronald Figureid
Pfc. James F. Fischer
Cpl. Willie S. Flores
2nd Lt. John Frech Jr.
Pfc. Lester E. Fulk
Pfc. Terrel J. Fuller
Pfc. Charles B. Garver
Cpl. Homer B. Gilley
Cpl. Gerald W. Glasser
M/Sgt. George R. Goetz r.
Pvt. Donald T. Grenier
Pfc. Arnold G. Gresser
Pfc. Robert L. Grimsley
2nd Lt. Douglas H. Haag
Pvt. Charles D. Hadnot
Pfc. Lawrence A. Harnage
Pvt. Fred W. Harpster
Pvt. Edward S. Harry Jr.
Pvt. Robert E. Haynie
Pvt. Sylvio L. Hebert
Pvt. Kenneth A. Hogan
1st. Lt. Crenshaw A. Holt
Pvt. Philip T. Hoogacker
Pfc. James L. Houston
Pfc. James Howell
Pfc. Donald C. Hoysradt
Pvt. Wayne G. Hughes
Cpl. Leonard C. Hull
Pfc. Donald L. Humiston
Pfc. Mitsuyoshi Ishida
Cpl. Carl E. Jarrett
Cpl. John E. Jennings Jr.
Pvt. Richard Jerome
Pfc. Leonard W. E. Jinks
Pvt. Donald R. Johnson
Pvt. Leroy Johnson
Pvt. Myron Johnson

Cpl. Ray Johnson
Pfc. Kassidy K. Jones
Sgt. Herbert Kalama
Pfc. Elmer C. Kidd
Pvt. Ralph K. King
Pvt. James F. Klinger
Pfc. Anthony Konze
Pfc. Stanley Kost
Pfc. Francis Krygowski
Pfc. John N. Lapointe
Pvt. Walter J. Levitski
Pvt. Orvill F. Linebaugh
Pgt. Billie Litchfield
Spec. 1 Ditlef J. Logoni
Pfc. Alfred Lopez[s] Jr.
Cpl. Ray V. Louviere
Cpl. Angelo S. Malanga
Pvt. Louis R. Masters
Sgt. Donald L. Mattingly
Pfc. William McDowell
Pvt. Clarence McClure Jr.
Cpl. Neil W. Meagher
Pfc. Robert E. Meyers
Pfc. Macario Mireles
Capt. Harry D. Moreland
Cpl. Russel F. Morris
Pfc. Moises Munoz
Cpl. John Nearhood
Cpl. Anthony J. Nicowski
1st Lt. John W. Nystrom
Cpl. Eugene Ottesen
Cpl. Elwood E. Overgard
1st Lt. Alfred G. Peiffer
Pvt. Lyle E. Peterson
Sgt. Maxie L. Pickard
Pfc. Albert G. Pierce
Pfc John W. Pitts
Pfc. Curlous M. Preas
Cpl. John F. Quigg
Pvt. Carl W. Ragin
Cpl. Charles L. Rausch
Sgt. Frank T. Reddick

Cpl. Walker F. Reimer
Pvt. Aggie L. Richie
Pfc. Tracy R. Roden
Pvt. Nokomis J. Rose
Cpl. Charles B. Royer
Pfc. John M. Rozear jr.
Pfc. Jose M. Samora
Spec. 1 James S. Sampson
Pvt. Royal W. Sanford
Pfc. Russell D. Schanck
Pfc. Paul W. Schnepper
Pvt. William D. Schonder
Pfc. Gerald G. Schuring
Pvt. William R. Seggie
Sgt. Luther D. Serwise
Cpl. James W. Sharp
Cpl. Robert A. Shepard
Sgt. Lawrence J. Smith
Pfc. Carol G. Snider Jr.
Pfc. Robert G. Snodgrass
Pfc. William R. Spiller
Pfc. William Springer
Pfc. William H. Steger
Pfc. John T. Sternad
Pfc. Walter Stoeber Jr.
Pfc. Neil H. Stone
Pfc. Marion F. Stumpf
Pfc. John R. Sweeney
Pfc. Contee L. Switzer
1st Lt. Sam O. Takahara
Cpl. George C. Tatarkis
2nd Lt. Mitchell C. Thomas
Pfc. Clarence A. Tish Jr.
Spec. 1 Marvin F. Tomlinson
Cpl. Arnold Toole
Pfc. Louis P. Torres
Pfc. Lloyd L. Tucker
Pfc. Raymond A. Vernon
Pfc. Anthony Vranic
Pvt. Casmir F. Walgzak
Pfc. James A. Wallen
Pvt. Raymond O. Ware
Pvt. Samuel K. Watkins
Cpl. James D. Watson
Pvt. Waddell White
Pfc. Albert Williams
Pvt. Merble E. Wilson
Cpl. Richard L. Wilson
Pfc. Howard W. Winrader
Pfc. Joseph H. Woods
Sgt. Audrey H. Wooster
Pvt. Frank Worley
Cpl. Edward C. Wright
Pfc. Kanji Yoshida

Cpl. Charles H. Young
Pvt. Russell V. Young
Cpl. Frank J. Zawacki

United States Navy
Ens. Thomas C. Biesterveld
Ens. William E. Brown
Lt. (JG) Billy E. Cochran

United States Air Force
1st Lt. Ernest M. Adler
1st Lt. Rolan M. Aikin
Capt. Jack V. Allen
1st Lt. Robert E. Anderson
Capt. Robert B. Andrews
2nd Lt. John W. Arms
1st Lt. Gilbert L. Ashley Jr.
Capt. Arthur M. Austin
Capt. Harold M. Beardall
1st Lt. Donald E. Bell
Sgt. Louis H. Bergmann
1st Lt. Wayne F. Black
1st Lt. Donald D. Bolt
T/Sgt. William J. Botter
A/3C John C. Brennan
Capt. Jackson A. Burrell
1st Lt. Woodrown Burton
1st Lt. Sterling J. Bushroe
Capt. Osborne T. Carlisle
A/2C James A. Cave
S/Sgt. Clarence M. Cherry
Capt. Robert W. Cogswell
Capt. Joseph S. Collins
A/2C Spencer R. Cooper Jr.
1st Lt. John R. Coulter
1st Lt. Alvin E. Crane Jr.
Maj. James F. Crutchfield
Capt. Gene A. Culbertson
1st Lt. Howard J. Davies
S/Sgt. Norman G. Davis
A/2C Willard M. Denn
1st Lt. Albert P. Derosier
M/Sgt. Patrick M. Differ
S/Sgt. Joyce M. Dorsey
S/Sgt. Joseph S. Dougherty
Capt. Victor L. Duer
S/Sgt. James H. Duncan
Capt. Malcolm B. Edens
1st Lt. Emmett O. Evans
Capt. Steve J. Festini
1st Lt. James W. Fleming Jr.
1st Lt. Robert R. Foster
Capt. James A. Foulks jr.

A/1C Alois A. Fuehrer
A/2C James A. Gallant
Capt. Fred H. Garrison
T/sgt. Winifred R. George
Capt. Robert D. Gibb
Lt. Col. Milton G. Glessner Jr
2nd Lt. Newman C. Golden
Sgt. John W. Grahan
T/Sgt. Robert F. Gross
1st Lt. Cornelius P. Guilfoyle
S/Sgt. Marvin L. Guthrie
2nd Lt. Edward S. Guthrie Jr.
T/Sgt. Robert W. Hamblin
T/Sgt. Keith E. Hammon
2nd Lt. Charles A. Harker Jr.
Capt. Guy B. Harrell Jr.
Capt. William T. Haskett Jr.
Capt. Luther R. Hawkins Jr.
A/3C Melvin B. Hays
2nd Lt. David T. Heer
Capt. Arthur Heise
1st Lt. Dewey R. Henry
1st Lt. Warren M. Hoff
1st Lt. William L. Holcom
1st Lt. Scott A. Holz
2nd Lt. John J. Horner
S/Sgt. Arthur W. Hoult
Capt. Howard D. Howell
2nd Lt. Laurence H. Hudson
Capt. Don Hyatt
A/2C Hidemaro S. Ishida
2nd Lt. Harrison C. Jacobs
2nd Lt. Paul J. Jacobson
T/Sgt. Morton H. Jensen
S/Sgt. Wayne F. Jensen
T/Sgt. Johnny M. Johnson
A/3C Gerald E. Johnson
A/3C James L. Jones
1st Lt. Oliver E. Jones
A/1C Jerome Karpowicz
Maj. Kassel M. Keene
1st Lt. Harold O. Keister
A/1C Robert P. Kelleher
Capt. Joseph C. Kepford
1st. Lt. Alfred H. King
1st Lt. Charles F. Kirk
1st Lt. Kingdon R. Knapp
Capt. Raymond J. Knueppel
1st Lt. Frederick R. Koontz
Capt. Robert M. Krumm
1st Lt. Gordon V. Kuehner Jr.
1st Lt. Robert H. Laier
Capt. Hugh F. Larkin
1st Lt. Laurence C. Layton

Capt. Jack Lewis
A/2C Wayne E. Lewis
Capt Lt. Wilbur E. Lewis
Capt. Samuel P. Logan Jr.
Capt. Joseph S. Long Jr.
1st Lt. Dominique K. Martin
S/Sgt. Clifford N. Mast
S/Sgt. Ernest R. McAdoo
1st Lt. John A. McAllaster Jr.
S/Sgt. Claude D. McFee
1st Lt. Robert E. McKee
A/2C Robert J. McLoughlin
1st Lt. Henry D. Miller
S/Sgt. Bernard Mitchell
1st Lt. Ara Mooradian
Capt. John G. Moore
Capt. Thomas E. Myers
2nd Lt. Lawrence A. Nelson
A/2C James L. Nichols
A/1C Rudolf Nikles
Col. Glenn C. Nye
Capt. Warren E. O'Brien
A/2C James J. O'Meara Jr.
Lt. Col. Julius E. O'Neal
A/2C Damian F. O'Toole
1st Lt. Ray W. Olcott
1st Lt. Arthur R. Olsen
A/3C Jess A. Osborne Jr.
Capt. Ernest R. Oyler
1st Lt. Alexander B. Padilla
2nd Lt. Alford C. Palmer.
A/1C Nicholas M. Palmietti
A/2C Charles E. Parham Jr.

1st Lt. James K. Peck
1st Lt. Roger W. Penninger
A/3C Norman W. Peterson
A/1C Ralph L. Phelps
2nd Lt. Duane M. Phillips
1st Lt. Herbert Pincus
A/2C James D. Pope
A/1C James H. Porter
1st Lt. Com F. Poyner
Capt. Charles W. Pratt
S/Sgt. Gerald W. Raymond
1st Lt. Harry M. Rehm
1st Lt. Charles W. Rhinehart
1st Lt. Herbert E. Ritter
A/2C Daryl E. Rodney
Capt. Fred D. Rountree
1st Lt. Gilbert J. Schaner
Capt. Norman W. Schmidt
A/2C Warren W. Schmitt
A/2C Edward A. Schwab
1st Lt. Clifford G. Selman
2nd Lt. John P. Shaddick III
1st Lt. Robert E. Sheenan
Capt. Thomas L. Shields
2nd Lt. James D. Smith Jr.
1st Lt. Johns E. Southerland
1st Lt. Charles R. Spath
Maj. Marvin J. Spence
A/1C Robert R. St. Mary
1st Lt. John S. Starck
1st Lt. Robert C. Steele
S/Sgt. Frank L. Stevenson
2nd Lt. Bruce A. Sweney.

Maj. Meach Tahasquah
2nd Lt. Charles R. Thompson
S/Sgt. Raymond Thompson
Sgt. Philip W. Tilch
M/Sgt. Horace N. Tiller
Capt. Archie P. Trantham
1st Lt. Harold P. Turner
1st Lt. James A. Van Fleet Jr.
A/2C William N. Vanwey
1st Lt. Edward C. Wahigren
A/2C Edward A. Webb
S/Sgt. Grady M. Weeks
A/2C Carl E. West
S/Sgt. William H. Whitman
S/Sgt. Kenneth E. Williamson
2nd Lt. Thelbert B. Wormack
Sgt. George W. Worth Jr.
2nd Lt. Joseph P. Ziegler

United States Marine Corps
Pfc. Gerald R. Bookamire
Col. Arthur A. Chidester
2nd Lt. Arthur D. Delacy
Maj. James K. Eagan
2nd Lt. James A. Gleaves Jr.
Pfc. James L. Green
Pfc William T. Lewis Jr.
Pfc. Billy J. Morrow
1st Lt. Forest A. Nelson
Pfc. Charles A. Taylor
Pfc. Raymond J. Tuttle
Pfc. Robert J. Young

[This document has been distributed through and corrected and edited by Mary and Chuck Schantag, of the POW Network. Located at http://www.asde.com/~/pownet]

266

THE FINAL HONOR ROLL KOREAN WAR CASUALTIES, 1950-1954

OFFICIAL LISTING OF THOSE WHO DIED WHILE IN CAPTIVITY

Abbott Charles L Pvt
Abbott Richard F Sfc
Abney Homer R Cpl
Adams Aubrey G Pvt
Adams Bosie Pfc
Adams Charles N Pfc
Adams Daryl T Pvt
Adams Harry L Pfc
Adams Raymond J Sfc
Adams Robert C Pfc
Adams Robert I 1lt
Adams Ronald H Pfc
Adams William H 1lt
Adams William R 1lt
Adams Willie G Jr Cpl
Adkins Clifford Pfc
Aetonu Litisoni Sgt
Agrell Carleton V Pfc
Aguilar Richard Pfc
Akers Herbert D Pfc
Akers Richard 1lt
Akins Willis L Pvt
Albrecht John Pfc
Ales Marion L 1lt
Alexander Charles Pfc
Alexander Jack D Pfc
Alexander Lonnie V Pfc
Alford Raymond K Pvt
Allemand Percy Pvt
Allen Charles Cpl
Allen Earnest Sgt
Allen Herbert L Pvt
Allen John A Jr Pvt
Allen Raymond L Cpl
Allen Walter E Pfc
Allums Morris Sfc
Ames William H Pfc
Ampon Joseph O Cpl
Anderson Billy N Sgt
Anderson Dewey R Cpl
Anderson Douglas R Capt
Anderson Ellsworth Pfc
Anderson John Msgt

Anderson Larry J Pvt
Anderson Norbert O Pfc
Anderson Omer L Cpl
Andino Perez Emili Pvt
Andring Arnold V Cpl
Angelakos Nick W Cpl
Angell Eugene L Pfc
Angevine Robert H Cpl
Antrom Joseph Pfc
Anzaldua Baldomero Cpl
Apodaca Abie L Pfc
Appenfelder Joseph 1lt
Archer Robert G Pfc
Arias Lawrence L Sgt
Arionus Lyman H Pfc
Armour James L Sfc
Armstrong John D Pvt
Armstrong William Pvt
Arpke Ray L Cpl
Arthur Patrick J Sgt
Asbury James W Cpl
Asher Ollie R Pfc
Ashworth Huey Pfc
Aten Fred W Pfc
Atherton Harold J Pfc
Avelino Domino T Sfc
Axtell Everett J Sfc
Ayen Donald J Sfc
Ayo Alberr J Pvt
Bach Richard B Cpl
Bailey Charles V Cpl
Bailey Earl T Cpl
Bailey James Pfc
Bailey Otis C Cpl
Bak Joseph Pfc
Baker Baxter L Jr Maj
Baker Donald L Pfc
Baker Frank Pfc
Baker Walter R Pfc
Bakie Donald L Pfc
Baldwin Lawrence Cpl
Balentine Ralph B Pfc
Balfour George F Pfc

Ballantyne James L Pfc
Balls James H Pfc
Bamford Charles M Sfc
Banach Stanley Pvt
Banks Earl Sgt
Barber Franklin H Pfc
Barchesky Lester V Sgt
Barder Billy L Cpl
Barker Ronald R Pfc
Barker William T Cpl
Barlow Duane F Pfc
Barnes David Porter 1lt
Barnes Herbert R Pvt
Barnes Len Cpl
Barnett George J Sgt
Barnett Ivey G Pvt
Barnett Murray W Cpl
Baron John Pfc
Barra Michael J Cpl
Barron Lawrence H Cpl
Barry Arthur Pfc
Bart Davey H Pfc
Barter Charles T Maj
Barter Frederick W Cpl
Basha Freddie Pvt
Bassett Henry D Pvt
Bauer Gerald Pvt
Baulk Richard E Pvt
Baxter Donald T Cpl
Beahm Thomas J Pvt
Bean Frederick B Cpl
Beard Harold E Jr Pfc
Beasley Clifford D Cpl
Beauchesne Alfred Sfc
Beaulieu Richard J Pfc
Becker Clarence R Pfc
Becker Ferrill Pvt
Beckham Larry E Pvt
Becklin Charles W Pvt
Beddingfield Fred Pfc
Beecher Wilbert C Pvt
Beed Milton M Sgt
Begley Frank E Cpl

267

Behringer Russell Msgt
Bell Charlie Cpl
Bell James M Cpl
Bell Thomas L Cpl
Bell Vesteen Jr Pvt
Bellamy Clyde Hughes A1c
Belton Wyatt H Sgt
Bender Ralph Pfc
Benefiel James W Pvt
Benner Warren W Pvt
Bensinger Alfred G Sgt
Berardi Thomas H Pfc
Berg Walter E Pvt
Berge Ralph O Pvt
Bergeron Joseph E Pfc
Bergman William J 1lt
Berrier Jackie G Pvt
Berry A D Msgt
Berry Bemnny Pvt
Berry James Pvt
Berry Richard W Pvt
Bevels Charles M Cpl
Beverley John H Jr Pfc
Beville Roger Cpl
Bevivino Bruno D Msgt
Bey Floyd T Cpl
Bienz Robert E Cpl
Bies Ronald S Pfc
Bilyeu Michael G Pvt
Bishop Arthur L Pfc
Bishop Lester E Pfc
Bishop Theodore C 1lt
Bissell James R Cpl
Bivens William F Capt
Black James E Pvt
Black James M Sfc
Black Vance Eugene Ltc
Blackwell Turner F Cpl
Blair Merviol W Pfc
Blakely Robert E Pfc
Blanchard Joseph L Cpl
Blahchfield Robert Pfc
Blataric Thomas J Pvt
Blevins Herene K Pvt
Blissenbach Joseph Sgt
Block Gerald V Cpl
Blosser David F Pfc
Blowers Ormar G Cpl
Blue Adelbert Pfc
Blue Clois M Sr Sgt
Blue George J Cpl
Bobbs John W Cpl
Bobovnyk James E Pfc
Boettcher Bruce D Pfc

Bogert John Jr Pfc
Bolden C G Pfc
Bolles Lloyd J Pvt
Bolton William M Maj
Bond Elihue Jr Pfc
Bonner William N Pfc
Booker George G Pvt
Booker Oscar L Pvt
Books Arthur H 1lt
Booth Ize Pvt
Boothroyd Albert E Pfc
Bordeau Alfred C Pvt
Borum James Pfc
Bostic David Jr Cpl
Boswell Elvin L Pfc
Bothwell Glenn R 1lt
Botsford Philip Pfc
Bounds Robert L Sgt
Bowen Edward M Cpl
Bowers James E Pfc
Bowers Lester J Pvt
Bowser Lemuel R Pfc
Bowser Roland L Pvt
Bowstring Benny Cpl
Boyd Alton C Pvt
Boyd Donald W Pfc
Boyden Melvin Pfc
Boyer Charles E Cpl
Boyiddle Silas W Pvt
Bradford Leonard C Sgt
Bradford Ulysses H Capt
Bradley Edgar N Pfc
Bradley Eldon R Pfc
Bradley George W Sfc
Bradley Oscar S Cpl
Bradley Thomas B Cpl
Brady John T Pfc
Bragg Clifton C Sfc
Branch Charles S Nsgt
Branch Melvin Pfc
Brandenburg Kennet Cpl
Brander Donald S Lpl
Brandt Arnold N Ltc
Branton J W Sgt
Brassfield Harry Msgt
Bratton Lewis W Hsgi
Braud Claude Pfc
Braun Sylvester Pfc
Bredeson Arlin S Cpl
Breeden Harry B Pvt
Breedlove Roy G Pvt
Bresett Lloyd H Pfc
Brewer Morris D Peg
Bridges Anice D Cpl

Bridgett James N Pfc
Briggs Raymond I Sfc
Bringe Donald P Pfc
Brockman Clarence Pfc
Brockman John J 1lt
Brooks Clifton E Pvt
Brooks Gilbert B Cpl
Brooks John W Jr Pvt
Brousseau Philip F Sgt
Brown Albert L Pvt
Brown Alfred R Cpl
Brown Andrew B Pfc
Brown Anthony E Sfc
Brown Arthur L Pfc
Brown Carlton H Sgt
Brown Charles O Pfc
Brown Dale E Pfc
Brown Daniel K Sgt
Brown David O Pvt
Brown Edwin E Pfc
Brown Garland S Sfc
Brown Harold M Sgt
Brown Isaac Pfc
Brown Joseph C Cpl
Brown Lawrence L Pfc
Brown Robert E Pvt
Brown Robert E Pfc
Brown Shelby B Jr Pvt
Brown William E Jr Pfc
Brown Willaih F Pfc
Brown William L Jr Cpl
Brucker Richard C Pfc
Bruno Lawrence Sgt
Brunson Jerome Cpl
Bryan Richard Pfc
Bryant David Cpl
Bryant Leroy W Pvt
Bryant Robert Sgt
Buchan Eldon R Pfc
Bucheit Robert C Sgt
Buckley Dennis D Pfc
Buckley James W Pfc
Buettner Bernard C Pfc
Buff Jack Y Msgt
Buford Gregory E Pvt
Buik Herbert E Pvt
Bulkowski George Capt
Bullard Jerry E Sgt
Bullis Milton T Pfc
Bullock Frank N Cpl
Bumstead Gerald F Pfc
Bunnell Hubert K Sgt
Bunnell Robert J Sfc
Bunting Worth L Cpl

Burchfield Riley Sgt
Burdue Wayne H Maj
Burgess Damon Sgt
Burgess Preston M Cpl
Burke David S Pvt
Burnett Raymond M Pfc
Burnett Robert R Cpl
Burns Francis T Cpl
Burns John J Pfc
Burns Peter J Pfc
Burr Donald K Cpl
Burrer Guenther Msgt
Burrows John K 1lt
Burton George R Pfc
Burton Robert C Pfc
Burton Samuel R Pfc
Buskirk George E Pvt
Bussiere Paul J F Pfc
Butler Billy J Pfc
Byers Charles E Pvt
Byrd Curtis P Cpl
Byrd James W 1lt
Byrom Delbert Cpl
Cabral Richard J Sgt
Cahalan Daniel E Cpl
Cain Sidney G Pfc
Caldwell Alvin O Sgt
Caldwell Howard O 1lt
Caldwell William S Pfc
Callahan Carlis J Sfc
Callahan Lewis R Cpl
Cameron Owen J Sgt
Campbell Booker T Pfc
Campbell Charles C Cpl
Campbell Clark G Ltc
Campbell Howard V Sgt
Campbell James E Cpl
Campbell Jimmie R Sgt
Cantrell Neal P Sgt
Cantrelle Joseph M Cpl
Cantu Arturo Sfc
Cantu Jesus R Sfc
Caperton Herbert Sfc
Capizzi John N Pfc
Capozzi Albert C Cpl
Cardona Orlando Pvt
Carey Gerald D Pvt
Carlson Norman G Cpl
Carlson Ralph W Cpl
Carman Lyle H Pfc
Carnes Harry Z Pfc
Carr Baldwin R 1lt
Carr Benjamin F Sfc
Carr Ralph R Sfc

Carr Thomas G Sgt
Carrier Charles L Capt
Carrouth Ralph N Pfc
Carter James E Pfc
Carter James R Pfc
Carter Lloyd L Pfc
Carter William J Pfc
Casey Raymond J Pfc
Casper Charles D Pfc
Cassidy Boyd W Pfc
Catlin David L Pfc
Catt Alva E Sgt
Catrell Merlin L Pfc
Caul Wilbur O Pvt
Caution William E Sgt
Ceasor James Pfc
Cecot Robert Pfc
Chambers Bennie E Pvt
Champion Felipe Pvt
Chandler Robert C Pfc
Chaney Dean D Sgt
Chang Albert S Cpl
Chapman Richard Pfc
Chapman Sam Sfc
Chapman Samuel Pfc
Chappelle James R Pvt
Charland Richard B Cpl
Charles Raymond M Pfc
Chatfield Fred T Cpl
Chavez Albert J Pfc
Cheatam John B Jr Cpl
Cheatem George L Sgt
Cheff Louis Pvt
Cherry R B Pfc
Chesnut Fred D Maj
Chezek James F Cpl
Childress Ernest Sgt
Childs Robert L Pfc
Chinn Leonard K Sfc
Chipman Herbert W Sfc
Choat Loyd L Pvt
Choate Joseph D Pfc
Cholewsky Alphonsu Msgt
Christensen Jerry Sfc
Christian Stuart B Pvt
Christiana John B Pfc
Ciucci George L Pfc
Clairmont Donald J Cpl
Clanton Robert W Pfc
Clark Basil L Sgt
Clark Glen J Cpl
Clark Glenn M Pvt
Clark Harold R Pvt
Clark James R Cpl

Clark Keith K Pvt
Clark Oc Jr Pvt
Clark Virgil D Pfc
Clarke Harry B Pvt
Clarkson Thomas Jr Cpl
Clarno Edward W Pvt
Clayton Claud Sfc
Clayton Phillip Pfc
Cleveland Hereford Pfc
Cline Charles J Pfc
Clinkscale Harold Pvt
Closson Archie J Pvt
Clouse Bernard C Cpl
Cloutier Robert J Cpl
Cloutman Rodney F Capt
Cobb Donald S Pfc
Cochenour James M Msgt
Cochran Billy G Cpl
Coers Burt N Ltc
Cohick Floyd E Pfc
Coke Richard B Jr 1lt
Coker Cecil Pfc
Coker Floyd T Pvt
Cole John M Jr Sfc
Coleman Gilbert T Pfc
Coleman Norris L Capt
Colford Wilbur B Pvt
Coller Raymond H Cpl
Collins Edward H Sgt
Colon Perez Jose S Pfc
Compton Charles T Pfc
Conaway Perry J Pvt
Conely Ulysses Msgt
Conger James M Sgt
Conlon Owen H Pfc
Conner Connie M Pfc
Connick Karl F Pfc
Connolly Mark Pvt
Connor Normand P Cpl
Contiliano Mario Pvt
Cook Eli W Pvt
Cook Harry W Jr Pfc
Cook James D Sgt
Cook Thomas H Pfc
Cooke Vincent H Pfc
Coon Ellis Sgt
Cooper Billie J Cpl
Cooper Joseph Cpl
Cooper Norwood C Pvt
Coraci Th0mas J Pvt
Corbin James W Pfc
Corder Doyle E Pfc
Cormier Ferman Pfc
Cornell Frederick Cpl

Cornell James H Sgt
Corney Samuel Cpl
Corona Jaime Pvt
Correa Jesus D Pfc
Coskey John H Pfc
Costa Anthony E Cpl
Coston Metro Msgt
Cotrill Robert E Pfc
Coulter Leon S Pfc
Counts Ernest Pvt
Court Thomas H Cpl
Cowan William W Pvt
Cox Calvin M Sgt
Cox Jansen C 1lt
Cox Lester Cpl
Cox Malcolm R Jr 1lt
Cox Robert C Cpl
Cox Walter J Pfc
Cox William O Pfc
Crater Willie Pfc
Crawford Charles E Sfc
Crawford Garland D Capt
Crawford Noland F Cpl
Crawford Paul D Sgt
Crawford Robert L Msgt
Crawford William L Pvt
Crawley Benjamin R Cpl
Crayton Thomas Sfc
Criswell Reed Pfc
Crockett John O 2lt
Crosby Lloyd B Pfc
Crowder Donald G Pfc
Crowell Allen B Pvt
Crutchman Roy S Pfc
Culpepper Bobby R Pfc
Cummins Zolton Pfc
Cunningham Jack J Cpl
Curley George A Jr Pvt
Currie John W Jr Pfc
Curry Maurice L Pvt
Curtis· Albert N Msgt
Curtis Harold L Cpl
Curtis Jack Pfc
Cushing Jess M Pvt
Cushman Richard G Sgt
Dagenhart Manville Pfc
Dally Kenneth H Sfc
Dalszys Joseph Pvt
Daly Wallace J Sgt
Damewood Louis Pfc
Daniel Richard Pvt
Daniels Curtis L Pvt
Daniels Hansel Cpl
Dankowski Alex Sgt

Dansberry Richard Pvt
Darmstadt Laurence Pfc
Davenport Henry Pvt
Davey Gerald J Cpl
Davis Alfred L Sfc
Davis Finley J Sfc
Davis George P Pfc
Davis John G Sfc
Davis Leo C Pvt
Davis Norman R Pfc
Davis Richard Sfc
Davis Sam H Pfc
Davis Weldon Pvt
Davis Willie Pvt
Dawson Norman F Pvt
Dawson Perry A Capt
Dawson Wallace J Cpl
Day Donald Pvt
Day Horace W Cpl
De Anda Daniel Pfc
De Cicco Leo N Pvt
De Luca Leslie J Pfc
De Young Reginald Pvt
Dean Alvin C Cpl
Dean CharlesPfc
Dean Ercel W Sgt
Deer With Horns Wi Pvt
Dehaan Joseph N Pfc
Dehner William W Cpl
Delauter Roy C Cpl
Demmin Dale Pfc
Demski Bernard Pfc
Dennard Ray Pfc
Dennis Vivan Sfc
Denson Lynwood L Pfc
Denson William M Pvt
Dentz James L Pfc
Desautels Richard Cpl
Detamore Robert G Pfc
Devone Goerge D Pfc
Dewey Delbert F Pfc
Dewey James D Cpl
Dewey Lee Pvt
Dews Joseph G Sfc
Di Domenico Mark R Pvt
Diaz Donald D Ltc
Dibble Donald E Cpl
Dick Myron G Sgt
Dickerson Dallas W Pvt
Dickinson Matthew Pvt
Didur Alexander Capt
Diekman Harold F Cpl
Diekmann Lester H Cpl
Dillard Floyd N Pfc

Dillon Frank A Jr Pfc
Dinerboiler Milton Pvt
Dingle Harry Waldo Capt
Dingman Wilbert I Cpl
Dirksen Abraham Jr Pfc
Dixon Charles R Pfc
Dixon Drryl D Pfc
Dixon Rooselvelt Jr Sgt
Dixon Willie F Pfc
Dobbie Robert B Msgt
Dobbs J B Pfc
Dobie King D Cpl
Dodgers Furman Pfc
Donaglia Vicenzo G Pvt
Donnelly William F Cpl
Donovan George T Sfc
Doolittle Norrie C Sgt
Dorrance James L Sgt
Doss Theodore R Pfc
Doucette Anthony C Pfc
Doufexis Th0mas L Pfc
Dougherty Bernard Pfc
Douglass William E Pfc
Downing Clarence C Pfc
Doxie Paul Sgt
Doyle Lawrence Pfc
Drainer John D Pfc
Drake Robert E Cpl
Drennen Hugh J Sfc
Dressler Carl W Sgt
Drew Charles F Pfc
Du Bose Clyatt R Pfc
Dudley Charles B Pfc
Duff Donald L Sgt
Duke Ray E Sfc
Duncan Lester Pfc
Duncan William E Pfc
Duncan Hyatt G Jr Sfc
Dungen Herman Pfc
Dunham Leland R Maj
Dunlap Alva F Pfc
Dunlap John G Pfc
Dunn Francis Pfc
Dupuy Glen M Pvt
Dutton Billie J Pvt
Dye Richard Cpl
Dyondya Michael Pvt
Dzienis John J Pfc
Eads Avon E Cpl
Eagan James Keyser Ltc
Earl James E Sgt
Early Elbyrne O Cpl
Eason James L Pfc
Easterday Charles Pfc

Eaton Edward D Cpl
Eaton John O Pfc
Eckhart Joseph H Pfc
Edgar William T Cpl
Edge Edward C Pfc
Edmonds James L Pvt
Edmonds Lester E Cpl
Edwards Coleman Cpl
Edwards Donald Cpl
Edwards Paul K Pfc
Eheler Donald L Pfc
Eide John Cpl
Eklund Edwin G Jr Capt
Eldredge Harry F Cpl
Elliott Roy E Sfc
Ellis Emanuel Cpl
Ellis John F Capt
Ellison Conwell G Pfc
Elmore Johnnie Jr Pfc
Emott Robert P Cpl
Emory Paul Jr Pvt
Encinas Richard C Cpl
Enfinger Edgar Sgt
Engelman Harvey G Pfc
England Cary J Cpl
England Horace S Sgt
Englehart Robert N Pfc
English Lemuel L 2lt
English Vernon R Cpl
Enlow Dale T Pfc
Enos Gordon F Cpl
Erickson Eugene L Pvt
Espelin Oscar E Ltc
Estes Edward E Pfc
Estes Robert V Pfc
Evans Alexander Cpl
Evans Edward R Cpl
Evans Floyd R Pfc
Evans Jess E Ltc
Evans Joseph K Sgt
Evans Joseph W Pvt
Evans Robert L Sgt
Evans Thomas B Jr A1c
Evans Vernon L Pvt
Evants Bobbie Sgt
Everhart Leonard V Pfc
Ewing Grant H Pfc
Fabbi Ernest Pvt
Fahrmeyer Kermit C Pfc
Falk Herman L Jr 1lt
Fallis Orson D Cpl
Fallon Richard L Pvt
Fallorina Pivo Pfc
Falls Eino E Cho

Fancher Harold S Pfc
Fanning Clyde Cpl
Farfan Lawrence B Cpl
Farler Hugh Phillip Maj
Farone William M Cpl
Farrell William T Pvt
Farthing Robert J Maj
Fastner Michael C Msgt
Faulkner Lynn R Pvt
Feder Walter C Pvt
Feenstra Raymond Sgt
Felton Thomas E Pvt
Fennell Isaac Jr Sgt
Fern James E Pfc
Ferry Richard P Pfc
Field Joseph F Pvt
Filarecki Edward J Cpl
Filler Donald L Pvt
Filloon Richard D Pfc
Findlay Edward H Cpl
Fine Richard M Pfc
Fink James W Sgt
Finley Green Jr Pvt
Fischer William R Pfc
Fisher John Pvt
Fitzgerald Edward Pfc
Fitzgerald John J Pfc
Flaherty Michael W Pfc
Flanagan Thomas E Pfc
Flauger Ervin J Pfc
Fleming Cecil L Pfc
Fleming Frederick Sgt
Fleming John Pvt
Fleming Ronald R Pvt
Fletcher John E Pfc
Fletcher Robert S Pfc
Flook Grady H Pfc
Florczyk Edward S Pvt
Flowers Henry E Sfc
Fluegel Martin C Cpl
Fluellen Elmer Sfc
Fochler Donald G Pfc
Fogle Billy G Cpl
Foley Charles T Pfc
Fontenot Joseph W Pfc
Foote Victor Gene Ssgt
Forbes Charles M Cpl
Ford James R Cpl
Ford Joe L Pfc
Ford John W Sgt
Ford Norman R Cpl
Ford Wilbert S Cpl
Forehand Thomas Sfc
Foreman Ira L Cpl

Fort Walter C Pfc
Fountain Andrew F Msgt
Fox Eldon E Pfc
Fox F C Cpl
Fox Louis D Jr Cpl
Fox Robert L Pvt
Franklin Hiram Pfc
Franklin John D Jr Pvt
Franklin Richard L Sgt
Frantz George Pvt
Frantzich Albert G 1lt
Frazier Hugh R Cpl
Frazier Reginald E Pvt
Frechette Charles Pfc
Fresen Richard D Msgt
Freund Aloysius J Sgt
Freytag Reuben W Sgt
Friday James F Cpl
Friley William P Pfc
Fringeli Ralph G Pvt
Frisk Robert D Pfc
Fry Jesse L Jr Sfc
Fujimoto Junichi Pvt
Fulk Lester E Pfc
Fullbright Gerald Sgt
Fullerton Harold O Pvt
Funa John F Pfc
Funkhouser Marvin Sgt
Furlow Robert D Pfc
Furman Walter F Pvt
Furst John Sgt
Futch Arvous Cpl
Gage Kenneth Leroy A1c
Gailey Robert G Cpl
Gaitan Jimmie J Pvt
Galberth Thomas P Pvt
Gallacher Donald J Cpl
Gallegos Frank R Cpl
Galloway Arnold C Sgt
Galt Robert L Jr Pfc
Gamble Calvin D Pvt
Gambrel Harry P H Pvt
Gantt Joseph E Sgt
Garcia Bennie Pfc
Garcia Charles M Cpl
Garcia Cresenciano Cpl
Garcia Roger B Pfc
Gardner Elmer D Pvt
Gardner Maurice P Pfc
Gardner William Cpl
Garrett George R Pfc
Garrison Charles Lt
Gary Louis Pvt
Garza Alberto B Sgt

Garza Nicolas C Pvt
Gass Bill B Cpl
Gately Donald W Pfc
Gayles Alvin Pfc
Gearhart William R Pvt
Geary Sterling Jr Pvt
Gedney Robert E Pfc
Gehman Robert Allen 1lt
Geisler Donald B Cpl
Geissler Richard J Cpl
George Edward Pvt
Gerrity Daniel W Pvt
Geurin M C Jr Pfc
Ghinazzi Mario R Pfc
Gibson Charles V Pfc
Gibson Hal T 1lt
Gibson Karl H Sgt
Gibson Hillard M Cpl
Gilbert Robert G Pvt
Gilford Robert J Pfc
Gill Charles L 1lt
Gill Eugene C Sfc
Gillette Robert L Pvt
Gilliam Volney H Cpl
Gipson Jim Sgt
Girona Emil J Sgt
Giroux Frederick J 1lt
Gladkowski Alphons Cpl
Glaise Edgar S Pfc
Glass Cecil R Pvt
Glasser Gerald W Cpl
Glenn Philip K 1lt
Glessner Billy F Pfc
Glover Ralph L Cpl
Goering Carl G Maj
Gohl Lavern P Pvt
Goins Martin L Pfc
Golden Alphonce Sfc
Goldsborough Paul Pfc
Gonzales Andrew L Pfc
Gonzales Henry C Pfc
Gonzales Joe Pvt
Goodall Robert Pvt
Goodin James L Msgt
Goodrum William E Pfc
Goody James E Sgt
Goosby Connie Pfc
Gordon Clarence J Cpl
Gordon Paul M Cpl
Gorman Kenneth J Sgt
Goss Patrick J Pvt
Goudlock David J Cpl
Gracey Burton Sgt
Graff Herman L Jr Pfc

Graham David L Cpl
Graham James J Pvt
Graham Robert P Pfc
Graham William M Cpl
Grahl Hans W Pfc
Gramberg Bernard M 1lt
Granillo Martin L Pfc
Grant Johnny W Pvt
Graveline Ernest L Capt
Graves Ben H Cpl
Graves Robert E Cpl
Graves Winston Sgt
Grazier Jack R Pfc
Greco Edward L Pfc
Green Elwood Msgt
Green George L Pfc
Green James L Cpl
Green Kenneth L Sgt
Green Walter W Pvt
Green Ward M Cpl
Greenwood Carroll Cpl
Greenwood Donald R Pfc
Gregg Levern Cpl
Gregory Robert S Cpl
Greis Raymond C Maj
Gressens Norman J Cpl
Grier Alonzo Sgt
Grieve John D 2lt
Griffin Charles W Sfc
Griffin Dower L Jr Pfc
Griffin James E Pvt
Griffin William J Pvt
Griffith Harold W Pfc
Griffith William G Pvt
Griffiths Jack D Capt
Grifford George P Pfc
Griggs Harry Pfc
Grimm Norman Sgt
Grissom Delmer R Pfc
Groleau Robert G Pfc
Groom Ivan W Pfc
Gross Myron E Pvt
Gross Walter F Pvt
Groves Alva C Pfc
Gualtiere Daniel P Pvt
Gudger Joseph D Cpl
Guerrero Julian Pfc
Guess Ray M Pfc
Guidry Joseph Cpl
Gunderson Raymond Pfc
Gunnell Arthur S Cpl
Gupton Willard H Pvt
Gustafson Dale R Sfc
Gustafson Harold W Pvt

Gustafson Henry L Pvt
Guynn John E Pfc
Haase Elvin W Cpl
Hackenberg Walter Pvt
Hagan James E Jr Pfc
Hagen Ronald W Pvt
Haggard Billy M Pfc
Haigh Raymond C Jr Pfc
Haker Gerald J Pfc
Halbert George R Pfc
Haley Richard Msgt
Hall Arthur J Sfc
Hall Arthur P Cpl
Hall Harold T Pfc
Hall John W Cpl
Hallum Leonard D Pvt
Halsor Kenneth N Pvt
Hamelin Marvin G Pfc
Hamershy Russell G Pfc
Hamilton Clyde Pvt
Hamilton James H Pfc
Hamilton Merlin J Sgt
Hamilton Raymond W Pvt
Hancock George R Pfc
Handley Danny J Pvt
Handy Raymond T Pvt
Haney Marvin 1lt
Hanke Robert H Pvt
Hannah Gordon L Sgt
Hannah Morgan H Pfc
Hannan Thomas F Pfc
Hannon Arthur T Pfc
Hansel Earl H Pfc
Hansen Dan H Pvt
Hansen Floyd M Sgt
Hansen Robert T Msgt
Hanshaw Harold C Pvt
Hansinger Nicholas Pvt
Hanson Harlan B Pvt
Hanson William W Sfc
Harbour Ronald E Pvt
Harder Norwood H Pvt
Hardman Kester B Cpl
Hardy David E Cpl
Hardy Edgar W Sfc
Hare James R Pfc
Harget James Cpl
Hargrove Oscar H Pfc
Harkness Harry E Sgt
Harmon John Sgt
Harper William L Cpl
Harrington James Pvt
Harris Artheria M Pfc
Harris Charles M Sgt

Harris Edward P Pvt
Harris Henry C Cpl
Harris John T Cpl
Harris Major M Pfc
Harris Max E Sgt
Harris Paul Cpl
Harris Richard L Sgt
Harris Robert C Cpl
Harris Robert L Pfc
Harris Rudolph Sfc
Harris Thomas W Pvt
Harris Walter Cpl
Harris William R Capt
Harrison Bannie Jr Pfc
Harrison Henry G Pvt
Hart Michael J Jr Pfc
Hart Robert H Pfc
Hartman Roger W 1lt
Hartmann Harry J Pvt
Hartwell George E Sfc
Harvey William R Cpl
Hastie John C Capt
Hastings Donald W Pvt
Hatch Gene N Cpl
Hatley William H Pvt
Haugen Richard D Capt
Havranek Erwin Pfc
Hawkins Julius W Sgt
Hawkins Ralph E Pfc
Hay Kenneth V Pfc
Hayes Randolph Pfc
Hayman James R Pfc
Hays Sandy Sfc
Head Richard G Pvt
Head Roy E Sfc
Healy Daniel E Cpl
Heard Sam Pvt
Hearn John E Pfc
Heath Leslie R Pfc
Heath Richard C Sfc
Hedgepeth Dollie Pfc
Hedges Edwin G Pfc
Hee Walter L Sfc
Heffley Edgar S Pvt
Hefta Kenneth Cpl
Heidelberg Willie Pfc
Heilman Ernest L R Pfc
Helman Glenwood C Pvt
Helms Eugene Pfc
Henig Francis B Pfc
Henness Jimmy E Pvt
Henry Leo Jr Pfc
Henslee Allan M 1lt
Hensley Bird Jr Ssgt

Henson Alfred Jr Cpl
Hernandez Luis Cpl
Herrick Virgil B Cpl
Herrin Donald R Cpl
Herrington Garland Cpl
Herrington Robert Pfc
Hess Edward J Jr Pvt
Hess Kenneth L Pvt
Hesseltine Herbert Cpl
Hester Joseph C Sfc
Hester Will H Pvt
Hetzler Thurman B Pvt
Hickenbottom Dougl Cpl
Hicks Chester S Pfc
Hicks Francis P Pfc
Hicks Kenneth A Sr Sfc
Hicks Tommy V Cpl
Hiers Ansel C Sgt
Higgins Frederick Pfc
Hilgenberg Earl E Sgt
Hill Donald G Pvt
Hill Melvin J Pvt
Hill Thomas L Pfc
Hill Xavier W Cpl
Hillen James W Pvt
Hinckley Homer C Ltc
Hoak Charles R Pfc
Hobart Richard H Pfc
Hobin Donald E Pfc
Hockaday Andrew B Sfc
Hodapp Arthur L Pvt
Hodge Virgil L Pfc
Hoffman Ernest Cpl
Hogan Paul E 1lt
Hohman Jack Pfc
Holencik Joseph P Pfc
Holland Frank J Pfc
Holland William K Pfc
Holley Thohas E Sgt
Hollis Robert L Sgt
Holloway Jimmie Msg
Holman Albert C Jr Pfc
Holman John H Sgt
Holmes James R Pvt
Holt Claude D Cpl
Holt Max S Pvt
Honea Charles H Pfc
Hood Walter L Sgt
Hook Bruce Pfc
Hooper Floyd E Pfc
Hope John G Jr Sgt
Horn Herman J Sgt
Hornung Frederick 1lt
Horton Leroy W Pfc

Houlihan Patrick J Sgt
Howard Edward M Pfc
Howard Joe W Pfc
Howard Ralph Pfc
Howard Robert W Cpl
Howe Jack D Pfc
Howell Elmer Cpl
Howell Martin L Pfc
Hoysradt Donald C Pfc
Hristopulos Clayto Pvt
Hubbard William Jr Pvt
Huber Ramon L Cpl
Hudson William J Pvt
Huff Glenn Cpl
Huffman Ronald C Pvt
Hughes Charles C Msgt
Hughes Ernest D Sfc
Hughes George L Sgt
Hughes Robert J Cpl
Hukill Paul F Pvt
Hume Thomas Maj
Hunnicutt James Sgt
Hunt Alexander Cpl
Hunt Duane H Pvt
Hunt Gwyn R Pvt
Hunt Ora Jr Pfc
Hunter Carson Cpl
Hunter David F Pvt
Hurst Francis J Pfc
Huss Robert F Cpl
Hutchinson W P Pfc
Huth William P Pfc
Hyatt Edward Cpl
Hyslop Kenneth C Capt
Imhof Charles H Sgt
Ingland Warren J Pfc
Isbell Richard Pfc
Iyotte Philip J Cpl
Izu Isamu Pfc
Jackson Clinton 1lt
Jackson Comer Jr Pfc
Jackson Floyd J R Cpl
Jackson Harold S Pvt
Jackson Herbert Pvt
Jackson Herbert H Cpl
Jackson James H Pfc
Jackson William L Pfc
Jacobs George J Cpl
Jager Edward J Pfc
James Davis E Cpl
James Jesse J Sgt
James John C Pfc
James Luther J Pfc
Jeanplong Paul Pfc

273

Jelly Stuart R 1lt
Jenkel James C Cpl
Jennings Alfred S Cpl
Jernigan Carl O Cpl
Jester William F 1lt
Jester William R Pfc
Jimenez Victor P Pfc
Jimerson Billie J Pfc
Joens John E Sgt
Johns Willie L Cpl
Johnson Dewitt W Pfc
Johnson Edward Pfc
Johnson Ervin M Sfc
Johnson Frank H Pfc
Johnson Gaynor T Msgt
Johnson Gudmund C Pfc
Johnson Harry W Jr Pvt
Johnson Henry F Pfc
Johnson Joe L Sgt
Johnson John B Pvt
Johnson John E Sgt
Johnson John N Capt
Johnson John R Pfc
Johnson Kenneth J Pfc
Johnson Lewis H Pfc
Johnson Norman R Cpl
Johnson Paul L Pvt
Johnson Roy C Cpl
Johnson Samuel Cpl
Johnson Samuel W Pvt
Johnson Varnell Pfc
Johnson Vernon G Cpl
Johnson William F Sgt
Johnson William O Pfc
Johnson William W Sfc
Johnston Frank S Jr Capt
Jones Arthur M Cpl
Jones Bertram E Pfc
Jones Calvin S Cpl
Jones Dale R Pfc
Jones Donald Cpl
Jones Donald J Sgt
Jones George J Jr Pfc
Jones James W Pfc
Jones John W Cpl
Jones Leroy Pvt
Jones Leslie J Cpl
Jones Lotchie J R Pvt
Jones Marvin W Cpl
Jones Thomas D Pfc
Jones Wilber G Jr 1lt
Jordan George A Jr Pvt
Jordan Warren H 2lt
Jordan Luther B Cpl

Jordan Paul H Capt
Joshua James L Pvt
Joslin Dale E Cpl
Joyce David Pvt
Joyce Thomas Jr Capt
Joyce William H Jr Pfc
Judd Vernon R Cpl
Jumper Joseph Pvt
Justus Bert W Jr 1lt
Kailianu Robert W Pfc
Kapaun Emil J Capt
Karpinecz Michael Sfc
Karty Dennis K Pfc
Kasarda Milton J Cpl
Katzman Ross W Pvt
Kauffman Clarence Pfc
Kearney Harry L Pvt
Keck Gerald P Cpl
Keirman Cornelius Cpl
Keith Curtis Pvt
Keith Edward L Pfc
Keith John W Jr Col
Kekoa Joseph K Pvt
Kelleher Francis Cpl
Keller John C Sgt
Kellum William H 1lt
Kelly Curtis C Pfc
Kelly Daniel F Pfc
Kelly Ernest M Sfc
Kelly James C Sfc
Kelly Robert T Pfc
Kemnitz Gilbert Sgt
Kenan Claude J Pfc
Kendall Richard Pvt
Kendig John P Pfc
Kenealy James R Pvt
Kennedy Gilbert C Cpl
Kennedy Leonard M Pfc
Keopke Elva L Sfc
Kerklin James H Cpl
Kessler George E Pfc
Kilby Thomas E III 1lt
Killam Hugh C Cpl
Kilpatrick Robert Pfc
Kim Chan J P Jr Pvt
Kimberlin John W Pfc
Kimbrough Colonel Sgt
Kinder Arthur S Jr Sgt
King Charles E Pfc
King Edmund 1lt
King Eldred H Cpl
King Franklin D Pfc
King George R Cpl
King Jimmy E Cpl

King Martin Pvt
King Ralph E Pfc
King Vernon R Pvt
King William J Jr Pfc
Kingsley Willie L Msgt
Kirchofer Roger B 1lt
Kirkner Clarence E Msgt
Kirkpatrick Ardell Pfc
Kirton Roy R Pfc
Kirwin John W Pvt
Kisela Joseph G Cpl
Kiser Henry G Sgt
Kish George J Cpl
Kitchens George T Pfc
Kittle James J Pfc
Kittrell James L Pvt
Klimsey Joseph W Pvt
Kling Harry J Pvt
Koch Kermit K Pvt
Koehler Robert H Pvt
Koenig Sammy G Pvt
Kolberg William V Pfc
Koch George W Sgt
Kornreich Gerald Cpl
Koroser Richard R Pfc
Koster Julius H Pfc
Kostuch Joseph J Cpl
Kotwasinski Willi Pfc
Kozer Michael P Jr Cpl
Kraft Roger J Pfc
Kralick Andrew P Cpl
Kreider Leighton G Cpl
Krepps Richard W Pfc
Kristanoff George 1lt
Kritzwiser Glen E Pfc
Krukonski Stanley Pfc
Krzyzaniak Raymond Sfc
Kubic Peter Pvt
Kubinek Roland W Capt
Kunkel William M Msgt
Kupraites Joseph J Cpl
Kvale Freddie Pfc
La France Delmar J Msgt
La Rose Robert J Sgt
La Roue Billy J Cpl
Labossiere Edward Pvt
Lackner Joseph C Wo
Ladell Simon Pvt
Laessig Kenneth F Pvt
Lambert Roland Pfc
Lambert Rudolph J Sgt
Lampson Harold L Cpl
Lander Lawrence E Cpl
Landy Theodore Pfc

Lang Melford H Pfc
Lang Raymond J Pvt
Lanier Claude Cpl
Lansdell Charles L Pvt
Larkin James N Pfc
Larkins William Cpl
Larson Durfee Maj
Lassiter Donald T Pvt
Laury Othello Jr Pfc
Lavasseur Louis J Pfc
Lavell Geoffrey Maj
Lavelle John G Jr Pvt
Lawlis Donald F Cpl
Lawrence Jack L Cpl
Lawrence John R Pvt
Lawson Aaron Pfc
Lawver Jack D Sfc
Layton Robert H Capt
Lazald John C Cpl
Le Matty Donald G Pfc
Leach Edward T 1lt
Leader Maple L Pfc
Lebiedz Joseph Cpl
Ledbetter Jack W 1lt
Ledesma Alberto Pvt
Ledford Aubrey Sgt
Ledger Ernest W Jr Pfc
Lee Charles S Pvt
Lee Clarence O Msgt
Leighton Edmond G Cpl
Leiviska Arthur W Pvt
Lejeune Kermit J Cpl
Lemaster James E Cpl
Lemay Ernest L Pfc
Lennox Richard N Pfc
Leonberger Karl Capt
Lewis Albert Cpl
Lewis Davis Cpl
Lewis George W Pvt
Lewis Lyman E Pfc
Lewis Olen Sgt
Lewis Warren G 1lt
Liebeg Robert W Pfc
Lien Ralph O Pvt
Lige Amos Cpl
Liggett James M Pfc
Lilly Ray K Pfc
Lindsay Homer F Capt
Lindsey Freeman Pfc
Lingle Keith L Cpl
Lingle William J Cpl
Linn Frank M Sgt
Lipe Billy D Cpl
Lipes Richard R Pfc

Lippert Kenneth W Pvt
Lipscomb William Cpl
Little Bear Melvin Pvt
Little Paul E Pfc
Littlefield Gary E Cpl
Lo Schiavo John Cpl
Lockett Eddie Jr Pvt
Lockett Isaac W Jr Pfc
Lockett Lindsey C Pfc
Lockwood William Pfc
Logston Edward R A1c
Long Charles M Cpl
Long Jac E Pfc
Longmire Chester Pfc
Loomis Otis W Sgt
Loomis Thomas H Pvt
Lord Charles H Jr Pvt
Lorenz Robert E Pvt
Lorrey David C Cpl
Lotis Thomas D Pfc
Lott George W 1lt
Love Robert J Pvt
Lovelady Wallace R Cpl
Lovett John M Pfc
Loving William N Pfc
Lowe Junior B Cpl
Lowe Milford G Pfc
Lublinski George S Pfc
Lucas Carl Pfc
Luebbers Daniel E Pvt
Luke Lee F Cpl
Lukitsch John J Pfc
Lundquist William Cpl
Luoma Allan E Cpl
Lusk Jesse M Sgt
Lutz John W Pfc
Lux Mortimer E Sgt
Lycan John S Jr Pfc
Lyedolph Robert M Pvt
Lynch James H Cpl
Lytle Jack W Sgt
Maas Melvin D Cpl
Mac Dougall Bernar Pvt
Mac Nair Raga Hect Pfc
Mack Alvin L Cpl
Macomber Wayne B Capt
Maddox Donald Pvt
Maddox James W Sfc
Maddy Allen T Pfc
Magee John V Sfc
Magnus Donald F Pfc
Magoon Robert L Sfc
Mahan Robert D Cpl
Maher Frank X Sgt

Mahon Kenneth R Cpl
Mahoney Kenneth R Pvt
Mahoney Thomas R Pfc
Main Harold L Sfc
Mairich Mark W 2lt
Majeske Arthur Jr Pvt
Major Charlie L Pfc
Makela Charles D Pfc
Malcolm Howard G Cpl
Malczewski Frank M Pfc
Maldonado Victor S Pvt
Mallette Donald J Cpl
Mancebo Richard R Cpl
Manegre Leo J Cwo
Mann William C Pfc
Manning Arthur E Msgt
Manning Bill D Pvt
Manning Lee H Cpl
Manross Thomas H Pfc
Mansell James E Pvt
Marchowsky Martin Cpl
Marion Christopher Sgt
Marquez Jasper V Pvt
Marquez Rudolph Cpl
Marrelli Joseph Pfc
Marsh Harold L Sfc
Marshall Alfred Pfc
Marshall Paul J Pfc
Martin Alfred J Cpl
Martin Charles R Pfc
Martin Elwin C Jr Cpl
Martin Henry C Sgt
Martin James Pvt
Martin James H Cpl
Martin James R Cpl
Martin John Cpl
Martinez Raymond R Cpl
Martins John Pfc
Maruk Zigmund H Pfc
Masko John E Pvt
Mason James L Pvt
Mason Joseph E Pfc
Massey Anthony Jr Pvt
Masterson Harold Msgt
Mathews Norman C Pfc
Matthews James L Sfc
Matthews Richard F Sfc
Maus William F Sgt
Maxwell Herbert R Pvt
Maxwell James Sfc
May Robert L Cpl
Maynard Edward W 1lt
Mayrand Charles E 1lt
Mc Allister John F Sgt

Mc Alpine Johnny L Pfc
Mc Bride Bobby G Pfc
Mc Bride Robert Pvt
Mc Cain James D Sfc
Mc Call John H Sgt
Mc Call Rufus Pfc
Mc Cartney William Pfc
Mc Caul Robert J Cpl
Mc Clatchey Herman Pvt
Mc Clellan Maurice Cpl
Mc Clintock John R Pfc
Mc Cloud Steve Sgt
Mc Clure Tom N Sgt
Mc Connell James W Pfc
Mc Coy Paul E T Pfc
Mc Coy Raymond H Cpl
Mc Cracken Kenneth Pfc
Mc Crary Curtis C Sfc
Mc Crea Verne L Pfc
Mc Cullers Charles Pfc
Mc Cullough Edmund 1lt
Mc Cullough John Cpl
Mc Dermond Robert Pfc
Mc Donald Charles Pfc
Mc Donald John D Pfc
Mc Donald Warren B Msgt
Mc Donnell Francis Msgt
Mc Donnell John J Pvt
Mc Dougal Charles 1lt
Mc Dougal Leslie D Sgt
Mc Dowell Junior R Sgt
Mc Elroy Joseph Cpl
Mc Evoy James C Pfc
Mc Gill William R Pvt
Mc Ginithen John M Cpl
Mc Gowan Donald Jr Pvt
Mc Grew James R Msgt
Mc Guire James P Cpl
Mc Intire Millard Sfc
Mc Intosh Henry Jr Cpl
Mc Intyre James T Pfc
Mc Intyre Warren H Cpl
Mc Kinley Ralph H Pvt
Mc Kinney Edward Sgt
Mc Kinney Richard Pfc
Mc Kinney Ronald E Pfc
Mc Klusky Frank D Pfc
Mc Knight Arthur L Pfc
Mc Lellan John W Sgt
Mc Leod Robert E Cpl
Mc Linko Peter J Pvt
Mc Master Joseph W Cpl
Mc Murry Joseph L Cpl
Mc Namara George W Pvt

Mc Nary Walter D Pvt
Mc Neil Robert W Pvt
Mc Neill Curtis Pvt
Mc Pherson Frankli Pfc
Mc Quade John P Sfc
Mc Queen Norman Sfc
Mc Shane Edward P Pvt
Mc Swain Leon Cpl
Mc Taggart John L Msgt
Mc Voy Carl R Cpl
Meacham Marion G Pvt
Meadows Emette S Sgt
Meehan Joseph J Jr Pfc
Mehmen Edward H Sgt
Meick Nick Sgt
Melchiorre Joseph Pfc
Mellinger James R Pfc
Melsness Earl W Pfc
Melton Richard D Cpl
Mensch Robert R Pvt
Mentzos Paul G Sgt
Mercer Earl S Pfc
Mesel Kenneth M Sgt
Meshulam Morris Pfc
Metkowski Edward Cpl
Mettert Raymond E Cpl
Mettler Allen L Pfc
Metzcar R Maurice Capt
Meyer Albert W Cpl
Michiel Max R Pvt
Mielke Robert C Pvt
Miller Bobby Pvt
Miller Donald M Cpl
Miller Gerald E Msgt
Miller Howard P Jr 1lt
Miller Kenneth R Pvt
Miller Lloyd E Cpl
Miller Milan E Sfc
Miller Paul Luther Sgt
Miller Raymond H Pfc
Miller Richard K Pfc
Miller Robert E Sfc
Miller Robert F Pfc
Miller Robert F Cpl
Miller Theodore R Pfc
Miller Wallace Pfc
Milligan Richard Pfc
Millon Johnny Sfc
Mills Ezekiel C Cpl
Mills Lawrence W Sfc
Minard Wayne Pfc
Miner Donald W Pvt
Minkin Jack R Pfc
Minniear Robert G Pfc

Misciagno Luke T Pfc
Mishler James E Pvt
Miss Ira Victor Jr Sfc
Mitchell Archie F Cpl
Mitchell Edwin L Pfc
Mitchell Jesse L Pfc
Mitchell Robert Pfc
Molenaar George Sgt
Mompher David P Pvt
Monaghan Eugene J Pvt
Monroe Napoleon Pvt
Montgomery Harold Sgt
Montgomery James R Pfc
Moody Charles R Cpl
Moody James Cpl
Moore Dexter Pfc
Moore Frank Msgt
Moore Jack S Sgt
Moore James L Pfc
Moore John D Jr Cpl
Moore Robert L Cpl
Morales Joseph S Pvt
Moreland Harry D Capt
Morelli Eugene M Pfc
Moreno Gilbert T Pfc
Moreno Raymond M Pfc
Morgan Albert Sgt
Morgan Clarence E Cpl
Morgan Enoch E Cpl
Morgan Frankie K Pfc
Morgan Melvin H Pfc
Morgan Roger L Pfc
Morgan Tommie L Sgt
Morris David W Pfc
Morris Stafford L Cpl
Morris Tom J Cpl
Morris William Cpl
Morrow Jack L Pfc
Morse Herman E Cpl
Moses Louis R Cpl
Moskowitz Edward Pfc
Moss Alonz Pfc
Moss Lawrence D 1lt
Moss William H Sgt
Moss William R Cpl
Mott Murel R Pvt
Moya Carlos B Pfc
Mrotek Lawrence M Pfc
Mulder Delano B Pfc
Mullins Cebert W Pfc
Mullins Thomas H Pfc
Mulock Arthur F 1lt
Munda Joseph F Sfc
Munger Graham B Sgt

Munoz Moises Pfc
Murdock Jackie L Pvt
Murphy Christopher Pvt
Murphy Edmund J Maj
Murphy Harry T Pfc
Murphy James D Cpl
Murphy Leonard Cpl
Murphy Michael D Cpl
Murphy Robert M Pvt
Murphy William F Pvt
Murray Bobby L Pfc
Murray Neil A Jr Cpl
Musick Lee R Cpl
Mutter Gene Pfc
Myers Guy K Pvt
Myers Robert H Sfc
Nagamine Hiroshi Cpl
Nance Robert C Pfc
Nash James T Pfc
Nava Adolphus Cwo
Nazelrod Earl C Pvt
Neary Richard Pfc
Neckers Edwin J Cpl
Neely Robert Jr Pvt
Neff Kenneth E Sot
Nelson Carl T Pvt
Nelson Forest Capt
Nelson James L Pvt
Nelson John H Sgt
Nelson Sam Jr Pvt
Nelson Woodrow W Pfc
Newton Earle C Jr Pfc
Newton William Pfc
Nichols Robert Pfc
Nichols Willis J J Pfc
Nicholson David L Cpl
Niemann Robert C 2lt
Niemann William H Cpl
Nixon Donald D Cpl
Nolan John Sfc
Nordin David T Jr Pfc
Nordyke Elwyn D Cpl
Novacek Donald W Pvt
Nowicki Kasmir E Pfc
Oaks Joseph S Pfc
Oboyle James M Cpl
Obrien Raymond J Pfc
Oden Willie E Sfc
Odom Lloyd B Pfc
Ohara Thomas J Pfc
Ohara William T Pfc
Ohme Otto Cpl
Olaker Freddy J Cpl
Oleary James P Cpl

Oles Peter Pvt
Olesiniski Robert D Pfc
Oliver Kenneth E Pvt
Ollero Luciano F Pfc
Olman Edward C Pvt
Olson Harold B Pfc
Olson Norman E Sfc
Olson Sigurd C Pvt
Olthan Charles R L Pvt
Olvis Leonard K Capt
Oneal Henry R Pfc
Phillips Orville P Cpl
Piatrelli Vincent Sgt
Pickard Maxie L Cpl
Pickering Fred D Maj
Pier James E Pfc
Pierce Leonard L Pvt
Pierce Orville W Maj
Piersee Howard E Pfc
Pilmer William T Pfc
Pina Frank J Pfc
Piner William E Cpl
Pinell Russell C Sgt
Piper Wallace R Pvt
Pitman Frank Cpl
Pitman William E Pfc
Pitre Charles D Jr Pvt
Pitierson John Cpl
Pleshek Roger W Pvt
Plocha Frank L Pfc
Plotner Gerald R Pvt
Plunkett Waitcell Sfc
Poe Robert H Pfc
Polk Warren Franklin 1lt
Polka Francis Sgt
Polzine Robert E Pfc
Pool Edward Pfc
Porter Earl G Sgt
Porter Henry M Pfc
Porter Henry N Sgt
Porter Mose Pvt
Posey Harold T Pvt
Posivak Michael J Cpl
Potts Richard Pfc
Powell Jackie L Pfc
Powell Willie Pfc
Prather Kermit Q Cpl
Pratt John L Cpl
Prettner Robert J Pfc
Provost Leonard E Pvt
Provost Robert Pfc
Pruitt Oliver L Pfc
Pruinier Harry C Cpl
Pryor George T Pfc

Pulley Jack C Cpl
Puopolo Joseph J Pfc
Putman Linzy L Pvt
Putzier Gene Pvt
Puzach Walter Pvt
Queen Gilmer D Cpl
Raboye Ronald Pvt
Raburn Cleon Msgt
Racich John Sfc
Radanovich Harry J Pfc
Railling Thomas E Cpl
Rainey William J Pfc
Raisbeck Sterling Pvt
Ramsey Troy O Pfc
Randall Elgin V Cpl
Randle Fred Sfc
Ransom Henry Jr Pvt
Rarick Rolan D Sgt
Raskin Alfred J 1lt
Ratcliffe Griffith Sgt
Raven Daniel J Pvt
Ray Duaard L Sgt
Reed Elvie J Cpl
Reed Lee B Pfc
Reed Melvin Pfc
Reed Ray W Pvt
Reed Robert D Pfc
Reeder Stanley G Cpl
Reedy Claude E Cpl
Reese Richard T Pfc
Reid Alexander Jr Cpl
Reiley Thomas P Sfc
Reinhart Noel F Pvt
Reisinger Walter L Pvt
Renner Thomas R Sfc
Resch Loyd Sgt
Rewis Dewey E Jr Pfc
Reynolds James H Pfc
Reynolds Stanley W Pfc
Reynolds Theodore Pfc
Reynolds William L Pfc
Rhine Vernon R Pfc
Rhoadman George M Sgt
Rhoads Edward W Pfc
Rhoads Vivan W Pfc
Rhodes Stanley Q Pvt
Rice Donald R Cpl
Rice Robert E Pfc
Richard Elmer G Pvt
Richards Edward F Pfc
Richards Flint B Sgt
Richardson Glen C Cpl
Richardson James F Cpl
Rickman Vincent R Msgt

Riddle Dock L Cpl
Riddle Hoyle T Sgt
Rights George L Pvt
Riley Charles D Pfc
Riley Charles L Pfc
Riley Howard C Sfc
Riley John F Cpl
Riley Lawrence T Pvt
Rines Raymond S Pvt
Ritter Joel N Pfc
Ritter Wallace Pfc
Rivers John E Pfc
Robare Norman J Cpl
Roberge Robert J Cpl
Roberts Everett R Pfc
Roberts Gordon Sfc
Roberts James J Pvt
Robertson Dewey E Cpl
Robertson James R Cpl
Robidoux Lawrence Cpl
Robillard Joseph Pvt
Robinson Ernest Cpl
Robinson George Pvt
Robinson James H Pfc
Robinson Jasper Cpl
Robinson Joseph C Pfc
Robinson Joseph W Pfc
Robinson Robert R Pfc
Rockwell Clyde T Pfc
Rodeischak Billie Pvt
Rodriques Roberto Pfc
Roe Stephen K Pfc
Roese Paul Pvt
Roffe Adolphus W Capt
Rogers Arthur H Pfc
Rogers George S Pfc
Rogers Harry L Pfc
Rogers Lloyd G Pvt
Rogers Raymond Jr Pfc
Roggow Walter W Pfc
Rohr Paul L Cpl
Rojas Raymond Pfc
Roman Joseph J Sfc
Romanek John V Msgt
Romeo Vincenzo D Cpl
Romo Angel P Pvt
Rooks Daniel F Maj
Roop Donald H Pfc
Roper Chester J Pfc
Rose Albert E Pfc
Rose Gilbert G Jr Pfc
Rose William Wilber A1c
Rosecrants George Sgt
Ross Andrew C Pfc

Ross Donald R Pfc
Ross John H Sfc
Ross Joseph B Pvt
Ross Tommy E Pfc
Ross Ulysses Sfc
Ross Walter A Jr Sgt
Roth Bernard F 1lt
Rothlauf Donald G Cpl
Roush Robert L Pfc
Rovello Salvador J Pfc
Rowden Thomas W Jr Ssgt
Rowe Willie Cpl
Rowland Ernest J Pvt
Roy Charles Sgt
Roy Floyd Sgt
Roy Roberts S Pfc
Rubel Charles D Pfc
Rubideaux Donald J Cpl
Ruddell James C Jr Capt
Rufeher John F Pfc
Ruffule Joseph Cpl
Ruggero Ciro J Pfc
Rushton James B Pvt
Russell Charles P Pvt
Russell Gordon C Sgt
Russell John W Sfc
Ruud Wayne C Peg
Ryan Vincent M Jr Pfc
Salmon Donald W Pvt
Sambol Paul Jr Pfc
Sampson Rudolph Pfc
Samsel Denzil G Pfc
Samuel George Jr Cpl
Sanders Ozell Pfc
Sanders Tony M Pfc
Sandoval Frank L Pfc
Sangster Caswell L Pfc
Sargent Claud C Jr Pfc
Saunders Edward Cpl
Saunders Frederick Pvt
Saunders Jack J 1lt
Saunders James R Jr Tsgt
Saunders Louis Pfc
Saunders Norbert B Pfc
Sayre Fred B Pvt
Sayre Herbert G Cpl
Schaekel Walter J Pfc
Schantz Addison Jr Sfc
Scherdin Hubert C Pvt
Schinkal Harvey T Sgt
Schipani George R Cpl
Schlegel Charles B Cpl
Schmollinger James Pfc
Schoenmann Glenn S Pfc

Scholten Donald E Cpl
Schoonover George Sfc
Schoulthies George Pvt
Schultz Richard J Pfc
Schluman John H Cpl
Schuster Merlin N Pfc
Schwartz Lon Cpl
Scofield Lowell D Pfc
Scott A V Pfc
Scott Amos L Pfc
Scott Floyd E Pvt
Scott Gerald F Sgt
Scott Jessie L Pfc
Scott Jimmie Jr Cpl
Scott Lawrence H Pfc
Scott Neil R Pvt
Scott Samuel L Cpl
Seadore Richard J Pfc
Seaton Arthur L Pfc
Sebastian Henry H Cpl
Sechman Gene Pvt
Sedlow Donald G Pfc
Seigle Joseph C Pfc
Seiler George D Pfc
Selby Donald H Pvt
Self Albert Sfc
Seminara Vincent C Pfc
Sesler Philip K Pfc
Settle Alain L 1lt
Sewell Nathaniel Cpl
Sexton Talmage J Pfc
Shackelford Howard Pfc
Shaffer George L Pfc
Sharp John T Pfc
Sharp Raleigh T Pfc
Shaw Glenace H Pfc
Shaw James P Pvt
Shaw Ralph L Cpl
Shedd Harold Cpl
Shee Robert W Pfc
Shelton William B Cpl
Sheppard James W Sgt
Shertzer Gordon R Pfc
Shippen Charles H Pfc
Shirley Alton E Sgt
Shirtz Alton L Sgt
Shisler Glen R Sfc
Shorman James G Msgt
Short John W Pfc
Short R V Leo Pfc
Shorter James W Pfc
Shreeve Charles D Sgt
Shults Rembert D Pvt
Shyne Eugene F Pfc

Sidney Alfred H Cpl
Siedler Edwin P 1lt
Sifling Thomas E 1lt
Silva Jesus Cpl
Simmons Gene Pfc
Simmons Leon F Cpl
Sims Clemmie Msgt
Simonson Ernest V Pfc
Simpkins Herman I Sgt
Simpson Grant W Capt
Simpson James C Pfc
Sims Holly B Pvt
Sirman Donald S Capt
Sitton Lester R Jr Sgt
Skeens Irvin K Pvt
Skero Charles M Pvt
Skinner Kenneth L Pvt
Skwierawski Joseph Cpl
Slaughter Lum L Cpl
Sloan Harold Cpl
Sloat Richard F Pvt
Sluss William R Pfc
Smalley Gail W Cpl
Smith Albert W 1lt
Smith Allen W Pfc
Smith Billy R Pfc
Smith Charles L Pfc
Smith Dayle L Pfc
Smith Dewitt R Capt
Smith Edward W Pfc
Smith Fred H Jr Pfc
Smith George R Pvt
Smith Howard F Cpl
Smith James E Jr Cpl
Smith James M Cpl
Smith Jerrold R Pfc
Smith Jesse C Sfc
Smith John Sfc
Smith John D Msgt
Smith John F Sgt
Smith Joseph W 2lt
Smith Leland F Pfc
Smith Leonard J Jr Cpl
Smith Paul R Pvt
Smith Paul V Pfc
Smith Richard W Sgt
Smith Robert Pfc
Smith Roger B Pfc
Smith Vernon D Cpl
Smith William D Pfc
Smith William L Pfc
Smithers Ferman T Pfc
Smithson Donald Cpl
Smoak Harvey H Sfc

Sholinsky Frank S Pfc
Snider Glenn Msgt
Snock Joseph M Jr Cpl
Socha Ernest T Pfc
Solem Joseph J Sfc
Solis Adelaido M Pvt
Solomon Richard W Cpl
Sonnier Louis Jr Pfc
Spain Francis E Pfc
Sparks Harold Cpl
Sparks James R Cpl
Sparks Ronald C Pfc
Sparks Ronald M Pfc
Spears Henry F Pvt
Specht Wilfred G Cpl
Spence John W Pfc
Spence Richard L Pfc
Spindler Frederick Pvt
Spinks Willie F Cpl
Spitzer Everett W Pfc
Spoon Manuel J Sfc
Spraggs David J Cpl
Springborn Robert Pfc
Spurlock John W Pfc
Srogoncik George J Pfc
St Julien Paul E Sfc
Stacy Clyde T Cpl
Staffen Frank G Pfc
Stallings Vernon D Pvt
Stancel Joseph E Sfc
Stankus Frank K Pvt
Stansbury William Pfc
Stedman Daniel Pfc
Stedman Gerald F Sgt
Steele Clyde D Pfc
Steele Dean Cpl
Steele Harold M Pfc
Steinberg Joseph D Sgt
Steinle Robert E Pfc
Stephens Harry E Pfc
Stephens Leon B Pfc
Stephens Robert D Pvt
Stephens Russell L Pvt
Stephens Wesley Cpl
Stepina George Sfc
Stepp Mermon J Pvt
Stevens James E Cwo
Stevens Simon J Maj
Stewart Edward F Cpl
Stewart Howard Cpl
Stewart James W Pvt
Stewart Raymond A Jr 1lt
Stewart Richard H Sfc
Stewart Robert E Pfc

Stewart Roy Pfc
Stewart William S Pfc
Stewart Wilson W Pfc
Stiles Earl C Cpl
Stiles George W Pfc
Still Edgar H Pfc
Stockman Richard W Pvt
Stoliker Thomas H Pfc
Stone Edward J Pfc
Stoney Oliver Jr Cpl
Stopa Dewey 1lt
Story Leroy Cpl
Stout Johnnie O Pfc
Strawser Paul P Pfc
Streeter Karl J Sgt
Strickland William Pfc
Strong William Pvt
Struble Britton R Sfc
Stumpf John L Sfc
Sturm Donald R Cpl
Stutlien Francis E Pfc
Suliman Frank J Cpl
Sullivan Clinton V Pvt
Sullivan Harold J Pfc
Sullivan James F 1lt
Sumner William G Cpl
Sund James N Pfc
Sund Roland V 1lt
Sunsdahl Roy L Pvt
Surber Harold P Pfc
Sutton Frederick G Pvt
Swain Vincent Jr Pfc
Swanson Richard P Pvt
Swarmer William R Sfc
Sweet Richard L Pfc
Sweitzer William C Pvt
Symons John O Sgt
Szweda Thaddeus T Cpl
Tablante Richard Cpl
Tadlock Alvin J Cpl
Tadlock Iva B Sfc
Tait Robert J Pfc
Takai Tohoru T Cpl
Talbot Edgar H Pvt
Tanker Arlond M Jr Pfc
Tanner Bobby D Pfc
Tanouye Kiyoshi Pvt
Tatar Michael R Pvt
Tate Hershel L Sgt
Taylor Douglas L Sgt
Taylor Earl W Pvt
Taylor Ira N Msgt
Taylor John J Pfc
Taylor Michael Pfc

Taylor William E Pvt
Teague James W Cpl
Tedford John W Pfc
Teeters Joseph L Pvt
Teixeira James C Sfc
Tenley Howard C Sfc
Tennille James E Pvt
Terrell Benjamin F Pfc
Terry Jimmie Pfc
Tessin Willard N Sgt
Tharp George W Cpl
Thayer George L Sgt
Theisen Norbert J Pvt
Thibodeaux Clement Cpl
Thieme Jack J Cpl
Thomas Ezell Sfc
Thomas Gerald Cpl
Thompson Elmore M Cpl
Thompson Jerry Pfc
Thompson John E Cpl
Thornburg Clyde Sfc
Threet Fred Sfc
Thurman Ruben Jr Cpl
Tice Clinton C Pfc
Tick Stanley M Pfc
Tillman Richard H Cpl
Tingle Paul L Pvt
Tinsley Cecil E Jr Cpl
Tinsley George M Pfc
Titus Robert E Pvt
Toatley Alexander Cpl
Todd Blanton Cpl
Todd Phillip J Pfc
Toler Robert S Cpl
Tolley Harry C Pfc
Tolliver Robert E Pfc
Tomaszewski Waclaw 1lt
Tomkovich Andrew Pfc
Tondreau George Pfc
Toney William H Pvt
Toomey Joseph D 1lt
Torhan George Pvt
Torres Phil Cpl
Toth Edward J Cpl
Totland Mical M Pvt
Towne Charles E Pfc
Tracy Theodore P Pfc
Trail Joseph H Cpl
Travers Joseph R Pvt
Treacy Edgar J Jr Col
Trent Donald C Cpl
Trent James L Cpl
Trent Jebru Pvt
Treptau Kenneth W Sgt

Tricomo John Pfc
Triplett Lowell C Pvt
Tripp William Sfc
Troche Maximo Pvt
Tross Eugene F Pvt
Trotman Robert C Cpl
Truelove Bobby L Pvt
Truett Ray E Pfc
Tugman Richard J Pvt
Turley James E Pfc
Turner Joseph L Pvt
Turner Winston M Cpl
Tuttle Allen H Cpl
Tye Jack O Sgt
Tyler Charles R Pfc
Tyler Robert L Pvt
Tyndall Bradford E 1lt
Ullmer Lavern C Pvt
Underhill Virgil E Pfc
Uurtamo Stephen T Capt
Vaillancourt Alber Msgt
Vaillancourt John Sgt
Vaillancourt Leo J Pvt
Valentine William Pfc
Van Dine Donald F Sfc
Van Draska Dale E Pvt
Van Newhouse Rich Pvt
Van Steenvoort Eug Pfc
Van Winkle Calvin Pvt
Vanderkooi Charles Pfc
Vaneekhoven Richar Pfc
Vanicola Pompey J Pfc
Vann Harvey T Msgt
Varkett Charles Pvt
Varner Alvin L Cpl
Varner Edmund S Pvt
Varney Basil Jr Pfc
Vaughan Wilson H Pfc
Vaughn Aubrey D Pvt
Vaughn Cleveland Cpl
Vazquez Joseph T Pvt
Vega Thomas P Pfc
Vercolen Albert L Sgt
Vergara Eliseo C Pfc
Vernon Raymond Pvt
Vester John W Capt
Viars James E Pfc
Vicaldo Robert Pfc
Vickers Wendell Cpl
Vickery Roy M Pfc
Vincent Albert Pfc
Vincent William E Pfc
Vink Lawrence E Cpl
Vinyard Bobby D Pfc

Vitello Robert J Pfc
Voight Paul T Jr Cpl
Wagner James R Pfc
Wagner Richard H Cpl
Wailes Ardean R Pvt
Wainwright Billy J Pfc
Walker James I Pvt
Walker James W Cpl
Walker James Y Pfc
Walker Leroy M Msgt
Walker Walter Pfc
Walker William H Capt
Wallace Clyde L 1lt
Wallace Earl Jr Pfc
Wallace Mitchell Cpl
Wallace Pendleton Pvt
Wallace William K Pfc
Walsh Robert C Pfc
Walter John G Pfc
Walters James C Sgt
Walters Leland R Pfc
Wancoski Frank P Pfc
Warren Edgar O Pvt
Warren Everett Pfc
Warren Samuel Cpl
Warrick John E Cpl
Warthan Dillon E Pfc
Washington John M Pvt
Waters Eunis G Pfc
Waters Luther N 1lt
Waters Raymond L Cpl
Watson Clarence E Cpl
Watson Leonard S Cpl
Watson Robert B Cpl
Watson Thomas H Pfc
Watson Walter J Cpl
Watts Hugh Jr Pvt
Wear Elmer C Cpl
Weary N D Sgt
Weaver Edward P Pfc
Weaver James M Pvt
Webb Donald K Pfc
Webb Stclair Jr 1lt
Weems Randall M Pfc
Wegrzyn Chester J Pvt
Weichhan Bernard E Pvt
Weingarth Howard R Sgt
Weister Jack Pfc
Welch Arthur R Sr Cpl
Weldon Harold D Pfc
Welker Harold M Pfc
Werhan Glen E Pfc
Wesley Walter H Cpl
West Donald L Pfc

Westfall John F Sgt
Westphall Johnie Cpl
Whaleh John R Sgt
Whaley Elwin I Maj
Whaley Henry N Jr Pfc
Wheeler John N Sgt
Whisler William L Pfc
White Billy R Pvt
White Charles Pfc
White Delbert L Pfc
White Frank M Capt
White Franklin H Pfc
White Robert L Pfc
White William F Pfc
White William K Pfc
Whitecotton Orbi Sgt
Whited Roy N Sgt
Whitman Lankford L Pfc
Widel Leigh W Pfc
Widener William J Sfc
Wilcox Robert B Sgt
Wilder Harold D Pvr
Wiley Farrel K Pvt
Williams Billy J Cpl
Williams Charles O Pfc
Williams Chester L Pvt
Williams Dale E Sgt
Williams Ezr Cpl
Williams James B Msgt
Williams James E Pfc
Williams Kenneth B Pvt
Williams Leo H Pfc
Williams Leonard J Pvt
Williams Percy E Pvt
Williams Stevens Cpl

Williamson Bennie Cpl
Williamson Claud H Pvt
Williamson James Pfc
Williamson John Jr Cpl
Willingham Joseph Pfc
Willis Charles Pfc
Wilner William H Pfc
Wilson David H Pvt
Wilson Earl T Pvt
Wilson Elmer T Pvt
Wilson Forest M Pfc
Wilson Hallie W Jr Pfc
Wilson Harry L Pvt
Wilson Samuel Pfc
Winchester William Pvt
Windom Clifford J Pfc
Wing Richard L Pfc
Wingard Lewis M Pvt
Winn Archie D Sgt
Winnie Richard Pfc
Winter Frederick W Maj
Winters William W 1lt
Wirschinger Claren Pfc
Wise Arthur F Pvt
Wise William L Sfc
Witt Robert V Pfc
Wofford Lawrence R Sgt
Wolfe Robert O Cpl
Wolfe Thomas F Cpl
Wolff Roy Cpl
Wood James L Sgt
Wood Kenneth E Sgt
Wood Lyle E Cpl
Wood Ronald C Sfc
Woodard Russell E Cpl

Woodring Raymond L Pfc
Woodroof Edward C Sfc
Woods Wilfred E Cpl
Woodworth Richard Sfc
Woolford William L Cpl
Worthington Henry Pfc
Wright Benjamin H Cpl
Wright Chester Pvt
Wright Robert J Jr Pvt
Wright Robert L Pfc
Wright Roy C Pfc
Wright Theodore Cpl
Wright William G Cpl
Wyda John P Pfc
Yarrish Gerald V Pvt
Yaw Billy G Pfc
Yde Erik F Capt
Yeley James H Pfc
Yonts Robert B Sgt
Young Gerald R Cpl
Young Howard W Msgt
Young Kenneth Pvt
Young Nelson E Pvt
Zak Robert W Cpl
Zamora Anselmo Pfc
Zebrowski John W Pfc
Zidelski William F Pfc
Zmeskal Charles L Capt
Zoellick William M Pfc
Zoller Jack R Pvt
Zumar Charles Pvt
Zuver Robert L Pvt
Zwilling Louis J Pfc

[THIS LIST WAS CONTRIBUTED BY MARY AND
CHUCK SCHANTAG OF THE POW NETWORK.
Located at http://www.asde.com/~/pownet]

SOURCE: KOREAN CONFLICT CASUALTY FILE,
1950 -1957
RECORDS OF THE OFFICE OF THE SECRETARY
OF DEFENSE RECORD GROUP 330,
NATIONAL ARCHIVES, WASHINGTON, DC.